Brightest and Best

Brightest
and Best

A Companion to the
Lesser Feasts and Fasts

Sam Portaro

COWLEY PUBLICATIONS
Cambridge ✦ Boston
Massachusetts

Published in the United States of America by Cowley Publications, a division of the Society of St. John the Evangelist. No portion of this book may be reproduced, stored in or introduced into a retrieval system, or transmitted, in any form or by any means—including photocopying—without the prior written permission of Cowley Publications, except in the case of brief quotations embodied in critical articles and reviews.

Library of Congress Cataloging-in-Publication Data:
   Portaro, Sam Anthony.
     Brightest and best: a companion to the lesser feasts and fasts / Sam Portaro.
            p.   cm.
     Includes bibliographical references.
     ISBN 1-56101-148-7 (alk. paper)
     1. Christian saints—Sermons. 2. Fasts and feasts—Episcopal Church—Sermons.
     3. Episcopal Church—Sermons. 4. Anglican Communion—Sermons. 5. Sermons,
     American. I. Title.
     BX5937.P59   1997
     242'.37—dc21   97-32498
                                                                  CIP

Scripture quotations are taken from *The New Revised Standard Version* of the Bible, © 1989 by the Division of Christian Education of the National Council of the Churches of Christ in the USA. Used by permission. All rights reserved.

Cynthia Shattuck, editor; Vicki Black, copyeditor and designer
Cover art: *Beatus Apocalypse.* Spain, ca. 950.

This book is printed on recycled, acid-free paper and was produced in the United States of America.

Cowley Publications • 28 Temple Place
Boston, Massachusetts 02111
800-225-1534 • http://www.cowley.org/~cowley

*For the communities at Brent House,
the University of Chicago, and the Diocese of Chicago*

my companions and partners in ministry

Contents

Foreword

The Most Reverend Frank T. Griswold III

Hagiography is a dangerous discipline which often produces worthy but somewhat wooden representations of the saintly persons it seeks to extol. This certainly cannot be said of Sam Portaro's efforts set out in the pages of this volume. His spirited and sometimes unsettling reflections upon the lives of the men and women commemorated in the calendar of *The Book of Common Prayer* give us food for thought while at the same time dislodge us from our bland pieties and oblige us to think again what it means to be living limbs of the risen body of Christ.

Flannery O'Connor once observed that a serious writer "must track down the Holy Ghost through a tangle of human suffering and aspiration and idiocy. It is an attempt which should be pursued with gusto." Sam Portaro has pursued his task of tracking down the Spirit in the lives of his subjects with gusto. The worthies of our past leap off the page with a startling freshness that engages us at once. I can see his reflections used in a variety of ways: liturgically at Morning or Evening Prayer; as inspiration for a homilist; as vehicles for personal reflection and prayer; as a means of coming to a deeper appreciation of the wonderful diversity and variety of ways in which the risen Christ seeks to "Easter" in the flesh and blood reality of our lives.

Preface

As I collected these meditations on the lesser feasts and fasts, I was reminded of an old gospel hymn by Philip Paul Bliss that we often sang in the rural Methodist church of my childhood.

Brightly beams our Father's mercy
    From His lighthouse evermore;
But to us He gives the keeping
    Of the lights along the shore.

Let the lower light be burning!
    Send a gleam across the wave;
Some poor fainting, struggling seaman
    You may rescue, you may save.

The lyric was inspired by a story told by the legendary Dwight L. Moody:

On a dark, stormy night, when the waves rolled like mountains and not a star was to be seen, a boat, rocking and plunging, neared the Cleveland harbor. "Are you sure this is Cleveland?" asked the captain, seeing only one light from the lighthouse. "Quite sure, sir," replied the pilot.
"Where are the lower lights?"
"Gone out, sir."
"Can you make the harbor?"
"We must, or perish, sir!"
With a strong hand and a brave heart the old pilot turned the wheel. But, alas, in the darkness he missed the channel, and with a crash upon the rocks the boat was shivered, and many a life lost in a watery grave. Brethren, the Master will take care of the great lighthouse; let us keep the lower lights burning![1]

---

1. Ira D. Sankey: *Sankey's Story of the Gospel Hymns* (Philadelphia: The Sunday School Times Company, 1906).

The individuals and events commemorated in the Episcopal Church's calendar of lesser feasts and fasts are, borrowing from another hymn, the "brightest and best" representatives of that vast community of "lower lights" whose gleam provides an essential supplement to the orienting signal of the lighthouse itself. These are the people and occasions of our own experience, touching the ordinary, earthbound stuff of our daily living. They are our companions in the way and though they are called "lesser," like the lights along the shore, so too without them we would likely perish. In countless ways they illuminate the way as we navigate our lives.

This collection itself began in the ordinary duties of midweek services in a university chapel for a small congregation of Episcopal students, faculty, staff, and their non-Episcopal friends. Usually only a dozen or so in number, dwarfed by gothic architecture designed to accommodate more than ten times that number, there was ample room for that vast company of witnesses to join us and, not infrequently, their presence was keenly felt. My words intended an intimacy to offset the expansive context and over the years a cohesive community formed; we met each week during the academic year, and gradually to that community were added each of those whose stories are included here. There were special moments of communion when we commemorated our namesake, Charles Henry Brent, and Julia Chester Emery, whose legacy lives on in our ministry at Brent House at the University of Chicago, a ministry begun nearly a decade after her own death but with resources we, and the church, owe to her service.

And there were fortuitous juxtapositions as I liberally shuffled dates to accommodate the vagaries of the academic calendar, relocating commemorations that would otherwise have been lost to holidays, term breaks, and the summer recess—moving, for example, the nativity of John the Baptist (June 24) into Advent, where his birth is juxtaposed with that of his cousin, Jesus. Or transposing Clare of Assisi (August 11) to early October, where she offers counterpoise to the images of the more dominant Francis. The happy accidents that resulted often provoked new and fascinating insights into old texts and the stories of those remembered.

Those homilies have been distilled here. Their content is often more dense than the original, their focus foreshortened. But in every case, these meditations are meant to be a starting place, not a final word. The collection is keyed to *The Proper for the Lesser Feasts and Fasts* published in 1994 by The Church Hymnal Corporation (now Church Publishing). That publication contains a one-page biography or commentary for each person or event commemorated, along with the collect and the lectionary (scripture citations) for that day; the full text of the biblical readings is available in a separate book from the same publisher, but the citations allow the reader to use a favorite Bible or translation. In nearly every case where I have used a scriptural reference it has been given in parenthesis and conforms to one or more of the readings appointed for the occasion. An additional volume, *They Still Speak: Readings for the Lesser Feasts*, edited by J. Robert Wright and published by the Church Hymnal Corporation, provides readings by or about all the persons commemorated in the calendar of lesser feasts and fasts.

While this collection may be used alone and/or with a Bible, the additional resources will greatly enrich any devotion or meditation. I recommend reading the biography first, the collect and readings next, and ending with the meditation provided here. Those who pray twice daily might read the biography, collect, and readings in the morning, then return to the readings in the evening, followed by the meditation, and ending with the collect again. Try a variety until the right combination and sequence serves; spiritual discipline ought to be a help and not a burden to our lives.

Among the lower lights along my own shore, I acknowledge and thank Cynthia Shattuck and Vicki Black at Cowley Publications, whose friendship and encouragement inaugurated, sustained, and polished this project; my bishop and friend, Frank Griswold; my partner and keeper, Chris; and, lastly, those to whom this work is affectionately dedicated: the many members of the community at Brent House, the University of Chicago, and the Diocese of Chicago who share this ministry.

The
Lesser Feasts
and Fasts

Saint Andrew

Apostle   *November 30*

The Thanksgiving Day parades and games are over. I am inundated with catalogues and my resolve is breaking down. I ought to be resistant to this virulent opportunistic infection, but the techniques get more sophisticated every year. How shall I express affection and respect for those I love? The merchants have many suggestions. But the story of Andrew suggests another.

In the Christian narrative, Andrew lives in the shadow of an older brother, Simon Peter. But it was Andrew who excitedly dragged Peter through the streets to a house where Jesus was staying, declaring that he and his friends had found the Messiah. So Andrew was the one who brought Peter to Jesus, a fortuitous introduction, to say the least. Peter grew prominent even as younger Andrew faded into the background of the Christian story. But when Andrew does appear, his actions are consistent with this vignette of sibling relationship.

Some strangers came to two of the disciples, requesting that they be allowed to see Jesus. It was Andrew who took their request, and probably took the men to Jesus, as well. The two men were Greek and this quiet little act of mediation set the stage for a ministry that would move beyond the confines of Jesus' own Judaism to become an inclusive, embracing, expanding mission.

And later, overshadowed by miracle is the tiny detail that it was one of the disciples who found a small boy among thousands and brought that child with his fishes and loaves to Jesus. The disciple was Andrew, a disciple motivated to give others over to God. Andrew seems always to be bringing friends, relatives, and strangers to Jesus. Andrew suggests a different kind of gift-giving.

As Christians, we know the importance of having Christ in our lives and the evangelical task of bringing Christ to others. But is it not equally important that I be in Christ's life? That Christ may dwell in me is but half the picture, the other half being that I also might dwell in Christ. That is the beauty of the manner and mission of Andrew; bringing others to God, he paid each of them the highest honor and accorded them the greatest dignity. Can there be any higher compliment, any greater token of esteem and worth, than to be reckoned a fit gift for God? What more endearing and loving gesture can one make on behalf of another than to say, "You are worthy of presentation to God"? And what more pleasing offering could one make to God than the gift of lives reconciled and reunited with the Source of all life and love?

It is time to start making lists and checking them twice, worrying about what to get family and friends. Andrew numbered among his gifts a brother who became a giant of faith and the foundation of the church, some strangers from Greece whose encounter with Jesus revealed the gospel as a gift for all the world, and a small boy whose meager lunch became the food of a multitude. Andrew gave Christ, and life, to others simply by giving others to Christ. Who will we bring to the manger this year?

Nicholas Ferrar

Deacon, 1637   *December 1*

Nicholas Ferrar is credited with founding a religious community at Little Gidding consisting of Ferrar's own household and such friends as attached themselves to that household. In truth, Little Gidding was of God's making, not Ferrar's. What Ferrar did was call that community to be fully what God intended it to be, and in response they devoted themselves to spending time together, being family and friends, being community.

Some of that time they spent in prayer and fasting, some in celebration and teaching, some in helping and healing. Their uniqueness was not their devotion to religious observance; such devotion had long been the staple of monasticism and continued, if only a little less rigorously, in most pious households of their day. Their novelty was their devotion to a *common* life in an age when our present-day inheritance of individual freedom was emerging, on the eve of a century that would see revolution sweep the European and American landscapes. Their distinction was a commitment to living closely with one another, relying upon one another. They knew a family's unity.

Community disaster, death, and certain jubilations and joys are family affairs. Those burdens too great to be borne individually are shared, pains too intense to be endured alone find company, fun too good to keep to oneself ripples and redoubles as it washes over each person and unites us in laughter, and the fear of the unknown becomes adventure when we join hands and sally forth encouraged in companionship.

It is not values that give rise to family or community, but the other way around. Out of relationships our values are born. Faith begins not with prayer, nor with action, nor with idealism, but with the real, incarnate presence of others. Community begins by awakening to the families and the friends into whose company God has called us, those among whom and through whom God gives us life.

Soon we will embark upon the pilgrimage to the manger where, in Bethlehem's stable, we see the true image of family: gathered around that infant we find a woman who conceived not in marriage but betrothal; a father made by covenant, not coitus; shepherds reeking of earth led by angels clothed in light; wisdom and wealth come to pay homage alongside simplicity and poverty.

In Nicholas Ferrar and Little Gidding, as at the manger itself, we are reminded to look around at what God has given us, to look more closely at those with whom God has called us to share our lives, and to make ourselves at home.

Channing Moore Williams

Missionary Bishop in China and Japan, 1910   *December 2*

Any consideration of Channing Moore Williams would gravitate quite naturally to patience, a virtue the man must have possessed in vast quantities. Perhaps his upbringing in the rural South, acquainted with the slow process of agriculture and the formidable setbacks imposed by natural circumstance, fitted him for what was to become his ministry. But patience seems too light a word to describe Williams's profound surrender of control.

Offering himself for ordained ministry may not have seemed so great a sacrifice in Williams's time. To offer oneself for service in China, however, was to sign one's life over to the mercies of God in a strange culture. To labor as he labored and against such great odds with apparently so little result—seven years of hard work for a *single* convert—is nearly inconceivable today, yet that is precisely where the lesson lies.

Our need for control is painfully evident in modern mission and evangelism. If our efforts do not translate into more members, more pledge commitments, we count them a failure. Yet nowhere in scripture or Christian tradition do we find our love of numerical success extolled, much less practiced. When Jesus sent seventy evangelists, they were commissioned two by two, told to move modestly, take up residence in a single town, within a single household, and to eat what was set before them (Luke 10:1-9). They were to content themselves with the habits and practices of the culture, to surrender control and expose themselves to the risk of assimilation. They were to risk the possible loss of all they held sacred for the sake of preaching the gospel.

On another occasion, when the apostles were gathered with the risen Jesus, they asked, "Lord, is this the time when you will restore the kingdom to Israel?" (Acts 1:6). They are asking about control: Would they now be in control as a nation? Would their time of living as transients, subject to the hospitality or the hostility of strangers, now be over? Jesus refused to confirm that such control was likely, then told them that in any case there was no possibility of their knowing the time of its coming. Instead, they were told to live "out of control."

Channing Moore Williams made a career of surrendering control, of giving his all to God in China and Japan. He gave unstintingly, prodigally—and without thought of recompense. How could he have stood it otherwise? So far from home for so long, working day in and day out for seven years with only a single baptism to show for it! Today he would lose all funding and respect; our ancestors made him a bishop.

As long as we maintain control, what we offer is not really a gift. It is only a gift when we relinquish our hold, when we render the gospel without thought of gain or return, giving it wholly into the care of others. When we eat what others eat instead of packing our own lunch, listen to what they have to say instead of telling them what to do, settle in and live in the midst of them instead of demanding they pick up and move to where we are—only then do we begin to see how very near the dominion of God is to us, how close is the household of God's making.

John of Damascus

Priest, c. 760   *December 4*

John of Damascus, a priest who lived in the eighth century, found himself in the midst of the iconoclastic controversy, a dispute over the proper place of images or icons in religion. It seems amusing at best, and petty and inconsequential at worst, that learned people could work up an intellectual sweat over such things. But what may now seem a waste of time was, in fact, an exercise of considerable wisdom.

In John's day careful attention was paid to details because they understood that small things can tell much about larger things. Behind a little thing—like the role of artistic images in church—is a whole set of assumptions and presumptions about God and about humanity. A small symptom can sometimes indicate the presence of a disease: in the case of the iconoclastic controversy, John of Damascus helped expose and rout the dangerous assumptions behind taking offense at images and icons.

One argument found images and icons offensive because they attempted to render the wholly divine nature of Christ in material substances. Another went further and found all material itself evil; any material representation of the physical body of Jesus was thus doubly offensive, since both the medium and its subject were odious to them. John saw in such arguments a fundamental denial of the Incarnation, for any denial of the humanness of Jesus or the sanctity of matter itself challenges the tangible benediction upon the world manifested in the person of Jesus.

Christianity has long fought but not yet won this battle. Denial of the Incarnation is often confined to subtle expressions as innocuous as attitudes over the place of art in church. Inattention to the little things leads to the gradual loss of the larger ones. Eventually we wonder why our tent is filled with proverbial camels, forgetting that once we allow the nose of the animal through the tent flap the rest of the beast is bound to follow.

John of Damascus prevailed and icons were allowed in worship. But we do not remember John of Damascus for his patronage of art; we venerate his memory for his insistent demand that we examine details for the premises behind them—an important consideration in this season, at the center of which is a baby, a teenaged mother, and an aging working-class father.

Within those details we glimpse the divine presumption. No broad gesture or display of power, no bold statement reveals God, only the manger. In the inconsequential birth of an insignificant child, in an inconspicuous place surrounded by the innocuous and ingenuous, the ineffable was incarnate. In the smallest was revealed the greatest, and nothing would ever be the same.

Clement of Alexandria

Priest, c. 210 *December 5*

Sitting in the synagogue at Capernaum, John's gospel tells us, Jesus struggled to express the meaning of his life. Drawing upon analogy and metaphor, he spoke to his disciples and followers of the manna in the wilderness, the "bread that comes down from heaven" (6:50). His life, he told them, was that bread. They murmured, dissatisfied and angry. "This is too much," they complained. "Are we to stomach this?" And scripture says that from that time many of his disciples drifted away from him (John 6:66).

At first glance it would seem that Jesus was unnecessarily complicating his gospel. The image of bread from heaven is very poetic, but does it really tell us anything? How are we to understand what he meant? Like all poetry, much is left to the imagination and each of us must work our own minds to make meaning of it. Images draw us out of ourselves, where we can meet Jesus in the midst of every parable, every metaphor and analogy. We cannot remain detached from his words and find understanding. This kind of communication invites us into communion, and in that communion we find meaning.

Clement of Alexandria shared a common consternation with the author of John's gospel. Their nemesis was the rising phenomenon of gnosticism, which posited—among other things—that salvation was attainable through secret and esoteric knowledge. Salvation was, therefore, reserved for an erudite few who could control the dispensation of that knowledge and its graces. Gnostics believed there was a single right interpretation and understanding, a clear way, and those who puzzled it out and possessed it held the power to include or exclude others from participation in the life of God. In their eyes Clement was too liberal, for he welcomed into the Christian dialogue the full realm of secular knowledge.

In the exchange between Jesus and his disgruntled followers we see the parting of the literal from the liberal, and the literal are left wanting. To their grumblings about his images of bread and flesh and blood Jesus replied, "Does this offend you? Then what if you were to see the Son of Man ascending to where he was before?" (John 6:61-62). In other words, "Does it shock you that I use metaphorical imagery? Must you actually see the literal reality? Have you no powers of imagination?" In other discourses he tersely summed up his chastisement with "How dull you are!" and likened that dullness to lack of faith.

Clement believed that ignorance and error are the fundamental human sins; because Adam and Eve could not imagine God, they sought to be God. Because they could not imagine, they sought to imitate, setting the stage for the human drama. "It is the spirit that gives life," said Jesus. "The flesh is useless" (6:63). It is not by the literal, but within the intuitive and imaginative that we find communion with God and one another.

Can we see within the manger the image of a God so tender and vulnerable as to be like an infant? Can we find the fullness of heart and the openness of mind to step into the poetry, enter the ambiguity, move within the spirit, and there find the reality of God? Could we but see within that infant Jesus the parable of God, we might meet in the imagination of our hearts, arriving at the manger to find a child who is one of our own, the better to see within all that is human and vulnerable that which is truly divine.

Nicholas

Bishop of Myra, c. 342 *December 6*

No one seems to know much of certainty about Nicholas. He was Bishop of Myra in the fourth century; beyond that meager fact most everything else is speculation or outright fabrication. Be that as it may, Nicholas became the patron both of sailors and seafarers and of children, eventually finding his way to America via those early Dutch pioneers who disembarked on these shores to begin a new life.

How is it that this obscure saint known for his generosity and giving of gifts is charged with watching over both sailors and toddlers? What could possibly be more different than those who go down to the sea in ships (a ribald and randy bunch to be sure) and those fresh-faced innocents who scramble upon Santa's knee? Perhaps their common connection is to be found in the helplessness they share.

Anyone who has ever spent any time in, on, or around great bodies of water will attest to their incredible power. To place oneself upon the ocean in even the largest vessel is to be at the mercy of one of the most savage elements on the planet. Can it be any wonder that those who had survived the crossing of an ocean to the awesome strangeness of a new world filled with unknowns might pray with fervent sincerity to a patron who remains even to this day the personification of benevolence? They knew that surrender of control lies at the heart of human life.

This is what it means to be human, to live upon the earth, to be a creature whose life is bounded by mysteries of birth and death, powers over which we have no real authority and only the illusion of control. In the midst of this reality we better understand the melancholy shadow of this Advent season, the unsettling uneasiness that accompanies every joy and the bittersweet pain within every pleasure. Within this reality we glimpse the profundity of a gospel that proclaims God's love in the gift of a son, and more particularly, an infant.

In Mark's gospel we are told that people—probably most of them women—brought little children to Jesus to be blessed (Mark 10:13-16). Children were brought to the adult because they were powerless to come themselves. The power-brokers—the disciples—rebuked the women and children until Jesus saw what they were doing and swept away their restrictions, even as the tide destroys the most intricate sand castle or pulls down the most impressive building. In a moment the current changed and the children were in his arms, safe and happy.

We are children always, for no matter our strength, we are forever at the mercy of powers beyond us. We are seafarers and sailors, traversing a powerful sea. And in this season we worship this truth of who we are, as we worship a child born of woman even as we are, this Jesus who set sail upon our sea. We celebrate Jesus surrounded by images of Nicholas.

Only one thing more is known: that Nicholas was tortured and imprisoned during the persecution of Christians under the emperor Diocletian. Thus Nicholas represents the fullness of benevolence to the most vulnerable human creatures amidst the cruelest and most unpredictable of worlds. He represents gifts and goodness in the midst of powerful uncertainty, the very icon of God to a modern world. As Santa Claus he has the power to transform us for a brief time each year, helping us acknowledge that the vulnerability we share is a blessing that opens our hearts to know the fullness of Love, who dares to be born of us, to live among us, to die with us, that we might know the ultimate gift of eternal life.

Ambrose

Bishop of Milan, 397   *December 7*

Judgment is a prominent theme in Christianity; fear of God's judgment is believed by some a motivation to more holy living, more loving devotion. Unfortunately, there is little evidence that fear motivates anything except death or destruction. Fear of incarceration or even death, long thought to deter crime, is challenged by criminal recidivism. Moreover, it is the fearful animal—human or otherwise—who is most inclined to attack and bite. Fear can provoke paralysis and death of another kind.

When fear overtakes the soldier, agility and clear reasoning are sacrificed, and so is the soldier. When fear seizes the nervous system it can ravage and destroy the mind, inducing paranoia or severe depression. When fear strikes with the force of shock, it can kill. There is little within fear itself to lead us to closer relationship with God. How, then, are we to interpret the seasonal admonition to be alert and waiting, always watchful for the day of God's appearing (Luke 12:35–37)?

In one moment Ambrose was a layman arbitrating a dispute between warring Christians and in the next he found himself elected their bishop. Devoted to his job as governor of upper Italy, Ambrose was following in the footsteps of his father, who had been governor of Gaul. A dispute between Arians and rival Christians over the election of a bishop demanded mediation. So fair and effective was Ambrose that, even though he had never been baptized, the people proclaimed him bishop on the spot. His love of his neighbors distinguished him, called him to the attention of the people, and commended him as their leader. He went on to serve well, using love instead of fear to meet the many challenges of a difficult time and a fractious community.

In his life and ministrations, Ambrose evidenced a profound understanding of the Incarnation. He understood that a God who wanted to be feared would never have been born into the world as a helpless child; such vulnerability engenders not fear but care, and love. Babies usually bring out the very best in us. The helplessness and tenderness of Tiny Tim ultimately moved the heart of Scrooge to relent from his meanness. The vulnerability of a baby—in the case of Jesus, a vulnerability emphasized by the contrast with the harsh political context and crude surroundings of his birth—moves us to want to embrace and protect. As one author, writing centuries before Jesus, expressed it, "Let us fall into the hands of the Lord, but not into the hands of mortals; for equal to his majesty is his mercy" (Ecclesiasticus 2:17).

The judgment of God is evidenced in the hands of a child, hands that reach out and hold without distinction. The majesty and the mercy of God is the manger; in the infant Jesus we see that judgment may be *for* even as judgment may be *against*. God has made a judgment in choosing us, in choosing to be one of us. Ambrose lived, loved, and proclaimed this positive judgment of God upon the human race, judgment written in an infant's face.

Saint Thomas

Apostle   *December 21*

Often remembered as a simple man whose insistence upon tangible proof of the resurrection made him rather literal-minded, Thomas is not always seen as a model character. Still, when Jesus proposed a trip to Bethany to be with his friends, even after he had been banished from the Jerusalem area on threat of stoning, it was Thomas who revealed a depth of affection for Jesus—and courage. He insisted that all the disciples go, too, "that we may die with him" (John 11:16). At table with Jesus for the last supper, Thomas listened as Jesus predicted his death and resurrection, and told them he would go and prepare a place for them. Then he responded with candor and a reasonable question: "Lord, we do not know where you are going. How can we know the way?" (John 14:5). And after the resurrection, it was Thomas who refused easily to accept the accounts of the others. In his earthy pragmatism he held out for a personal encounter with the risen Jesus—and his persistence was amply rewarded (John 20:24-29).

Take the Bethany business. Jesus had been threatened with death if he should return to the region; he had left an angry mob of dissatisfied people behind him there. Thomas is downright savvy; it would be much harder for a mob to rise up against a group of them than to ambush a solitary Jesus. Thomas's suggestion that they go with Jesus in order that they might die with him seems as much a challenge to the others' faith as it is a chilling prediction of their eventual martyrdom.

Thomas's remark at the last supper comes in the midst of a very confusing and convoluted discourse between Jesus and his disciples about the events they would encounter soon afterward, in Gethsemane and beyond. Using heavily veiled references and highly symbolic language, Jesus waxes eloquent about going away, coming again, and houses of many rooms. The interjection from Thomas seems a bold challenge to obscurity, placing Thomas in a long line of those whose primary ministry has been to call us back to clear and simple truth.

Finally, there is the incredulity with which Thomas greets news of Jesus' resurrection. Remember that Thomas was in the midst of a community in total disarray, hiding in fear and riddled with rumors made from some eyewitness accounts and the inevitable embroidery attached to them. Holding fast to his skepticism, Thomas demands what would become the cornerstone of all Christian faith—a personal experience of the resurrected Jesus. For his pains, he is rewarded. Jesus grants his request, for he has asked the right question, demanded the right thing.

Christianity is a shared, communal religion and a corporate faith, but at the heart of this faith and tradition is a personal encounter with the risen Lord. Christian faith is based not upon scriptural or traditional witness alone, important as they are. Reason also plays its part, and reason demands the personal experience of Jesus. Only after that personal meeting does Thomas declare the definitive lordship of Jesus, for it is not until that personal experience that such a claim can be made.

Thomas the pragmatist reminds us that our life as Christians and as the church has ultimately to be practical, pragmatic, practicable—all have their origin in the same root, which means literally, "do-able." Faith is not an idea; it is do-able, because it is based on a living relationship with a living God, a relationship manifested in a living person named Jesus. Faith is shared and transmitted not as an ideal or argument, but as a living relationship with God manifested in what we are, what we say, what we do, what we practice. Call that simplicity if you will, but count it as the profundity it is, and give Thomas his due.

The Nativity of Our Lord

December 25

We are once again at the manger, making a big, symbolic fuss over someone else's baby. But what do we see when we gaze upon this child, Jesus? To some, Jesus is of the past, a great historical figure whose life revolutionized art, music, architecture—and merchandising. Advocate of a humanistic philosophy, he lives in the past, in a time of dusty camels and no plumbing; in a world peopled with crotchety old saints, pious peasants, religious academicians, and zealous monks singing Gregorian chant in great Byzantine and Gothic cathedrals redolent with incense. Or he lives in the world of grandparents and great-grandparents who read the Bible and quoted it freely, in recollections of childhood years when every day ended with "Now I lay me down to sleep...."

To others, Jesus is of the future. He is a dim, shadowy figure who will comfort us in death; a grand and glorious soldier who will avenge injustice. He lives in a future when Arabs will be at peace with Israelis and Serbs will love Croats. He lives in a future when all will share the abundance we know in this land, and life's mysteries will be open to benefit every race. He lives in a utopian future of perfect political systems and just economies.

To those of his own time—Jews and Romans alike—as to still others today, Jesus was just another baby, nothing very special at all. Concerned with things past and things future, the babe in their midst was of little consequence. Preoccupied with what used to be, obsessed with what might yet be, they and we fail to see and savor what simply *is*.

Those who lingered around the manger in Bethlehem knew somehow that God was present, that a powerful reconciliation was beginning, a gap bridged between what has been and is yet to be. Come to the manger again today, hold the baby in mind and heart, and realize once again that God is with us.

Saint Stephen

Deacon and Martyr December 26

It is ironic that we should clothe this season in nostalgia and sentiment, the antidotes to change and the signs of our resistance to life's challenges. The manger accommodates our romance; the powerful days that follow bring us back with a terrifying jolt to the import of what we celebrate at Bethlehem. The romantic relief of the nativity only prepares us for the breathtaking descent into Stephen's death.

"We have heard him say that this Jesus of Nazareth will destroy this place and will change the customs that Moses handed on to us," witnesses declared against Stephen (Acts 6:14). That was the charge brought against him, but that was not why they stoned him. Those were the trumped-up charges put forward to buttress the case of the Cyrenians, Alexandrians, Cilicians, and Asians whose anger against Stephen prompted this furor.

Answering his accusers, Stephen unmasked their ruse and unleashed their anger. After rehearsing the history of God's people, Stephen concluded, "You stiff-necked people, uncircumcised in heart and ears, you are forever opposing the Holy Spirit, just as your ancestors used to do" (Acts 7:51). They fulfilled Stephen's testimony even as he spoke. Yet it was not Stephen they stoned, but Truth itself. Stephen, like Jesus before him, did not take the stones personally; he was only a surrogate for God, the real target of the mob's anger.

This is the darker side of Christmas. The coming of the Light into the world in the birth of Jesus at Bethlehem is always challenged by those who prefer to remain as they are, the turning of time into a new year is resisted by those who do not want to let go of the old. Stephen's martyrdom indicates how ill-prepared we are for the answering of our prayers for justice, how poorly we accept the coming of God's truth. Behind the shabby charges of Stephen's sedition against tradition, perversion of custom, and disloyalty to the sacred memory of Moses lay the naked reality that those who brought the charges would rather murder the messenger than accept the message.

The challenge is no less for us. We are asked to confront the truth that the customs we honor and the traditions we maintain can harbor and hallow human sin. Custom and tradition have their dark side, especially when they excuse our evil and impede God's justice. It is justice, not tradition, that determines the shape of our lives. That was the message of the child in the manger and the faithful deacon struck down in his youth.

In a season glazed with sweetness and almost sickeningly rich in tradition, in sacred and social ritual, the martyrdom of Stephen is a timely reminder of the sin of custom. It is a reminder that our traditional response to truth and justice is neither reverent nor tender, but angry and violent, that few traditions are so old or established as our traditional sinfulness.

The romance of the manger only momentarily distracts us from the truth that the very veneration of tradition itself eventually led to the trial and death of this infant whose message was justice, that tradition itself was called as witness against him. An all-too-common human violence stoned Stephen; there is no tradition so old as our deadliness. Kneeling before the answer to our prayers cradled in the manger, remember that his last prayer—and his deacon's—was the prayer that we be forgiven, forgiven our tradition.

Saint John

Apostle and Evangelist   *December 27*

The interplay of darkness and light in the opening paragraphs of the first epistle of John takes on a new character in this Information Age. To be in the dark these days means not that we sit in an unlighted cavern plotting evil, nor that we skulk in the shades of night doing mischief. To be "in the dark" is simply not to know. It is tempting to cultivate a willful ignorance, to go with the flow and let the tide carry us. So we drift easily into conformity, letting popular opinion, or its manipulators, decide for us.

It happens in the church, too. We may go through the motions of baptism and marriage and communion with no real appreciation of the serious and substantial consequences of what, to some, are little more than social conventions. There is a bliss in ignorance, a bliss all the sweeter when cloaked in the guise of innocence. Tomorrow we commemorate the slaughter of the innocents; today we confront the death of human innocence. And a violent death it is.

The penetrating light of the glory of God's presence is so scorching as to be fatal: "You cannot see my face," the LORD says to Moses, "for no one shall see me and live" (Exodus 33:20). It was not out of vainglory but compassion that God would not be revealed to Moses. Similarly, in the visible presence of Jesus we welcome the fullness of God's truth, but we cannot see the fullness of that light and live. To come within that light is to invite a death—the death of our cherished ignorance and the violent martyrdom of our beloved innocence. To walk in the light is to share a common life, to open our lives to the scrutiny of community, to surrender the comfort of social conformity: "If we walk in the light as he himself is in the light, we have fellowship with one another" (1 John 1:7). Nowhere is that quite so clear as in the closing paragraphs of John's gospel, paragraphs that bring into focus the strange, and strained, relationship between two communities of early Christians, those who followed Peter and those who followed John, personified in the story as their namesakes.

Peter has just been called to discipleship for the second time in his life. It is after the resurrection and Jesus has shared breakfast with the disciples. Echoing the passiontide denials that marked Peter's lowest ebb, Jesus asks Peter three times, "Do you love me?" and thrice Peter replies, "Lord, you know that I love you." "Feed my sheep," says Jesus, concluding with the clear command, "Follow me" (John 21:15-19).

The narrative continues, "Peter turned and saw the disciple whom Jesus loved following them. . . . When Peter saw him, he said to Jesus, 'Lord, what about him?'" Jesus gives a most enigmatic response, the best summation of which is probably, "What's it to you?" (John 21:20-23). And the gospel ends.

Even though it be at Peter's expense, the episode is the Johannine last word—a reminder that to follow Jesus is to come away from cozy conformity, and even comforting companionship, accepting responsibility for a personal conviction. Peter responds to Jesus' invitation with a look over his shoulder and the question, "Uh, what about him?" And Jesus says, "Never mind about him. It is you I am calling."

The coming of Jesus into our lives challenges us; in the light of the manger we stand exposed. The particularity of that birth drives home to us our own particularity. In the light of the manger we stand alone, bearing the burden of personal responsibility, pinned to the cross of our own particularity where we are savaged and ravaged by truth. We suffer the death of innocence to be born anew to God's truth, a violent and painful cleaving from the comforting refuge of conformity's anonymity—and entrance to life in and with a God who takes us personally.

The Holy Innocents

The martyrdom of the Holy Innocents completes a trilogy of post-Christmas observances. Our ancestors are to be commended for their unflinching juxtaposition of this story with the feast of Jesus' nativity. It is hard to think of the grim murder of children so close to the manger. The tragedy of this story is that it continues unchanged, that even as the redemptive act of God in Jesus lives, so too does our deep need of that redemption.

An adult Jesus told those who would follow him that they were to receive the gospel and dominion of God as a child (Mark 10:15). One reading of that directive suggests that we are to receive God with the childlike perception of innocent childhood. But within the circle of the manger there is another, more literal, possibility. Might Jesus have also meant that we are to receive God in the shape and person of the child?

That God chose to be revealed in the birth of an infant in Bethlehem is the miracle and the mystery of the Incarnation. But for reasons we shall never fathom, the *childhood* of Jesus—which may have been of surpassing importance to us—is lost. We hear from many pulpits, even on Christmas itself, sermons that hastily yank us from the manger to the cross, as though to remind us that, of course, it was the *adult* Jesus who accomplished our deliverance.

Yet God chose to come to us in innocence, in openness, and in the very incarnation of possibility. An infant—any infant—may remind us of past passion and of present tenderness, but the overwhelming sensation engendered by a baby is the fearsome mystery of possibility in a future that is yet unseen. How shall this baby grow, and into what kind of person? What shape will this incarnate future take, and how shall I be equal to the responsibility of that maturation?

We are not comfortable with mystery, yet despite our attempts to eliminate God from our lives, we have never fully succeeded in killing off the reality of God's possibility. It is relatively easy to distance ourselves from past notions of God. It is also increasingly easy in our independence to move through this life without reliance upon or acknowledgment of a God present to our experience. But in the dim recesses of a future we cannot control, God lives—like a child in a manger. And neither we, nor Herod, can live with that. We want no part of that which we cannot control. We are uncomfortable with the notion of the infant God, the gift of

God in the infant. Herod simply stands in for us in this instance and acts our part. It is telling that in the United States we possess a neglected educational system in the midst of an intelligent culture and an appalling rate of infant mortality in a land of unparalleled economic and medical advantage. Something within us despises the child, despite our every protestation to the contrary.

Our wars take no heed of children, for wars are not concerned with the future but the present. For the sake of his own power, Herod slaughtered Bethlehem's future. For the sake of present pride and comfort, we wager whole generations. We look back in wonderment at Herod and ask how it could have happened.

Thomas Becket
Archbishop of Canterbury, 1170   *December 29*

Thomas Becket is easily the most romantic figure of Anglican martyrdom. His story, dramatized in T. S. Eliot's *Murder in the Cathedral*, is the tale of a man whose friendship with a young prince led to high office in state and church. As Chancellor of England under King Henry II, Thomas complied with the will of his royal friend, and was rewarded with the see of Canterbury. As archbishop, however, Thomas proved less amenable to Henry's demands, and when the tension between them over matters of taxation reached a white-hot pitch Thomas fled to France to escape punishment.

Exile only increased Thomas's popularity. He returned as a public figure and the object of rivalry with the king himself. In a moment of passionate rage, Henry voiced a heartfelt desire to be rid of this friend who had so betrayed him. Four of the king's knights who heard him, eager to please their king and win their own place in his affections, rushed to assassinate Thomas, murdering him in his cathedral on the afternoon of December 29 in the year 1170. His death unleashed an outpouring of popular veneration of Thomas and anger directed at the king.

Henry was justified in his frustration with Thomas, for prior to his appointment to the see of Canterbury Thomas had offered little evidence of piety or integrity. He had played the king's friend convincingly and had certainly given Henry reason to trust in his loyalty. Even if his religious convictions were sincere, he had for too long shared the king's intimacy to make his conversion seem anything but stubborn obstructionism. Once ordained, Thomas used the power of his office to strike back at Henry, even threatening to place the realm under interdict—the equivalent of excommunicating the entire nation. Each man was stubborn and willful, and each was powerful, playing out a drama of mammoth proportions.

The story of Henry and Thomas, when stripped of its pageantry and romance, reminds us that each and every one of us shares the central flaw of pride. Our faith reminds us that every facet of our lives is touched by imperfection in a creation that has fallen short of God's intention for it. Even our best intentions seem to go astray and land us in places of profound pain.

The friendship of Henry and Thomas was of epic proportion, as were their anger, their contention, and the sad end of their argument. So also was their forgetting, for each seems to have paid insufficient heed to the power of sin, and their own susceptibility to its corrosion. In a recent *New Yorker* Edward Conlon, reflecting upon contemporary abuse of power and the paradoxical "mutation of heroism into the basest brutality," observed, "Belief in one's own exceptionalism may be a cultural cliche, but it is also the manual for tragedy." We are given their story, as every heroic tragedy, not that we might worship or revere either man, for each in his own way was culpable, but that we might discern their tragic flaw in ourselves, and learn from them.

The Holy Name of Our Lord

January 1

There is something subtly humorous in the reading from Exodus about the image of Moses standing at the entrance of the tent of meeting, addressing the mysterious pillar of cloud, his hands empty, the tablets of the Decalogue in pieces. God explains patiently that if Moses will come back to the top of Sinai with fresh tablets, he can have a duplicate of the original. Having lost his temper and destroyed the first tablets, Moses is given a second chance.

On the mountain, God—whom we might expect to be angry over the broken tablets and annoyed at having to write them all over again—takes Moses back to the beginning. There, says the story, God came and stood beside Moses and pronounced the name YHWH. Then, in very patient tones, like the exemplary teacher laboriously toiling over the dull student, God spells out the meaning of that name:

> The LORD, the LORD, a God merciful and gracious, slow to anger, and abounding
> in steadfast love and faithfulness, keeping steadfast love for the thousandth

generation, forgiving iniquity and transgression and sin, yet by no means clearing the guilty, but visiting the iniquity of the parents upon the children and the children's children, to the third and the fourth generation. (Exodus 34:6-7)

Because that last phrase is not entirely consistent with the ones before it, one wonders if Moses added that little embellishment for the edification of the shamefaced Israelites who, considering the celebrations of the previous night, should have been nursing one doozey of a hangover.

In Luke's recounting of the shepherds' visit to the manger we see a repetition of this naming, this time in Bethlehem. By the time of the birth of the child, the name of the LORD, while still a powerful force in the life of the people, had lost the compassionate tenderness so beautifully articulated in that scene with Moses. In the midst of an outbuilding, in the company of simple animals and slow-witted humans, the patient explanation begins again. Often portrayed by dramatic artists as rather stupid figures, even from the times of the earliest morality plays, the shepherds are the comic relief of the story of the Incarnation.

They are of simple means and childlike minds, led by the voice of angels to see the child long before the wise ever appear on the scene. What they find is only a baby, a child whom the angels name Jesus, or more accurately, *Yeshua*—Joshua in Hebrew—a word meaning "The Lord is salvation." It is as though God, standing beside them even as God stood with Moses, begins again the patient explanation of who God is: a God as compassionate and gracious as the child who receives all without distinction, as long-suffering as the child who spends hours at a simple task without boredom, as constant and true as the child whose affections are fiercely loyal even against reason, as forgiving as the child whose memory swiftly erases hurts far greater than the petty indignities begrudged by adults.

This is an excellent beginning for a new year, to ponder the name of God and learn again what it means; to begin anew, tablets fresh and clean, in the company and in the name of God.

The Epiphany of Our Lord

January 6

The magi may not have been what we have thought them to be. The number of the magi, now accepted as three, is logical conjecture, based upon the number of gifts recorded in Matthew's gospel, but there is no specific number in the text. Is it not possible that there were only two magi and that one brought an extra offering? Or might there have been more—say, six—all of whom pitched in to pay for the three gifts? We cannot even be sure that they were kings; the term *magus* was often a contemptuous name for itinerant magicians and entertainers.

I rather like the notion that the magi might have been traveling entertainers, members of a class commonly accepted as fools in every sense of that word. Of course, such a possibility radically alters the asymmetry of the creche, where the exotically adorned kings clearly upstage everyone, including the winsome animals and the Holy Family itself. In that regard, the magi are the most modern of all our religious symbols, sympathetic icons of power and wealth that draw more attention than a child born in poverty, more attention even than God.

There is something right about a troupe of wandering artists whose whim to follow a star brings them to the cradle of Jesus. That might explain their unthinking stupidity at dropping in on Herod, asking the whereabouts of his local rival. Surely a genuinely learned person of the period would have known enough of local politics and human nature to surmise that no one in Herod's position was going to countenance a second king within his own borders. That they may have been itinerant entertainers is also a likely explanation of their later mistrust of Herod and their ability to slip out of his territory quickly and without incident, even as they probably skipped town on other occasions when the heat was on.

But above all else, the possibility that the magi were really pretty simple people fully accords with Paul's notion in Ephesians that God's revelation is a truth often hidden from the learned and the wise, only to be revealed most fully to the simple. There is then no reason why Matthew or any other gospeler would have had cause to call these people kings; had they been kings, would not those who recorded the story have surely marked that detail with some pride?

Yet, we want the story the way tradition gives it to us. As it stands, the story suggests that the rich and powerful, the learned and the astute are the first to recognize and name the infant Jesus a king. This validation accords with our own belief that superior intellect and study produces insight, that truth is suspect until it is acknowledged by power and wealth. That's the way it's supposed to be, not only at the manger but in life.

What is more difficult—and hence more exotic, mysterious, and wonderful—is the possibility that some simple and foolish people, drawn to the side of the manger, might surrender everything to the unknown child therein. How these travelers came by their gifts, we cannot know. But is it so strange that entertainers and magicians should possess gold, frankincense, and myrrh? If we lavish material wealth on their modern counterparts, is it not conceivable that they might have come by those gifts in the course of their travels, as recompense for their own talents to amuse?

There is only one thing about this story that we can hold with any certainty: whoever these people were and wherever they were from, they were henceforth called "wise." Their wisdom was not necessarily the precondition of their visitation, but it was certainly the one gift they took with them from that stable.

Wisdom, then, is not the prerequisite to relationship with Jesus, but the product of knowing the Lord. Those who encounter God come away with more, and better, than what they bring. And is this not always the case in every relationship? If we ever come to know wisdom in our relationships, are we not always wiser on the way home?

Julia Chester Emery

Missionary, 1922 *January 9*

Julia Chester Emery is not the kind of person one expects to meet in a calendar of religious commemorations, in part because of the nature of her accomplishments. Her story does not involve extraordinary feats of courage, neither was she tortured or executed for reason of her faith. She was only twenty-four years old when she assumed the only ecclesiastical post she would ever hold, secretary of the Woman's Auxiliary of the Episcopal Church. In that office Julia Emery served for forty years, a faithful lay woman.

By the time Julia Emery left her post in 1916, she had helped organize branches of the Woman's Auxiliary in nearly two-thirds of the eighty-five hundred parishes of the Episcopal Church. Moreover, the Auxiliary itself dispensed many dollars in financial aid to missions and raised the awareness of the larger church to the important work of outreach.

Today only a handful of foreign missionaries remain in service, their work frequently overlooked. When we do think of mission, at home or abroad, our knowledge is often out of date and our preconceptions erroneous. Julia Emery reminds us that the most difficult and demanding work of mission is the most mundane, the work of administration and education. Increasingly, missionary work involves not exotic travel or rare courage; far less does it involve a zeal for conversion to one's own ideals or methods. Instead, modern mission demands just those qualities Julia Emery devoted to service—gifts for educating, organizing, and administering.

We remember Julia Emery for raising funds, organizing volunteers, administering institutions, and educating lay members of the church. Apparently, her only training for this ministry was a willingness to try it, for she possessed no special education or preparation. Her only authority was collegial, for being a lay woman, she had neither the office nor the perquisites of ordained status to buttress her leadership.

Julia Emery reminds us that we all possess the resources we need to be effective missionaries, except perhaps the two most important qualities exemplified in her—a willingness to try and the commitment to stick with it, even for a lifetime.

William Laud
Archbishop of Canterbury, 1645 *January 10*

How are we to commemorate one of the key figures in the terrible works of the Star Chamber—that instrument of torture employed in the name of religion—in the season of the Star of Bethlehem, the guiding light of God's Epiphany? What are we to think of William Laud, religious advisor to Charles I, whose attitudes toward the practice of religion cost him and his monarch their heads?

> Do not think that I have come to bring peace to the earth; I have not come to bring peace, but a sword. For I have come to set a man against his father, and a daughter against her mother, and a daughter-in-law against her mother-in-law; and one's foes will be members of one's own household. (Matthew 10:34-36)

In that difficult saying Jesus addresses what many of us know to be natural enmities: father and son, mother and daughter, in-law and in-law. The common element uniting these tensions is that each is an enmity rooted in divergent expectations. The familiarity that breeds the hottest contempt is the familiar (or familial) relationship that surprises us by doing or being something suddenly unfamiliar.

The failure of the daughter-in-law to be like the mother-in-law (or the son-in-law like the father-in-law) breeds the embittered opinion that one's child has picked a loser. And whether it be within our family of origin, the family of our baptismal birth called the church, or that generic family named the human race, we are ill-prepared and ill-tempered when confronted by those who diverge from our expectations. Some of our worst tantrums can be attributed to our anger at being unpleasantly surprised, our anger at being crossed by someone whose individuality conflicts with our own.

The discipline exacted upon the child, says the author of the letter to the Hebrews, is to endure the trials of such challenges and to learn how to balance one's own self with and within larger communities of equally independent selves. Indeed, the struggle to reconcile our differences, to take such surprises in stride, is the sign of our legitimacy as God's children. Matthew rightly likens the struggle to that of bearing a cross. It is a hard discipline to learn and to practice.

Like most of us, William Laud had both his good points and his bad ones. Suffice it to say that he—like us—was very complex. The true measure of his commemoration may simply be in what it says of our community and in what it suggests we should be. For despite the reality that there is within William Laud something to offend everyone, he is included and revered as one of our own. Surprise is a demanding disciplinarian. The only surprise greater than finding him among those worthy of remembrance is what finding him here suggests of the other disagreeable people I meet each day, and of the disagreeable person I myself can be.

Aelred

Abbot of Rievaulx, 1167　　　　　　　　　　　　　　　　　　*January 12*

Aelred grew up in the royal court of Scotland and knew the joy of intimate friendship with the children of the king's household. Years later, his friendship with Bernard of Clairvaux shaped his ministry and encouraged him to found a Cistercian community marked by a profound emphasis upon friendship.

Friendship is a form of love that seems antiquated and even suspect today, all but subsumed by the inflationary use of that word in our daily vocabulary. Just as one can profess love for anything and everyone, loving one's wristwatch and brand of laundry detergent with a fervor equal to love of one's spouse or even of God, so now we can call anyone "friend." Not only does this debase our notion of true friendship, it also impoverishes our theology. For at the heart of the Christian tradition lies a deep and abiding respect for friendship. To be a Christian was, and still is, to be a friend of Jesus and, consequently, to be a friend of God.

The importance of the word "friendship," then, is that it is a profound expression of the relationship of choice. For while we confess in our creeds that we are the handiwork of a single Creator, and thus children of the one God, such bonds do not exhaust the limits of relatedness. Families related by blood can be fractured by disrespect and void of any but the most vicious affections. To say we are children of the same parent does not say it all; it is equally important that parents choose to love their children and that children choose to love their parents. We occasionally see families that are more than family—they are friends. Indeed, families are made of the union of friends of different blood who choose to love one another. This is the basis of marriage and committed partnerships.

Friendship is more, however, than mutual affection; it is also an arena of growth. In Luke's gospel Jesus offers insights into the nature of true friendship in three strange exchanges with others. To the person who offers to follow Jesus wherever he goes, Jesus replies, "Foxes have holes, and birds of the air have nests; but the Son of Man has nowhere to lay his head" (9:58). Could it be that Jesus was saying to this person that while he was free to follow, he could not expect to find security, or a home, in that following—that such was an unrealistic expectation of friendship?

To another Jesus said, "Follow me," but heard in reply a request for time to bury a father. Jesus replies somewhat harshly, "Let the dead bury their own dead; but as for you, go and proclaim the kingdom of God" (9:60). Did Jesus see in this person a slavish devotion to duty, a soul-numbing attachment to obligation? Is he suggesting that devotion to duty may be used as an excuse to avoid the consequences of friendship? Is Jesus' command to "go and proclaim" a penance aimed at directing the dutiful recluse outward, a challenge to embrace life with purpose and in service to others?

To the one who asks leave to say farewell to those at home, Jesus seems particularly harsh: "No one who puts a hand to the plow and looks back is fit for the kingdom of God" (9:62). If we are concerned with saying good-bye to what we have left behind, we cannot be fully present to what is at hand.

In each case, Jesus was truly a friend, even though he was not particularly warm. In each case, Jesus loved the others too much to leave them where they were; he loved them enough to challenge them to larger life. True love and genuine friendship demand more than uncritical affirmation; I love my friends not only because they affirm me but also because they encourage me to be more. In contemplating the mysteries of human affection Aelred wrote of four qualities that characterize friendship: loyalty, right intention, discretion, and patience. Perhaps he pondered these qualities in the light of these three who came to Jesus as strangers and departed as friends.

Hilary

Bishop of Poitiers, 367   *January 13*

There are few experiences in life as painful as betrayal. Who has not known the pain of a broken heart, when the one who has claimed our most intimate friendship denies us in public? No apology can assuage the hurt and no explanation can soften it. There can be no secret friendship. Friendship is joyful, and joy is to be shared. Yet the belief persists that one can be a secret friend of God.

Many of us believe ourselves to be religious, even faithful, people; we say so in our creeds. Yet, despite this profession at worship, some of us take no active part in the ongoing life and relationships of the church. Others of us maintain an active affiliation with a congregation and faithfully participate in its programs, yet never betray any indication of that life beyond the walls or associations of the parish. Some of us find in small circles of intimate friends moments of profound fellowship and faith, depth of prayer and personal commitment, but emerge from these groups only to disappear into the masses on the streets, indistinguishable from all others. And some of us draw very close to God in solitary meditation and prayer, enjoying a mystical communion with the divine, but like trysts with a lover locked away in an obscure retreat, our religion is a secret affair no one knows about.

Hilary would be an embarrassment to most of us. He was very public in his faith, suffering exile for his courageous stand against his foes. He knew the cost of friendship with Jesus, of maintaining his faith even in exile. In Epiphanytide, the season for public manifestation of God, the season of mission symbolized by the star that guided others to the baby who was the ultimate expression of God's intimate friendship with the world, it is appropriate to consider how—and how often—we break that friend's heart.

It is easy to stand by the manger, quietly loving the baby. It is far more difficult to walk unashamedly beside that baby when he is fully grown, through hostile territory and beyond. It is easy to get caught up in the warmth of friendships for a brief season lasting only from December to the new year, to stand around the punch bowl and sing carols. It is harder to stand by those friends in time of need, to sit with them and share their pain. It is easy to read printed prayers out of a prayer book within the ordered calm of worship. It is much harder to frame words of faith and hope and love from the heart when surrounded by the chaos and uncertainty of unruly human relationships. It is always easier to be a friend in fair weather than in foul.

And there is no creature so low as the one who apologizes for or denies his association with one called "friend" in any other setting. Yet I have done it and so, probably, have you. As we in this Epiphanytide praise the God who has brought us out of darkness into light, how can we consign that Friend to the shade?

Antony
Abbot in Egypt, 356   *January 17*

A wealthy young man approached Jesus. He obviously did not know Jesus well, since he addressed him twice using only the formal titles "Master" and "Teacher," not his proper name. "What must I do to inherit eternal life?" the man asks (Mark 10:17). In response Jesus repeats six of the Ten Commandments but omits the four that pertain to relationship with God—the singularity of God, the prohibition of idols, the taking of God's name in vain, and the keeping of God's sabbath. The man enthusiastically affirms that he has kept the six commandments in question, kept them faithfully all his life.

"You lack one thing," said Jesus to the man. "Go, sell what you own, and give the money to the poor, and you will have treasure in heaven; then come, follow me" (Mark 10:21). There was no virtue in selling his riches and giving to the poor; eternal life is not to be bought. A radical redistribution of his goods would, however, move this man's investments from goods to people; instead of investing in things he would be investing in other people, in relationships. And that, as Jesus seems to have been hinting, was the man's blind spot. Anyone who asks what he must "do" to inherit anything obviously does not understand that the prerequisite to inheritance is relationship. He had been a very good man, if we are to judge by his actions, but he was still a very poor man for he lacked the relationships that truly enrich life. And chief among those relationships is relationship with God.

Antony in the desert was apart but not alone. Except for very brief times of retreat, Antony lived in community. He and his companions were dedicated to some of the hardest work we know: singing, fasting, praying, loving, and making peace. Their work was not for their own welfare, but in order to provide alms for others. Their energies, therefore, were wholly devoted to their relationships with one another and their relationship with God. They were nurturing this life and the next.

Eternal life is unendurable punishment if unaccompanied by relationship. What good is everlasting life if it be given only for everlasting solitude? Antony only withdrew from the world; he did not withdraw from life. There is a difference. That difference, it seems, was lost on the eager young man who went away because he could not buy his inheritance, not empty-handed but empty-hearted.

Confession of Saint Peter the Apostle

January 18

This day marks the commencement of the annual Week of Prayer for Christian Unity. Ironically, the gospel reading appointed for this commemoration includes a foundational text of Christian division—Jesus' designation of Peter as the rock upon which the church would be built and upon which Rome bases its claim of primacy. Moreover, Peter's confession itself, proclaiming Jesus as "the Messiah, the Son of the living God" (Matthew 16:16), divides Christians from Jews. It is difficult, then, to understand why Jesus would commend Peter for this confession of faith, unless we consider that Jesus may have been commending not the correctness of Peter's response, but its originality. Peter was commended because his reply was his own.

We are not the church simply because of a professed allegiance to a common cause; that is a club, not a communion. The church is a vast and varied family of individuals, each unique and precious, yet united by a common bond not just with one another, but with and in God. It is my relationship with my parents that is the foundation of my relationship with my sisters and brothers; without the former, there could be no latter. For Christians, it is not our agreement with one another that makes our relationships and establishes our kinship, but our confession and acknowledgment of a primary, prerequisite relationship with the God who made us all.

Peter confessed what he experienced in communion with God. Peter's relationship and the confession that emanated from it were uniquely his and cannot be imposed upon anyone else. For to impose my relationship with God upon another, to demand that her relationship look in every way the same as mine, is to rob the other of her own unique relationship.

My younger sister's relationship to our parents could never be the same as mine. She sees them from a woman's perspective; I see them from a man's. She missed twelve years that I was privileged to share with them by virtue of my elder status. But when I went away to college, she saw them in ways I could not. Yet they are still our parents and we share them in common. So it is with the family of faith.

We see with our own eyes, touch with our own hands, walk our own paths. Each of us sees God in a different and particular way. We learn from one another and grow with one another when we share those vantages with one another. Those of us who know and share the western Christian tradition will find many affinities in our relationships with God, but we dare not exclude others of God's family simply because they do not see with our eyes. We, like Peter, are responsible for one confession—our own. That confession is our rock, our contribution to the foundation and structure of God's church. We can only offer it to the Builder.

Wulfstan

Bishop of Worcester, 1095   *January 19*

Most of us think of servants as workers who are not expected to have initiative or a will of their own, but are to carry out the desires and designs of their overseers unquestioningly, obediently, and exactly. The word "servant" is frequently used to describe the relationship of the believer to God, but God has called us to something other than unquestioning and mindless obedience. We are no longer to be servants; we are to be friends. "I do not call you servants any longer," Jesus tells his disciples, "because the servant does not know what the master is doing; but I have called you friends, because I have made known to you everything that I have heard from my Father" (John 15:15). As friends we are appointed and encouraged to join God's creativity, and a life built not upon the regimentation of servitude but upon the relationship of colleagues.

Wulfstan refused to observe the strict ordering of eleventh-century political, social, and religious life. A humble man, disparaged by some for his lack of education and only reluctantly appointed to episcopal rank, Wulfstan was an unlikely candidate for influence among the powerful. Yet, without apology for his origins and without compromising his integrity, Wulfstan earned the trust of those who might well have scorned and spurned him. He became the friend of kings.

Working with William I, William II, and Lanfranc, the Archbishop of Canterbury, Wulfstan helped to put an end to the slave trade that sold Englishmen into Irish bondage. His loyalty in friendship to rulers and prelates, as much or more than any skill, enabled him to accomplish much for others. To be a friend of God means, as Wulfstan learned, to find ourselves in the company of the strangest people, in the least likely places.

Walking with God, we find ourselves well beyond the limits of our well-reasoned design, in places where all reason says we cannot be. We find ourselves where we never dreamed we would be, seeing things we never dreamed we would see, saying things we never dreamed we would say, doing things we never dreamed we would do, accomplishing what we never dreamed we could accomplish. We find ourselves by God's side as God's friend. If we are truly wise, we will not ask how or why. We will just be thankful, and keep on walking.

Fabian

Bishop and Martyr of Rome, 250   *January 20*

In the year 236 Fabian found himself in Rome, a layman visiting from elsewhere in Italy. An assembly of clergy had gathered to elect a successor to their deceased pope. As one might expect, especially in Italy, the open-air assembly drew a throng of curiosity seekers, Fabian among them. As he stood with the crowd, a dove flew over them and alighted upon Fabian. The clergy declared this a sign from God and elected Fabian their pope.

After he had recovered from his shock and the several subsequent liturgical rituals of Christian initiation and office, Fabian served ably and faithfully. He organized the city of Rome and the church within it—impressive accomplishments in their own right, but even more so in a time when the persecution of Christians was particularly acute. Indeed, Fabian himself was eventually martyred in a campaign of hostilities against the faithful.

It is unthinkable that episcopal, much less priestly, ministers might be elected from the laity today, but it is exciting to contemplate the creative possibilities of such happy accidents as befell Fabian. The laity is the first, and primary, order of ministry; neither Jesus nor his disciples were professional (or even devoted) members of the religious establishment. Jesus himself relied upon a cohort of strangely peripheral people now revered as apostles; the only religious enthusiast among them was Judas, and we know the story of his end.

The stranger's ministry is the source of the church's greatest riches. Fabian's election and his subsequent gifts encourage us to trust the power of a God who sometimes gives to the church its richest gifts and its most valued leaders on no stronger recommendation than the whimsy of a dove.

Agnes
Martyr at Rome, 304   *January 21*

At twelve years of age, the age of her death, Agnes embodies that awkward time when one is more ensnared than poised between the innocence of childhood and the experience of adulthood. Yet to our sensibilities, and those of her adoring biographers, Agnes seems the helpless victim to power and violence. Portrayed as a virgin undefiled, her name echoing the Latin word for "lamb," she is made to seem meekly passive. But to perpetuate this image is to add insult to the injury inflicted upon her by those who took her life. Where are the powerful energies of a young woman in the most explosive and expressive stages of youth? Where is the zeal and the grit that could provoke the kind of death she suffered?

The humility of the saint is not innate; it is a discipline. Do we assume that because Agnes was twelve and female that she was incapable of standing firm in her convictions? After all, in her society, a person of twelve was less a child than a young adult, for maturation came quickly where lives barely spanned four or five decades. Women of her age were at least betrothed, if not wed and nursing. Our romance—or our chauvinism—demean both the child and the woman in Agnes.

Jesus has more respect for the child; he does not say that one humbles oneself in becoming like a child. Rather, he says that "whoever becomes humble like this child is the greatest in the kingdom of heaven" (Matthew 18:4). Childhood is not a humble status in itself; even children are subject to pride and must exercise discipline to embrace humility. Such innocence and humility as Agnes possessed were due not to her gender or age or status, but were hers by choice, by discipline and dint of character.

Challenging our presumptions, Agnes remains, after nearly seventeen hundred years, a dangerous woman. Her witness is a force with which to be reckoned; she remains a woman who raises questions and challenges our assumptions, a woman with power both to witness and convert, if we will let her.

Vincent

Deacon of Saragossa, and Martyr, 304   *January 22*

If the lives and deaths of martyrs are to be instructive to us we must move beyond the sensationalism of their exploits and ends to the fundamental affinities we share with them. This is certainly the case with Vincent, a fourth-century Spanish deacon. His primary service was that of spokesperson for Valerius, Bishop of Saragossa, whose remarkable gifts for ministry were so appreciated that his profound speech impediment was not counted against him. When Valerius and Vincent were arrested in one of the many waves of persecution common to their time, Valerius was dependent upon Vincent to speak for him.

The governor challenged the two to renounce their faith or face torture and possible death. Vincent, of course, turned to the senior bishop and sought his will. Valerius responded by telling Vincent that just as he had been entrusted for years with the proclamation of the word of God, so now did the bishop entrust his deacon with the vindication of that same faith. Vincent was entrusted with responsibility for both their lives.

Vincent could well have fashioned a reply preserving the bishop's integrity while yet saving his own skin. Or he could have offered his renunciation and the bishop's, disavowing the Christian faith and mission. But Vincent responded emphatically and without hesitation. While Valerius was only exiled, Vincent was tortured painfully until death in angry retaliation for his unshakable and fearless demeanor before a governor who undoubtedly thrived upon his power to hold others in thrall.

While such a story holds a sympathetic and even timely message for those who profess their faith in the midst of political oppression, as some today do, for many of us our experiences and situations are different. Vincent challenges us in his willingness to accept full responsibility for who he was, for what he had done, for what he confessed and believed.

Arthur Miller's *All My Sons* is an electrifying play, an epic tragedy set in a world we can understand. It is the story of an industrial manufacturer who, in the midst of wartime, approved the shipment of defective materials for airplane assembly. His defense is that it was a question of profit, a tactic of survival. He confesses the truth of his deception and says that he always believed that someone else—someone in the assembly line, in the receiving room, or in the inspection process on the other end—would find the fault. He had abdicated responsibility, and the subsequent life he made for himself was built upon a succession of lies and deceptions, all intended to circumnavigate his responsibility. As the play unfolds and the fabric of lies unravels, the far-flung consequences of his betrayal are revealed in a legacy of death and destruction. Twenty-one planes with their crews, his business partner, his family, and eventually he himself are all destroyed by that one lie. It is a tragedy that lends new and lively power to the gospel admonition not to "fear those who kill the body, and after that can do nothing more" (Luke 12:4), but rather to fear those forces that have the power to create a living hell for ourselves and all touched by our lives. We are to fear and respect the power of moral consequences, the burden of responsibility that C. S. Lewis called "the weight of glory."

The power and authority entrusted to us, even in seemingly small acts and activities, is awesome. We are entrusted with the co-creation of this world, invited to serve God as Vincent served Valerius. We are called to speak and live and love with God and on behalf of God. It is our portion of divinity, this weight of glory.

Phillips Brooks

Bishop of Massachusetts, 1893   *January 23*

The tenderness and warm friendliness of Phillips Brooks is familiar to all who know the much-loved Christmas carol "O Little Town of Bethlehem." This magnificent preacher and poet echoed his own carol elsewhere when he wrote, "Whatever happens, always remember the mysterious richness of human nature and the nearness of God to each one of us."

Jesus warns his disciples against false prophets who try to direct us to find God's Messiah "in the inner rooms" or "in the wilderness" (Matthew 24:26), as though God were elusive and distant, to be found in the depths or the deserts. Phillips Brooks reminds us that we are blessed with a mysterious richness in our human nature. It is both burden and glory, this human nature which makes us other than God, apart from God, but also allows us—in that distinctive otherness—to enjoy relationship with God. Brooks reminds us that alongside this rich nature we have the nearness of God. Therefore God is in the solitude and the loneliness, in the conflict and the commitment. God is near at hand. It is not an original or even dazzling insight, but then the homely truth of God rarely is, this God who comes to us, abides with us, our Lord, Emmanuel.

Conversion of Saint Paul the Apostle

January 25

The scriptural story of the transition that changed Saul, the zealous persecutor of Christians, into Paul, the apostolic cornerstone of the church, is a rare first-person narrative amidst texts far less intimate and personal. As such, it makes a nice companion to the confession of Peter. Together these feasts frame the octave of Prayer for Christian Unity. If Peter's confession reminds us of the uniquely personal dimension of one's commitment to God, Paul's story treats us to what such a commitment can require of us: conversion.

Though it happened in midday and in the company of others, the change wrought in Saul that rendered him Paul was intensely personal and lonely. He was, after all, struck blind—in sense and symbol a special isolation and helplessness. Moreover, the word of God that comes to him in his helplessness is hardly comforting: "I will rescue you from your people and from the Gentiles—to whom I am sending you" (Acts 26:17). He will be rescued not only from strangers but also from familiars, set on his own, alien to all, welcome nowhere.

Like Jesus before him, Saul entered his vocation through wilderness. What Saul learned in darkness was less mystical or magical than practical. He learned how much he needed others to live. He learned all over again what it means to be born, to emerge from and enter into a world in which enemies and friends alike are indistinguishable. He learned to give and receive all over again without the ability to discriminate; as *persona non grata* to friend and foe alike, all his relationships had to be remade.

Failed experiments in ecumenism and social politics suggest that unity is not to be found in mass movements of like-minded people sharing common perspectives and policies. Faithful witness seems not to depend upon uniform or even conforming testimony, for even the four gospels contradict themselves and each other. Experience suggests that unity embraces the multitude of our differences, that community is often far from cozy, and that conversion does not mean changing others to our point of view but perhaps just the opposite—weaning each and every person and institution from the arrogant exclusivism that prevents genuine conversation.

We may not have reached Damascus yet, but neither are we lost in the darkness. It may be dim, chaotic, and difficult to find our way, but this is where

God came to Saul and where God comes to us, to rescue us not only from our enemies but also from our friends, not only from strangers but also from familiars, that we might see beyond these discriminating distinctions to a new way of relating. In helplessness we learn anew the help we need and the help we can offer. God invites us, calls us, to engage the powerful conversion—and the conversation—of the world.

Timothy and Titus

Companions of Saint Paul   *January 26*

Timothy wept. Titus was probably equally disheartened. Each was young in years, even younger in the Christian faith. Their conversion and subsequent discipleship, as is so often the case, had begun with their attraction to a charismatic figure, Paul, who even in his own time approached legendary status and conferred upon these young adults his own protection. They had assisted him in the field, traveled with him and enjoyed his company and mentoring. The heroic leader is letting go of the disciples, who must now walk unassisted. Each is a difficult task, and this tension illuminates the enigmatic sheepfold of the Good Shepherd in John's gospel.

John's metaphor is flawed and its flaw prevents, even forbids, a literal interpretation. No shepherd literally leads the flock to life abundant, but tends the flock for a single purpose, the end of which means sacrifice for the sheep. The sheep are going to give up coat and life, either for the economic or the spiritual gain of the owner. Whether stripped of wool and butchered into chops for the owner's table or the market, or offered in bloody sacrifice on the altar of the owner's religion, the sheep inevitably die.

The shepherd obviously sets aside such considerations. Even as we must leave questions of life and death, judgment and justice, to God, so the shepherd must care for the sheep neither weighing their merits nor considering their ends. Nor does the shepherd hover protectively; the shepherd is often absent from the flock, seeking the wayward stray or richer pasture.

The thief and robber may be the person who only pretends to shepherd, who cares nothing for the sheep but sees them only as commodities to serve a selfish end—to feed the thief's own hunger, or to be fenced for cash, or even sacrificed to fulfill the thief's religious obligations. The thief in the modern ministerial sheepfold, then, is the one whose ministry consists largely of feeding the personal hunger for adulation, or the need to be needed. Selfishness is always a temptation; more difficult is life-giving leadership. It is hard on the leader and upon the follower. So it was that Timothy wept and Titus had to be reminded of why he had been left in Crete.

We are bound to models of dependent discipleship, tethered to the notion that ministry is what we do with one another and among one another within the community we call the church. When we are cut adrift from those models and habits, we weep for fear like Timothy and lose sight of our purpose like Titus. We forget that Christian ministry began without a written corpus of scripture, that there was a time before tradition, and that the earliest communities of believers were denied the physical presence of Jesus and often the company of their own members in the conduct of their work.

Forced by circumstance to move out on their own initiative and often denied the security of community, they learned not simply to imitate Christ but to incarnate the gospel. They ventured as pioneers into new pasture, into a ministry that separated them as it called upon their different abilities to perform diverse tasks. Reunions of the scattered were genuine occasions of communion instead of the endless round of committee meetings, commiseration, and congratulation they would one day become. Denied visible leaders to take them by the hand and the comfort of like-minded companions to encourage them, they learned the confidence of their own gifts and the power of their own faith in the footsteps of Timothy, Titus, and Paul.

John Chrysostom

Bishop of Constantinople, 407   *January 27*

The commemoration of a great preacher only accentuates the erosion of our facility for speech. It is rare to find a person who can speak thoughtfully or clearly, and rarer still to find those who will listen carefully or critically. The strength, vitality, and propagation of our faith are based upon the telling of a community's story, the ability to communicate to one another and with one another from generation to generation, from day to day. The measure of John Chrysostom's preaching—any preaching—is the power of that preaching to inspire and assist others to tell the story, to make the living Word live in words.

No preacher can tell your story for you. And the story is not complete without your version, your testimony, your witness. We are deeply indebted to all those who in their own words and experiences, either written years ago or spoken just yesterday, open our eyes to deeper insights, newer expression, and greater clarity of the story. But seldom do we hear, in the pulpit or out of it, the simple exposition of God's presence and activity in our lives. We have grown fearful, afraid that we shall not know how to speak or that others will not know how to hear, fears that we hold in common with the prophets and disciples who have gone before us. Fear that stops our tongues threatens the continuity of our faith; silence, the disappearance of words, is the death of the story.

That John Chrysostom was a great preacher I accept on the evidence given by those who knew him. But there is an interesting and telling irony in the historical witness. He was exiled, it seems, because the empress Eudoxia "believed" he had called her a "Jezebel," suggesting that the circumstances of his exile were motivated by hearsay, the miscommunication or convolution of words. That he seems neither to have disputed the charge nor apologized only lends credibility to the likelihood that John Chrysostom sullied the name of the empress with a word and that he both magnified and aggravated the exile by his refusal to speak in response or defense. The golden-mouthed patriarch died in an exile made by a word and marked by an enigmatic silence. There's a sermon in there somewhere.

Thomas Aquinas

Priest and Friar, 1274   *January 28*

We can attribute to Thomas Aquinas only the *discovery* of reason as a component of the faithful life, for there is ample evidence that from the beginnings of religious faith as we know it reason was assumed to be a legitimate vehicle of revelation. Jesus himself, in the strange parable of the nets full of fish, seems to assert a certain reasonableness as essential to faithful discipleship.

An indiscriminate seining fills the nets with all manner of fish. Jesus points to the necessity of separating what is useful from what is not; Hebrew fishermen separated from their catch all sea creatures forbidden by their dietary laws. Those fish were neither marketable nor edible, and were discarded as useless. Jesus then asks the disciples if they have understood the necessity of the sorting, to which they respond, "Yes." Jesus then explains that those who teach of the kingdom must work out of a treasury of knowledge that includes both old and new, strong and weak. In short, education for the kingdom must include a wealth of knowledge and experience as indiscriminate as the net (Matthew 13:47-52).

What Jesus seems to challenge is a standstill of the human imagination, tradition entrenched and unwilling to admit any change or reevaluation, despite daily evidence of continual evolution, growth, and God's progressive revelation. But he also challenges the opposing extreme: a fiery zeal that espouses every fuzzy-headed notion that comes down the pike. Offering a middle ground, Jesus commends a wisdom attentive to all of life's experience and discriminating in its judgment. Wisdom, Jesus seems to say, will be gleaned from the whole of life and in the midst of the swirling tides of time.

Wisdom is a treasure and those who hold it are stewards. "I learned without guile and I impart without grudging; I do not hide [wisdom's] wealth" (Wisdom 7:13). What does it mean to "learn without guile"? It means to learn without thought of gain, without cunning or design, to learn simply for the sake of learning, with no ulterior motive in mind. Thomas Aquinas reminds us that reason, like the revelation it facilitates, is a gift of God. We speak of knowledge as power; our Hebrew forebears—as well as our Christian ones—teach us that knowledge is gift. And those who learn without guile teach without grudging. Those who appreciate that knowledge and wisdom are gifts willingly share; those who guard knowledge as power fear that new knowledge will threaten or destroy their status. They revere only history's knowledge and hold institutions hostage. They hoard education's bounty and shape the destinies of races and generations.

It is time to set sail with the spirit of Thomas Aquinas, to toss the net far and wide, open to the wonder of this world, sweeping the vast ocean of life's generous wealth of experiences. It is time to go fishing, to get ourselves some wisdom.

Brigid (Bride)

February 1

The branches of our family tree are a wild and tangled lot. It is both humbling and refreshing that we count pagan ancestors among the saints and that, in truth, the shape of our liturgical and seasonal life is grounded in older, non-Christian religion and custom. "Now remember what you were," says Paul, "…when God called you" (1 Corinthians 1:26, TEV). When Brigid remembered what she was when God called her, she remembered her Druid past.

Paul reminded his own generation that God makes use of every aspect of their lives as an integral part of a most creative ministry. They were not, then, to repudiate, demean, or deny what they were when God called. They were to remember what they were in order that they might recover and celebrate the diversity they once brought to God's service in response to God's call.

What one was when called by God might actually be the gift God seeks in us. There is no need for religious testimony that rejects our past, no matter how sinful. Shame and self-denigration have their proper place in our personal pilgrimage toward true humility, but they are too easily turned into destructive weapons. Even the negative memories of addiction, abuse, or other human struggles are useful to God in a diverse human community, for such perspectives as we gain in these experiences are shared by others who need our genuine care and understanding if they are to hear God's call in their lives. Brigid offers a glimpse of how God uses what we were to enhance what we are, of how her pagan past became part of her Christian experience, and ours.

Brigid founded a convent in the fifth century at Kildare, the center of the cult of a pagan goddess. A sacred fire said to be maintained by that goddess served as an object of devotion and there is no indication that Brigid extinguished it. More likely she used wisdom and creativity to reclaim the flame for God's use. Such unconventionality is certainly consistent with this woman who established the only known Irish double monastery, uniting women and men in a single religious community. Moreover, it is consistent with the kindness for which she is remembered, a kindness that refused to douse the flame of faith in any person.

Jesus did not mean for us to shame, insult, or bully others into companionship. And even though the evangelist reminds us that we are not to be terribly mindful of life's externals (Matthew 6:25-33), there is little evidence that pagans run after externals any more than we Christians do. Christian or otherwise, behind our preoccupation with such externals, our materialism and careerism, lies a deeper human need for validation, some welcome place to be who we are, some appreciative and useful way to make our lives count.

There is in many a parish church an old and venerable habit of waiting in reverent silence until the candles upon the altar have been extinguished. Never mind that candles were placed on altars only for the purpose of illuminating the pages of the liturgical text and are oddly incongruous in this age of electric lighting. This quaint custom of waiting seems superstitious, an odd ritual of fire-worship more Druidic than Christian. But it is also a reminder of Brigid and her community that commingled Druid and Christian influences, the flame a reminder that what she was has become something of who we are, and all are a part of the richness of life in God.

The Presentation of Our Lord

February 2

Today is the fortieth day after the Nativity. After forty days, the Jewish woman who has been delivered of a child is considered ritually purified, restored to the fullness of her health and vitality, her body rested from the ordeals of labor and the trauma of the birth itself, and her natural cycles returned to stability. She may now be received in the Temple precincts and return to the public life of corporate worship.

On the fortieth day, the child and family enter the Temple to redeem this new life. Because all creation, and thus all children, belong to God, parents of Jesus' day offered the first male child to God as the first-fruits of the harvest of their marriage. But alongside the child are offered the sacrificial animals whose lives are taken that the child might live. Joseph and Mary probably saw nothing extraordinary in the ritual they kept. The minimal requirement of the law established that at least two turtledoves or young pigeons be sacrificed. Joseph and Mary could barely afford the minimum; one suspects they secretly wished for a quick, quiet ceremony and a safe retreat from attention. But Simeon and Anna took over.

They are a wonderful pair, these two old-timers. Simeon was one of those men who seems always to have been around. No one, including himself, could probably recall his true age. His eyes had seen everything, the worst and the best. Anna, too, had lived a full life. She had known marriage and a long widowhood. Her days spent in the Temple confines, she knew its corruption, the emptiness of its halls and of those who filled them. She had seen many rituals, and many babies. But this child gave Simeon and Anna joy and filled them with hope.

What did they see that made them carry on so? They probably saw nothing, and everything. They saw a family of humble means and demeanor, a young and tender mother and her awkward, aging husband—the essence of simplicity. Their meager resources prevented any display of ostentation and their very plainness made them the kind of people who, sadly, leave no impression whatsoever. Maybe that is what all the fuss was about.

Simeon and Anna had seen plenty of people come and go from the Temple. What they had not seen was the simple truth this ancient ritual of presentation proclaimed. When the infant Jesus was brought, it all came together. In their simplicity and plainness this family represented all that it means to be human—just plain human. They had neither the arrogance that pretends to greatness, nor the brooding hostility that hates the human condition. They were just plain human, neither better nor worse than any of God's creatures, and they came to make an offering.

It was enough for God. Simeon and Anna saw, perhaps for the first time in their long lives, that this offering of humanity was ample to fill the Temple with holiness, and the heart of God with joy. Simeon, who had seen all the world has to offer, and Anna, who had seen all the human soul seeks, took one look at the child and saw the truth. Simeon did not say he had seen the Messiah, only that he had seen "deliverance...made ready in full view of all the nations," and Anna proclaimed that this child was "destined to be a sign" because of whom "the secret thoughts of many will be laid bare" (Luke 2:31, 34 NEB). Those eyes that had seen it all, for the first time saw all that God desired, and it was a little child.

This sight filled them with joy, filled their life with meaning. Their love, their faith, and their hope fulfilled, they could go to death in peace. They saw at the end of long and very full lives, in the blessedness of life's wisdom and God's grace, that God requires far less than we may think, only what we are.

Anskar

Archbishop of Hamburg, Missionary to Denmark and Sweden, 865   *February 3*

On my worst days, many of which seem to come in February, I need to know of people like Anskar. Anskar was a dud. He labored long and hard, but saw few, if any, accomplishments. His efforts only began to pay off long after his death. I need the memory of Anskar in this hurry-up-and-get-there culture where the bottom line is all that counts for anything; Anskar is the antidote to our demand for instant results.

Little is said these days about the importance of the seemingly small contribution to the world. Shoddy workmanship, cheap goods, and tolerance of mediocrity are our monument to our lack of patience. Yet life is lived and changed in the small things. Our world is made one life at a time, our lives ordered one day at a time. How can we look at this world, and at one another, and not appreciate the care God has lavished in our creation? After all, we Christians claim to have seen the face of God in the face of a child, and to have found our way by the light of a single star out of all the spangled heavens.

God, by whose power this world might be transformed in the twinkling of an eye, has such patient love for us and such admiration for our abilities that all creation awaits our handiwork. God patiently attends our halting attempts to help, even as God waited for Anskar.

Cornelius the Centurion

February 4

Just days before meeting Cornelius, the book of Acts tells us, Peter had a puzzling vision. While at noonday prayers, Peter grew hungry. His mind wandered; in a dreamy trance Peter saw a great cloth lowered from the skies, a picnic spread within its folds. This banquet contained all the foods forbidden by Peter's Jewish law. Three times the feast was lowered before him and thrice he was commanded by a voice to kill and eat this forbidden bounty. Three times Peter refused. Struggling between obedience to the law and obedience to the vision, Peter was challenged to change.

As Peter puzzled over his dream, messengers arrived from a stranger named Cornelius, a Roman military official, asking him to come to Caesarea to meet with Cornelius. Peter saw a direct connection between his vision and this opportunity to respond. He did not have to go to Caesarea. In fact, his better instincts might have told him to be more cautious, lest he walk into a trap. He did not have to tell anyone of his strange dream. He could have just observed the law and stayed put, and Christianity might have remained a sect of Judaism. But Peter ventured beyond the protective confines.

In years to come, when he related the story of his meeting with Cornelius in Caesarea, Peter would tell his listeners that only the day of Pentecost itself had so moved and shaped his faith and life. Each of us has at someplace in our lives a challenge to grow, to change. Each of us is challenged to move beyond our prejudices and into those areas where even our deepest convictions stay our feet. Not every instance is so dramatic, but each is of equal importance.

Peter was not asked to convert the entire Gentile populace, only to go to Cornelius. Later, when called to stand in the midst of his Jewish critics, Peter would recall his visit to Cornelius, the unclean Roman outsider. He would recount the vision of forbidden food, the command to eat, his threefold denial, and his change of heart, adding only, "If then God gave them the same gift that he gave us when we believed in the Lord Jesus Christ, who was I that I could hinder God?" (Acts 11:17). Who, indeed!

The Martyrs of Japan
1597   *February 5*

Whenever we think of martyrdom, we usually think of innocence under attack. Violence seems more tragic when perpetrated against those who desire no evil. Yet nearly all martyrdom is provoked. Even the death of Jesus upon the cross is more than a simple clash of good and evil; it was a complex political event provoked by Jesus' return to Jerusalem after he had been ordered out of the city. And bearing a cross is more than punishment: it can mean losing one's life for the sake of gaining one's soul (Mark 8:34–38).

Bearing the cross is the final gift of human dignity accorded the condemned. Literally shouldering full responsibility for the consequence of one's actions, the condemned person is allowed this gesture as a final act of integrity. The cross was the shape of Jesus' response to God, the consistent, integrated outcome of a life of fidelity to God. Had he toed the line or compromised, he might have avoided execution. But any other course would have been evasion, betrayal of the vocation to which he had dedicated himself. The Franciscans and their followers who were hanged from crosses above the fields of Nagasaki in 1597 were similarly dedicated and they, too, were caught up in a complex political struggle.

These early Christian missionaries represented a rival religion to the spirituality of Japan. Moreover, they represented intruding nations and aroused the suspicions of a people who had much cause to be wary, for the Japanese had been dominated before. We do not remember these martyrs for innocence; surely they knew the threat their presence and their witness represented to the Japanese. We do not remember these martyrs for sacrifice, but for a tragic symmetry.

Nagasaki is now a name so infamous it eclipses the memory of six friars and a handful of followers. The atomic destruction visited upon that place in this century not only literally seared the ground of that earlier execution, it obliterates the sixteenth-century loss. But they are connected. Nagasaki is part of our cross. Clumsy, weighty, and uncomfortable, it is burdensome and bothersome to bear this cross. Yet bear it we must, not for punishment but for integrity—as an integral reminder of our power and responsibility.

It is not our luxury to lay this cross aside, nor to justify it. We may not embrace it with eagerness, but neither can we evade it with ease or excuse. We can only bear it, with dignity and with God's grace.

Absalom Jones
Priest, 1818   *February 13*

One evening recently I watched two television documentaries scheduled in consecutive hours on the civil rights movement and the volcano Vesuvius. In retrospect I discerned that in a way both of these programs were concerned with the same thing: the volcanic forces at the heart of the earth and buried within the hearts of its people, forces that occasionally break the surface, venting steam and gas or worse and destroying everything in their path.

On the slopes of Vesuvius, the volcano that destroyed Pompeii and Herculaneum, there is a little town called San Sebastiano, devastated in 1944 by the final treacherous blast from the last eruption, but rebuilt and thriving, as it has been for centuries. It remains a testimony to the indomitable spirit of a people who believe the power of humanity greater than the power of the volcano. It also represents the foolhardiness and pigheadedness of my own Italian ancestors and relations, for only indomitable stubbornness and raw stupidity would so tempt fate and the elements. But is this spirit so different from successive generations who struggle to rebuild society in the wake of racism's ravages?

Absalom Jones and those like him who lead the way to justice possess a comparable tenacity in the face of racism that erupts violently with hot blasts of hatred, touching our deepest fears and threatening to destroy us. Born a slave, Absalom Jones secured his own freedom in 1784 and eventually challenged the Episcopal Church to take its earliest steps toward equality; he continues to challenge us today not to retreat from this hard and potentially volatile work.

Absalom Jones encourages us to stand fast upon the slopes of Vesuvius. Racism is as hot and intractable as earth's molten core. We cannot rationally decide not to be racist, not to be afraid, for fear does not behave rationally. Jesus, speaking to his disciples of violence and hatred, told them they lived in a fearful world that would threaten to destroy them. Then he commands them to love one another; he offers not a rule but a response.

"Set us free…from every bond of prejudice and fear," we pray today, but our response to that fear is where we may make our own difference. We need not flee the volcano, but like the people of San Sebastiano, we must be prepared always to rebuild anew. Our prayer is not aimed at changing the world, but at shaping our own response to that world—a prayer to meet the violent and virulent racism of the world with a response of reconciling love, a steadfast and tenacious faith that dares to lay its foundations on the slopes of Vesuvius.

Cyril and Methodius

Monk and Bishop, Missionaries to the Slavs, 869, 885   *February 14*

The custom of giving love tokens on this day is a holdover from the pagan celebration of the Lupercalia and the mythology of Cupid, that chubby little Roman archer whose Greek counterpart was Eros. It has little to do with Cyril and Methodius, brothers and missionaries who left their home in Thessalonika in response to the King of Moravia, who sought teachers for his people. They had to start from the ground up and began by teaching the Slavs to read their own native tongue, Slavonic. They invented an alphabet and set about the daunting task of making a literate, and literary, culture. What followed was a scandal sadly familiar to Christian mission.

Cyril and Methodius ran afoul of the clergy in Germany, who objected that these missionaries were teaching, preaching, and writing in what was deemed a barbaric tongue. Cyril and Methodius were giving the people the gospel in a language they could understand and teaching the people to pray in their own tongue. The jealousy flared not from enemies outside the community of the faithful, but right at the heart of the church, among the clergy who held the authority and power of nearly all scholarly activity. Here, then, is where we encounter the difference between the love celebrated on Valentine's Day and the love exemplified in Cyril and Methodius, the difference between Cupid's passion and Christ's.

But in a sweet irony, the story of Cyril and Methodius brings us to the only word derived from Cupid's stock: cupidity. It is the word for the passion of possession, avarice and greed. The hallmark of Eros, this possessiveness laces every Valentine greeting beseeching that you be *my* valentine, or that I be *yours*. Possessiveness also marks the German response to the work of Cyril and Methodius. The German clergy were jealous; their possession—learning—was in danger of escaping their grasp and they feared loss of control.

Those who dare to free the gospel from language's limits are often harassed and hounded, accused of heresy and ostracized as traitors. The church is certainly no haven from jealousy. Paul wrote to the Gentiles in Ephesus not in freedom but from prison. He believed the Gentiles equal heirs to the gospel and thus ran afoul of those who claimed exclusive Jewish possession of that truth. The mission of the church has always had to contend with those who fear the change that outreach inevitably brings. Congregations and communities may insist loudly that they welcome new members, but then behave inhospitably when those newcomers appear. We may claim to want change, but resist that change when it comes.

Our mission as Christians is to empty ourselves, making room for all who would come in. We are to incline ourselves not toward possessive jealousy, but toward benevolent generosity. We are not to possess buildings, treasures, or one another. We are to possess no bibles, liturgies, or theologies. We are commanded to have but one thing—a life open always to the other person. Those who will may keep their Valentine; we revere Cyril and Methodius through whose open lives a people found the way, and the words, to God's love.

Thomas Bray

Priest and Missionary, 1730   *February 15*

When Jesus sent his disciples in pairs ahead of him into the towns where he would be traveling, he told them to remain in the place to which they had been sent (Luke 10:7). The temptation to move from place to place was great for the disciples, especially when the move offered a less difficult assignment, with less challenge and more comfort. But this admonition to stay put is equally applicable to other temptations in ministry; it is an antidote to our tendency to flit from idea to idea, and to neglect the translation of ideas into realities.

Thomas Bray made a brief visit to America in the seventeenth century. He stayed only two months, but what he saw remained with him for years to come. His impressive ministry gave the colonies numerous lending libraries, improved education, better clergy, relief to slaves, and a humanitarian alternative to debtor's prison (the colony of Georgia). Evidently, the impressions of this brief time in America were carried to the end of his life, visited and revisited day in and day out, until he gained insight into each, shaped a response, and exerted his influence to bring that response to life. Bray seems to have found the balance between the two extremes of idea and activity.

We are easily seduced by ideas; we too often think that because we have discussed an issue or problem, we have solved it. But at the other extreme, when we plunge into action unreflectively we believe that because we are actually doing something we are exerting a profound influence upon ideas and systems. At either extreme we are in danger of distraction, of being diverted from the hard work of keeping ideas and actions in balance. It is especially good to bear this in mind during Lent, when we are easily distracted by temporary disciplines.

As we ladle soup and tend shelters for the homeless, we might consider these brief sojourns our own little visits to the colonies. The harder discipline is devoting our energies to solutions to address systemic ills, solutions that elude the easy answer and whose nagging perplexities may be carried with us for a lifetime. Each of us is part of the system that has produced hungry and homeless people in a land of plenty. If and when we truly see that, we will not rest until we, like Thomas Bray, have struggled to meet that need with ideas and influence as powerful as these issues are challenging.

Pray for the diligence of Thomas Bray, whose ministry crossed the oceans more often than he, whose investment of two-and-a-half scant months continues to yield abundantly across the distance of two-and-a-half centuries. His was a diligent devotion, an unswerving dedication made of two visions carried a whole life long: the vision of God's people and the vision of God's realm—and his ceaseless effort to reconcile the two.

Martin Luther

Reformer, 1546   *February 18*

That the Protestant Reformation succeeded to the extent that it did is due not to the efforts of Martin Luther, but to the grace and activity of a God whose ways are clearly not like our ways and without whom no vine can bear any fruit whatsoever. I wonder how Martin Luther felt as he watched his original intention fail, for that is in truth what happened. What he intended as a reform of the Catholic Church became a separate body entirely. Reform of the Catholic Church was neither wanted nor appreciated; it was sloughed off like a snake might shed a skin. Only in this instance, the discarded skin took on a life of its own and prospered.

This simultaneous failure and success of the Protestant Reformation suggests that our fears of schism are ill-founded. Perhaps God intends us to be divided—not in any mean-spirited or destructive sense, but precisely because division is an essential component of otherness, of relationship, and relationship is the essential component of the faithful life. The measure of our faith and our orthodoxy, then, is not in how well we succeed in holding our institutions together, but rather in how gracefully we accept our partings and how well we relate to one another in our separation.

We, like the church described in John's gospel, are a vine of many branches. Each branch can and does bear fruit, but each also shares a common root. The root that joins us all in the human race is our common creation by God. The root is no more complex than that; it is not common creed or confession, save that common acknowledgment that all are made by and related in that one God who called Abraham and Sarah, Jesus and Mohammed, and perhaps many more. What we commemorate in Martin Luther, then, is no particular accomplishment, but rather a courage and a confidence that dared to question the limitations of human institutions and dared to trust in the expansive creativity of God. Luther was willing to upset and even abandon the relative safety and security of the established order, confident that God's order should and would prevail.

Luther's example and experience suggest that human institutions cannot truly be reformed, because we will always stand in the way of change. Some destruction is inevitable. The detractors of contemporary efforts at church reformation are only partly correct when they claim that our reforms are killing this institution. But the proponents of change are also only partly correct when they claim that their efforts bring new life. In truth, the institutional church (and a good many other human institutions) is dead. Such life as we see may not be evidence of reformation but of resurrection, for which only God may be thanked. If we are to survive these times, we must let go both of our fear of failure and of our zeal for success.

We must rest confident not in our institutions, but in our God. As Isaiah proclaims, the wicked must give up their ways, but so also must the righteous give up their plans; the life of the church depends upon neither our attempts to conserve nor our plans to reform. Our task, as John reminds us, is to abide—to abide in God's love, to place our confidence and make our dwelling not in institutions but in God. As Martin Luther boldly affirmed, we and the institutions we fashion are only wayfarers in time. Only in God are we truly at home.

Polycarp

Bishop and Martyr of Smyrna, 156   *February 23*

Ever had the experience of wanting something very much but not being able to afford it? The choices are simple—forego the desire, wait until you have saved enough to procure it, or lower your standards and buy an affordable substitute. And we all have those regretful compromises, clothes that fell apart in the washing machine, watches that stopped ticking the first week, and cars that never made it out of the repair shop. Polycarp was given a chance to compromise, but he did not take it. Besides having a rather funny-sounding name, Polycarp was something of an oddity—a gentle old man leading a feisty young church in the worst period of its infancy, when Christians were internally warring over the Gnostic heresies and externally attacked by the pagan culture around them. In the midst of this strife, Polycarp was given a choice: curse Christ or die.

The setting was a packed amphitheater in Smyrna. The crowd had been enjoying an afternoon of watching wild beasts tear Christians to pieces. The magistrate, to his credit, saw no gain in executing an elderly bishop, and sought to dissuade the crowd, but to no avail. Polycarp was steadfast in his confession of Christ, and the magistrate, fearing the crowd's anger, gave the order, adding variety to the festivities by sending Polycarp to his death in flames.

In the years since Polycarp died we have tried in vain to negotiate a settlement with the powers of this world. We have sought a church/state alliance that might obviate the necessity of sacrifice, but it grows increasingly evident that we have bargained ourselves out of our patrimony and shortchanged the state in the bargain. We Christians are different, and we must accept that difference, decide what we shall be, or lose ourselves in the process. If we settle for an imitation of anything long enough, we will forget what the real actually is. Or maybe we have fed upon the imitation so long, we have never actually tasted the real thing. Do we understand any better than the sons of Zebedee and their mother that taking a place beside Christ means not preferment but pain, not security but sacrifice (Matthew 20:20-23)? Can we understand that true witness to Christ's reign does not endear but instead endangers us within our present culture? Dare we face that danger as bravely as the octogenarian bishop we remember today?

These are hard questions that demand much of us. But it remains true that we get what we pay for. Polycarp reminds us that once upon a time there were

Christians who realized that if they wanted true life there was a price to be paid, an investment to be made. We want maximum benefit for the lowest price. By contrast, at the hour of his death, Polycarp thanked God for the gift of Jesus and for the incredible riches of a life devoted to the love of Jesus. He prayed to be acceptable, to be a worthy recompense for the treasure God had shared with him in and through Jesus, and for the promise of resurrection to eternal life. I am confident that Polycarp got what he paid for. And so shall we.

Saint Matthias

Apostle   *February 24*

Where is Matthias in the strange story in Acts of his election to succeed Judas? This small episode is the only reference we have of him. His invisibility is our legacy and all that we have to commemorate Matthias, a strangely silent figure touching our history only long enough to reveal our folly, and God's grace.

Peter insisted on the original structure of the apostolate; Jesus had called twelve disciples and that number must be maintained. So Matthias was elected, the dozen restored, but not for long. Like the tower of Babel this structure, too, collapsed in the happy confusion of Pentecost, a casualty of the Spirit. Affection, not administration, would ultimately shape the church and make it a living witness to the word of God in Jesus Christ.

We need the ghostly presence of Matthias when we are tempted to place tradition or structures ahead of relationship; when we confuse self-examination with self-exultation in a culture where everything, including our religion, conspires against our communion with one another. We need this gospel of human frailty and institutional failure in those times and places when and where our tradition and institutions threaten to grind up human lives, when so much that is destructive and hurtful, divisive and hateful, is done in the name of preserving orthodoxy and purity.

We can only conjecture what became of Matthias. I fancy he was a plain man, and shy, not given to outward show. I cannot imagine him as other than perplexed and a little pained at his election. It was a dubious honor at best, being selected to fill the space of Judas, who had so ignobly failed; being selected not by desire but by the draw of the lot, and for no function or merit save the fulfillment of one person's notion of propriety, procedure, and institutional symmetry. That Matthias disappeared I find not the least surprising.

I imagine he quietly withdrew, bearing within his heart the pain and sadness of it all. I would like to think he proved faithful to the Christ he had loyally followed for so many years. I would like to think he prayed in a place apart in peace, and grieved and wept for Judas, for Jesus, for himself, and for us.

George Herbert

Priest, 1633   *February 27*

Despite his literary renown, George Herbert was a simple priest in his own day. It was his misfortune to be related by blood or ideology to all the wrong people, distancing him from any hope of favor in a system where advancement was linked to preferment, not to performance. Once we wander past a cozy image of a country parson's life in the countryside of seventeenth-century England, we come to the inexorable truth of frustration and isolation that accompanied Herbert's life and ministry. He is the perfect patron saint of every intellectual who has ever been consigned to the exile of life beyond the stimulation of city or university, the loneliness that plagues every heart, mind, and soul that has dreamed great dreams.

The crowning achievement and a recurring theme of Herbert's poetry is the notion that "nothing is little in God's service." Words to cheer the farmers and hardworking women of his villages? I doubt it. These were the words of a pastor in need of some cheer of his own, in need of a reason for living in places like Fugglestone or Bemerton, some sense in a daily commuting and communion within so cramped and crabbed a confinement.

The first of the epistles attributed to Peter reminds us of the humility of our calling: "Do not lord it over those in your charge, but be examples to the flock" (1 Peter 5:3). They are words not for the ordained alone, but for every believer and minister. We, no less than Herbert, live in a world that values power and domination, that measures personal worth by financial gain and notoriety. Our greatest persecution is the torture of living in the midst of such expectation; the greatest persecution of the church is the threat of being ignored, being judged insignificant or irrelevant. Our only defense is a proper perspective.

"Nothing is little in God's service" is the only antidote to despair, the only hope for living. Herbert was only thirty-seven years old when he was sent to

Fugglestone and Bemerton. At a point when he might have expected to be at the threshold of a brilliant career, he was literally put out to pasture. There, not far from Salisbury, he tended his parish with devotion and patience, kindness and genuine love for his people. Three years later he was dead.

Forty years is not long to live; even in length of life, Herbert fell short. Still, read his poetry, sing his verse in hymns, hear his voice in the prose reflections on his life and ministry. Then set those words against the shortness of his life and know—as only the heart and soul can know—that "nothing is little in God's service."

David
Bishop of Menevia, Wales, c. 544   *March 1*

A modest monastic, David was literally pulled out of his monastery and into an assembly of bishops, where he was compelled to arbitrate a dispute fomented by theological controversy. His talents exposed, he was soon made Primate of Wales. I suspect he quietly resented it. To be uprooted from something one wants very much to do and plopped into the midst of some other task is an aggravation, at the least. When it becomes the work of a lifetime, it is an agony.

A God, or a gospel, so demanding is not an easy sell. Evangelism that attempts to cajole people into contentment through beautiful liturgies that merely entertain is so much more attractive. Who wouldn't prefer a spirituality that is a holiday from reality rather than perpetual relationship with a living, and often demanding, God—the God who would not let David go until his life had been emptied out in service to others?

Something of the same sort happened to Paul, as he lovingly recounts in his appeal to the Thessalonians. He neither flatters nor entices. Instead, he offers an incarnate gospel: "We are determined to share with you not only the gospel of God but also our own selves" (1 Thessalonians 2:8). More than the words of the gospel, true evangelism is the sharing of our very selves with others. The word "evangelism" does not appear in the Bible; only the word "evangelist" is found, the gospel never separated from a person—an embodied, incarnate expression.

The pandemic loneliness of our time suggests a scarcity of people willing to give themselves to others. But that is the evangelistic task, God grabbing us by the scruff of the neck as the people grabbed David, and pressing us into service. No matter where we hide, what our personal preference for peace, solitude, even isolation might be, the true needs of the world seek us out and grab hold of us, compelling us—inviting us—to be what God calls us to be: love incarnate, light to the world, finding and filling its darkest corners not with words, but with the living presence of God in each and every one of us.

Chad

Bishop of Lichfield, 672   *March 2*

Chad's irregularity in almost every aspect of his life is his charm. He stands out as one of those wonderful people whose ministry survived and flourished not because of the church but despite it. He gave up the trappings of institutional office for the work of ministry.

Chad was unheeding of structure; he was probably considered either free-spirited or dimwitted. He went wheresoever he was asked to go, by the most direct route and usually on foot. He carried out his work with concern for his people and devoted himself to the simplest tasks as though they were the greatest. He neither argued with authority nor quibbled with propriety. In truth, Chad would have conducted his ministry faithfully, as so many people do, without any recognition. He did not need the trappings of office, honors, or title. It mattered little to him whether he served a Celtic church or a Roman one, for he served neither; he served God.

In the gospel reading for this day Jesus enters the house of a ruler, a member of the Pharisees; he had come to dine but was perceptive enough to know that *he* was the main course. All present watched, waiting for Jesus to make some claim they might challenge with their institutional authority. Others anticipated that Jesus would reveal himself worthy of their admiration, adding cachet to their own standing, like those who invite presidential candidates to dinner, secretly hoping they are entertaining the next Chief Executive. They were not there simply to dine, nor to nurture a meaningful relationship; this was definitely a first-century "power lunch" and those present were concerned to exert the power and exercise the control.

Confining ministry to an institution or office subjugates God's power and authority to our own. Those of us who fear any relaxation of authoritarian control over ministry need to remember that the church has never bled to death, but it has in several centuries nearly succumbed to clampdowns that cut off circulation. It is no small irony that anatomists confirm Jesus did not bleed to death on the cross, but died of suffocation induced by the rigors of crucifixion.

Chad was one of those gentle and remarkable people who "go with the flow." He was neither impressed nor depressed by the church, caught up not in the power and politics of the church but in the life of God and God's people. It was not that he intentionally placed himself last, but that he placed God first. He did not set out to be humble, he just ended up that way.

John and Charles Wesley

Priests, 1791, 1788   *March 3*

Inheritors of Thomas Bray's legacy, John Wesley came to America as a missionary of the Society of the Propagation of the Gospel, and Charles as secretary to the colonial Governor of Georgia, James Oglethorpe. John and Charles were privileged children, denizens of an Anglican rectory, enjoying the benefits of station, education, and considerable innate talent. It is therefore surprising to find them in Oglethorpe's colony, comprised as it was of honest debtors deported from their native land to inhabit this colony of the New World.

How easy it would have been for John and Charles Wesley to remain in their places of privilege, building successful careers upon the firm foundation established by their father, with all their connections at Oxford. But a flame ignited within them at a Moravian meeting in Aldersgate revealed that God had a harder task in mind.

"It is too light a thing," said God to the prophet Isaiah, "that you should be my servant to raise up the tribes of Jacob and to restore the survivors of Israel; I will give you as a light to the nations, that my salvation may reach to the end of the earth" (Isaiah 49:6). That is a sentiment we seldom hear or heed. We examine our lives and measure our gifts seeking the perfect fit, and the easy one. Somewhere beyond the place where we fit just right is the place where we shall be stretched by God to fit a new challenge.

John and Charles Wesley were stretched to serve people who were paupers in every sense—without money, pride, or hope. They were stretched to proclaim the gospel in this new land. It was too light a thing that they serve God among a people established in privilege, a community already confirmed in its faith. Theirs was a weightier task; they who had been so blessed with ability were called to take those abilities where they were most needed, not where they would be most richly compensated.

From them we learn that the path of discipleship sometimes leads not to the obvious, but to the adventurous; does not soothe, but stretches. The fullness we seek for our own hearts may be found when we offer ourselves to fill the hollows of God's heart.

Perpetua and her Companions

Martyrs at Carthage, 202   *March 7*

The story of Perpetua and her companions is bloody and violent. These young Christians were brutally tortured in an arena, savaged by wild animals, and finally executed, their throats slashed. Yet when we tell their gory story it seems rather tame, even small—like suffering and death reduced to the size of a television screen. Reducing the enormous problems and overwhelming sufferings to words renders them less threatening. Distance shrinks even impressive mountains to molehills.

"Recall those earlier days when, after you had been enlightened, you endured a hard struggle with sufferings, sometimes being publicly exposed to abuse and persecution, and sometimes being partners with those so treated" (Hebrews 10:32-33). The blessed amnesia that fades the memory of pain, especially when accompanied by privilege and comfort, insulates us from hard realities. Life's acute pain and problems are reduced to little pictures in daily papers, weekly magazines, and television screens—shrunken images to touch the hearts and souls of a shrinking people.

Shrinking congregations are not as alarming as shrinking hearts. The author of the letter to the Hebrews, reaching back to an earlier prophet, sounds a contemporary note in the warning that God's "righteous one will live by faith. My soul takes no pleasure in anyone who shrinks back" (Hebrews 10:38). With different words, but no less intensity, Jesus reminds his disciples of the tribulation that waits them in this world, warning of a time when "the love of many will grow cold" (Matthew 24:12).

Buffered as we are from the violent crises that cost Perpetua and her companions their lives, passion shrinks to pettiness, and love grows cold. Many of us can protect, or at least distance, ourselves from the dangers of discipleship. We can switch the channel or turn off the set and make it go away. Yet life is as dangerous for some today as it was for Perpetua. And the deaths died today are surpassingly violent. There is no compelling evidence that the world or its problems have grown any smaller; the planet is much the same size it has always been and poverty, disease, and warfare are as rampant now as ever. I marvel that such a story as Perpetua's can be so reduced that I can hold it in my hand. How easily our hearts shrink.

Gregory

Bishop of Nyssa, c. 394   *March 9*

We Americans do not like limitations. We constantly push against them, seeking at all costs a life without boundaries, where all options are forever open, a life as limitless as the skies. For this reason the explosion of the space shuttle *Challenger* will remain a powerful icon for a whole generation of Americans, a generation who, having been taught that the sky is the limit, was surprised to see that limitation so tragically drawn.

Gregory of Nyssa had an unfailing sense of his own limitations. A man with the rare sense to be miserable at his own ordination, he knew that he was being propelled into something he was ill-equipped to handle. He was cautious in investing himself, his faith not inclined to move too quickly, or too lightly. Maybe the deaths of his brother Basil and his sister Macrina impressed upon him the ultimacy of life; one cannot suffer loss so intimate, both kin and contemporary, without a renewed sense of one's own finitude.

Lent begins with a somber imposition of ashes upon our foreheads, a solemn ritual reminder of the very real limitations upon all human beings. Yet from this symbolic truth we move into a season that seems hell-bent on disproving that affirmation, as we work at perfecting our self-disciplines and our piety, straining against the limits of that finitude. Taking upon ourselves an almost superhuman load of activities, are we not attempting to prove to ourselves, to our neighbors, and to God that we are inexhaustible, even invincible?

Compounding this reckless repudiation of human limits, we give up tobacco, alcohol, chocolate, or good nutrition even while adding extra prayer, worship, study, and service—as if to say, not only can I do *more* during these forty days, but I can do it on *less*. In the end, we arrive at Easter like the runner to the finish line, pleased as punch with ourselves for having endured. Lent can shape growth and become a powerful prelude to Easter only when it becomes a genuine embracing of our limitation. For Easter is not a celebration of the triumph of our will; it is a thanksgiving for the triumph of God's will.

Gregory the Great

Bishop of Rome, 604   *March 12*

Constantinople was an education in itself, opening Gregory's mind to a world beyond Italy. In Constantinople he learned the limits of the East, whose empire was quickly crumbling, and of the eastern church, whose influence was fading. His sense of the world's vastness and his knowledge of his own limitations contributed mightily to Gregory's integrity, and to his ministry as Bishop of Rome. The many demands upon Gregory might well have fragmented him and driven him to despair, but they became instead the foundation of his formidable force. His appreciation for the greatness in service and the service of greatness reveal his close kinship with Jesus.

Jesus and Gregory both worked within the world of human institutions and lived within the confines of human finitude, yet each was capable of transcending the limits—even of provoking and challenging the limits. Their greatness lay not in power accrued to themselves, but rather in the power they unleashed in others in their love, hope, and faith. Because others love us, have faith in us, entrust hope to us, we are inspired, encouraged, and enabled in our work and in our living. As we, in turn, trust in one another, love one another, hope in one another, others are strengthened to serve beside us. Little is as damning or destructive as the lovelessness, faithlessness, and hopelessness that says neither we nor the works of our hands are worthwhile.

The rebuilding of nations does not need dollars nearly so much as the faith, hope, and love that deems every human life a thing of incomparable worth. The revival of the church does not need expensive programs or more professionals so much as a thoroughgoing application of the baptismal promise to respect the dignity of every human being by loving, believing, and hoping that every member of this body is sacred and essential to the whole. The restoration of our lives does not need wealth or possessions so much as faith in ourselves, love for ourselves, hope in ourselves—a right sense of our worth as God's own.

Wholeness proceeds from a right understanding of the vastness of all life and the limitations of our own finitude. Those who walk with integrity are neither overwhelmed by the whole nor frustrated with their part. They are grateful for both, thankful for the abundance of God, thankful for the gifts they have been apportioned. This was Gregory's true greatness.

Patrick
Bishop and Missionary of Ireland, 461   *March 17*

His name alone connotes all that is Irish, the icon of a people and their faith. The life and legend of Patrick are so overshadowed by the jovial parades of politicians, shamrocks, and shillelaghs and the torrents of green-tinted beer quaffed in his honor that he seems more at home in taverns than tabernacles. Still, like the legendary Midas whose touch turned all to gold, it seems that everything Patrick touched became Christian. So for those who live by neat divisions of sacred and profane, religious and secular, Patrick is a problem.

Patrick's popularity was evidently something of a problem in his own day. He was criticized for lack of a proper education, perhaps because he relied more upon his own language and images than upon religious cliche, speaking of God from his own experiences and impressions instead of from the established canon. It would seem that popularity and personality are deemed by some gifts unworthy of holy service. This notion deserves to be challenged.

Some believe that in evangelism—proclamation of the gospel—personality should not intrude, nor our witness rely too much upon our own experiences. We are taught to rely instead upon the words of scripture and the formulas hammered out by learned ancestors or professional "experts." Yet in his first letter to the Thessalonians Paul appeals to that congregation out of the depths of self. His gospel, he says, has not been cloaked in fancy words, nor bounded by concern for politics. His gospel, and its proclamation, have been intensely personal (1 Thessalonians 2:2b-12).

Jesus claims authority for his own witness, then confers that authority upon others, encouraging them to make disciples of all nations. But he gives them no tools; they have only the gifts of their personalities to bring others into union with God. How can we pursue a mediating, reconciling ministry of evangelism and absent ourselves from the process? In order to make an introduction, to facilitate a reconciliation, we must be in the middle of things.

For our own day and culture this ministry demands reclaiming the pagan and secular dimensions of our life in the name of the God who created all things, inviting others to look more closely at the world with an eye toward discerning the image of God. It demands opening ourselves to others, becoming the place where others may meet the Christ who dwells in us.

Patrick's power and his persuasion were his personality, a life so open and expansive it welcomed an entire nation, the whole of Ireland. Today, on the occasion of his feast, mugs will be raised around the globe in toasts and all the world, if only for a moment, can be Irish. This is a rare, even eucharistic, image—this elevation in which diverse humans rise above their differences to meet as one. God grant us the ease and the expansiveness of Patrick, that we may be the place of happy meeting where earth and heaven touch, in toast and truth.

Cyril

Bishop of Jerusalem, 386   *March 18*

I have in my office a framed cartoon ripped years ago from a *Playboy* magazine, the gift of a friend who knows me too well. Along one side of the picture is a long chorus line of citizens from some exotic isle of vaguely Polynesian ethos. These happy natives, women and men, are high-kicking in a formation that would do the Rockettes proud. Standing before them on the sands of the beach is a young cleric in pith helmet and clerical collar, facing a rather dour couple with heavy Bibles in hand who have come to check on the young missionary's progress. The young missioner, his talented congregation arrayed behind him, their bright smiles and limber limbs lifted in exultation, looks somewhat shocked and nonplused as he reports to the bishop, "Christianity? I thought you said teach them choreography!"

King David transformed worship in Israel by giving thanks to God in song, placing singers before the altar to give "beauty to the festivals" (Ecclesiasticus 47:8-10). In the fourth century Cyril developed liturgies for Palm Sunday and Holy Week incorporating poetic expressiveness, movement, color, and hymnody to reenact Jesus' final days and make them accessible to human experience. I am in sympathy with those who complain they "just don't get anything out of worship"; people *should* expect at the very least to come away from worship with deeper insight into God and into their own human condition. If they do not, we are wasting our most precious resource for evangelism and neglecting our vocational obligation to teach.

Cyril was wise to comprehend that faith requires more than intellectual assent. Indeed, the great moments of profound religious understanding are frequently playful, more dramatic and experiential than intellectual. Jesus' own teaching employed stories, parables that still captivate and charm. He used nets and fishes, touch and tone, food and drink, basins and towels, and ultimately his own body to illustrate the truth of God's relationship with us and activity among us.

Cyril understood that we are called literally to act—to act out our faith—especially in those times and places where our own faith and devotion are wanting. As we stand around the altar and share the eucharistic meal, it is arrogant folly to assume that we are perfectly united as God intends; what we are about in this act is itself a dramatic action, a moment when we cease to be what we are and take up roles of what we are to be, in the hope that one day we shall become who we aspire to be. In short, we are acting.

In the midst of the world we people of faith become the largest guerrilla theater company on the face of the earth. On the stage of our daily lives we are called to consider well in every action the seriousness of our roles as people of God, people of faith. As for the little cartoon missionary whose steadfast presence in that framed picture both amuses and instructs me in the conduct of my own ministry, I can only hope that his bishop possessed the wisdom and grace of Cyril who, no doubt, would have reassured him that in teaching his flock choreography he was advancing nicely in the task of teaching them Christianity. The rest would be easy.

Saint Joseph

March 19

Tucked away in the recesses of Lent, this day commemorates a man who was asked in advancing age to take a child bride and, even in the betrothal, to accept the dowry of a child not his own. We must peer into the shadows, where he seems nearly always to have stood, to see this man who provided for a family while others were resting in the ease of years, who took upon himself the rearing of a boy who must have been in many ways a trial to him.

Joseph was not a sophisticated man, else he would not have put up with it. He was humble and maybe even a little simple, the kind of man who has a soft heart, the kind described as "the salt of the earth." He was probably a carpenter of sufficient competency to make a living at it, but there is no evidence that he was in any way exceptional—except that he was the kind of man who could take a pregnant, teenaged wife and a troublesome, temperamental boy and make a life with them. He was that remarkable person who could shrug off the gossip and the complaints, take them in stride, else he could not have stood what he was asked to endure.

For his labors he is rewarded with anonymity. There is benediction in that; for the self-effacing and shy, the simple and unschooled, it is a fitting heaven to be gently forgotten. What we know of Joseph we see only in Jesus: the influence of a father upon a son—a down-to-earth common sense, an appreciation for labor and laborer, an unflinching pragmatism. If to Mary we attribute the acute spiritual perceptions of the Lord of life, it is to Joseph that we attribute our Lord's deep and abiding commitment to the earth of which we are formed and to which our humanity is confined.

Lent, then, is the appropriate season to recall Joseph. It is he who reminded Jesus, and reminds us, that we are dust and that to dust we shall return. It is Joseph who taught Jesus to live and to love as one of us, as one with us. Mary may have encouraged his devotion to God, but it was Joseph who forged in Jesus an unswerving commitment to the human race. In the midst of those conflicting devotions Jesus lived. Stretched taut between those commitments, Jesus died.

Old man Joseph, the father of us all. God bless him, and in that blessing, us as well.

Cuthbert
Bishop of Lindisfarne, 687   *March 20*

Whether they are appearing to Jacob in the desert, to the shepherds on the hills above Bethlehem, or in the dreams of Cuthbert, angelic messengers tell us that we share a life with a world far larger than we think. They remind us that we belong to the life of God. It is this message that animated the ministry of Cuthbert.

His was a simple ministry of visitation and teaching in a land of superstition and idolatry, a place reminiscent of our own, where faith had been supplanted by magical remedies and disciplines. We may not think them similar, but our reliance upon self-improvement disciplines, exercise, and medications is not so far removed from alchemy. We have simply brought Merlin into the microwave era in our modern contention with mortality, our battle with the frustrations of human limitations and life's futility. Such a culture needs a Cuthbert.

We need those who recall us to the radical truth of the Incarnation, who remind us that our worth is derived from our relationship with God and not from the many things we run after, or set up in God's place. Cuthbert understood the eucharist as a continuing statement of our worth. Made of bread and wine, simple and natural elements necessary to our life, our eating and drinking are always a confession of our mortality; because we are mortal we must feed our bodies and give them drink. Thus every meal, even the most festive and frivolous party, is a confession of our finitude. To gather with Jesus and to celebrate his resurrected body in bread and wine is to find our true worth as welcome guests at God's table, where we not only ascribe to God all the honor God is due, but also ascribe to ourselves the singular honor that is ours—people worthy of God.

Thomas Ken
Bishop of Bath and Wells, 1711   *March 21*

He publicly rebuked the Prince of Orange for mistreating his wife and Charles II for trying to house his mistress in the royal chaplain's residence. He went to the Tower of London in defiance of James II. Thomas Ken impressed others as a person who actually stood for something.

The ability to stand for something is critical to relationship with others. It is very hard to have any kind of relationship with another person when boundaries keep shifting. To know where another stands is to know the limits by which the other person is defined, and knowing those limits is the beginning of relationship. That is why some of our best and most trusted friends and colleagues can be those with whom we live in fundamental disagreement.

That being the case, it is all the more surprising and saddening that we seem less and less able to appreciate differences as the basis of community and of communion. After all, it is precisely because God is *not* like us that we can have any relationship with God. Yet in the human sphere we seem incapable of relationship except with those who are in every way as we are—right down to the thoughts in their heads, the words in their mouths, the income in their accounts, and the clothes on their backs.

For a picture of the churchly tradition we have inherited and for a worthy pattern for our living, one would have to go far to improve upon the bravely opinionated Bishop of Bath and Wells, Thomas Ken, and his sovereign, Charles II. These two dared to stand in opposition to one another: the philandering monarch and his priggish, punctilious chaplain. Charles so respected Ken he made him a bishop; Ken so respected Charles he stood by the king's deathbed and administered final absolution. God grant us such grace.

James De Koven

Priest, 1879   *March 22*

Writing to a young Timothy, an older and more experienced Paul encouraged him to endure in the face of controversy, counseling him and his warring congregation "to avoid wrangling over words, which does no good but only ruins those who are listening. Do your best to present yourself to God as one approved by him, a worker who has no need to be ashamed" (2 Timothy 2:14-15). A modern advisor might add, choose well the ditch you wish to die in.

Twice elected and twice denied the episcopate, James De Koven refused to trade his convictions for a consecration. At issue was De Koven's defense of ritualism, a contentious matter in nineteenth-century Anglicanism. De Koven clearly defended not the externals of liturgy, but the devotion they symbolized. Nevertheless, he lost his argument and was denied the episcopate to which he had been duly elected, in Wisconsin first and later in Illinois. Tragically, both those who elected him and those who rejected him were probably right to do so.

Those who elected De Koven obviously knew him to be a man of integrity and conviction. They may not all have agreed with him, but there was likely very little doubt as to where he stood. And once he took a stand, he seems to have held it tenaciously. That is why those who were reluctant to confirm his election to the episcopate were wary. Conviction is well and good, even admirable. But personal conviction must be balanced, especially in leadership, with a heart open to compromise. Jesus' parable of the indiscriminate net that snares all kinds of fish and the conscientious laborer who sorts the good from the bad ends not with a moral, but a *non sequitur* about a householder who "brings out of his treasure what is new and what is old" (Matthew 13:47-52). He thus suggests the value not of strict divisions into distinct categories but a creative balance of opposites. Those who knew De Koven well knew he could bend quite easily before the blessed sacrament upon the altar; was he as pliable and respectful of a Lord who is sometimes revealed in ways and persons that challenge our deepest convictions?

That De Koven was gifted and gracious in many ways is evidenced in his accomplishments—his teaching, administration, and pastoral care. Was he the victim of partisan ecclesiastical politics? Quite possibly. But he may also have been an example of how vocation is exercised in the Christian community, of how God's call and human discernment, working together, order the life and the leadership of the community of faith.

The true measure of De Koven is that he seems not to have been embittered by these experiences, but rather accepted them as the vocational directions of the Holy Spirit. He offered whatever anger and disappointment he suffered (and being human, we can be assured he suffered them) back to God and the church in faithful service. He practiced the ministries to which he was called with integrity and skill and, in the end, all were well served.

Gregory the Illuminator
Bishop and Missionary of Armenia, c. 332   *March 23*

When King Tiridates became convinced of Christianity's claims, he made Armenia the first nation to experience Christianity as a state religion. We have Gregory to thank for this dubious achievement. No faith is well served by imposition from above, and the struggle to extricate religion from politics continues to be one of the most daunting tasks of modern ministry and diplomacy. We cannot commend the imposition of a ruler's religion upon his or her subjects, but we can admire Gregory for his determination to evangelize at home. Gregory, whose father fled Armenia (where he was wanted for assassinating the king), went back to Armenia after a sequestered childhood in Cappadocia and resumed his life in the halls of authority, where he managed to convert a king.

While we are relatively comfortable discussing matters of faith in the "safe" setting of our local congregations, we seldom share the gospel—the experience of God in our own lives—among those with whom we live and work daily. We overlook with embarrassing ease and frequency the fact that our most persuasive power is to be found in our relationships; thus we usually go about evangelism backwards, treating evangelism as something done to strangers, even something that initiates relationship, when the opposite is more often case.

When Paul shared the gospel with the Athenians he obviously had spent time among them. His knowledge of their faith and life is plainly evident in his remarks to them, remarks which seem to have convinced and converted many of them. Jesus, too, seems to have built upon relationships as the foundation of his own evangelization. Even on those occasions when he preached to large gatherings, those who had gathered were brought there by friends and colleagues expressly to hear what he had to say, which is rather different from what we conceive as evangelistic enterprise. If Jesus had used our designs, he would have gathered up strangers and worked to persuade them, but on no occasion does that seem to have been his practice. He speaks only to those who wish to hear him. Can it be any surprise that his audiences were more receptive, and his adherents more numerous, than our own?

Discipleship and evangelism have always rested upon a foundation of peer relationships. It seems so simple and so natural, yet is apparently the hardest thing for us to do. We would rather market religion to strangers than share our faith with a friend at work or in class, with a neighbor or acquaintance, even a sibling. While we may not commend the wholesale, hierarchical methods of Gregory and King Tiridates, we have ample and conclusive evidence in them that whole nations are brought to faith when faith is shared among friends.

The Annunciation of Our Lord

March 25

Signs and wonders make us uncomfortable and challenge our confidence in what we hold to be fact (though, of course, even what we hold as fact is always subject to being revealed a fiction). So there is something about the story of Ahaz that touches our own experience. Even when God's prophet, Isaiah, asks him for a sign, Ahaz declines. For his humility he is upbraided. "All right," God replies to Ahaz, "if you won't ask for a sign, I'll give you one anyway."

Ahaz seems properly deferential, even devoted, in his demurral. After all, scripture adjures us to refrain from testing God. But it is one thing to test God and yet another to shy from God's offer to engage our life. God attempts to initiate conversation with Ahaz, to which Ahaz in effect replies, "Thank you, but if it's all the same to you, I'd rather not."

The annunciation is given as a proclamation. A meek and somewhat inexperienced young woman is visited by an angel, who announces that she is about to conceive and bear the child of God. The consummation of this conception will be carried out through the offices of the Holy Spirit. The woman is compliant, even grateful, for this intrusion into her life and body. But in the conversation between Mary and Gabriel there are echoes of the earlier conversation between Ahaz and God's prophet.

The angel greets Mary with the assurance that she is respected and that God is with her, but she, like Ahaz, is wary. Hearing the angel's somewhat effusive greeting, Mary is deeply troubled and wonders what this greeting might mean, suggesting that Mary was not nearly so naive and inexperienced as we might have believed. She has obviously been around the block a few times and certainly knows that, wings and glistening raiment aside, a line is still a line and conversations that begin as that one did can lead to pretty strange, even disastrous, consequences.

So the annunciation was not an announcement after all. It was the beginning of a conversation, and that is a different proposition altogether. What we see in these exchanges between Ahaz and God's prophet, and Mary and God's angel is a painful attempt at conversation. And God seems clumsy at this business of social intercourse. God does not do light banter or polite chit-chat, so Gabriel sounds like a grade-B movie thug and Isaiah delivers God's message with an impatient pushiness. Is God really so awkward as to meet Ahaz's reluctance with a brisk, "Oh, just take the sign anyway," or to greet the dubious Mary with, "Hi, you're a terrific woman and I've chosen you to have my baby?"

God is certainly straightforward and blunt, especially for the kind of intimate and personal engagement experienced by Ahaz and Mary. And both Mary and Ahaz are right to be cautious with such invitations to engagement. Conversation is a dangerous business; it can change your life. Look at Mary and Ahaz. Neither was the same after their talks with God. Neither was God.

The angel's conversation with Mary is the last blunt angelic intrusion in the scriptural narrative; only an occasional voice is heard thereafter. Even God seems to have honed the social graces and realized that there must be a better way to enter the conversation than by playing awkward games with prophets and kings and sending intimidating angels crashing into other people's lives. After Mary we have the Word, and fewer words.

God enters the conversation at our level, in a helpless and vulnerable infant who grew into a precocious but thoughtful child who grew into a gentle, even taciturn, man who said very little but carried on the most intimate of conversations in a life open for all to see. No more annunciations, only conversation—and a child born not as sign or wonder, but as invitation to intimacy, opening a conversation with power to change us all.

Charles Henry Brent

Bishop of the Philippines, and of Western New York, 1929   *March 27*

Stretching unexplored parts of ourselves can make us uncomfortable. The new student away from home for the first time, faced with finding a place in a diverse collegiate environment, among strangers and in an unknown community, will naturally have moments of homesickness, times when that sense of self needs some connecting reassurance with those relationships that make us who we are. The more pluralistic our environment, the greater our need to know who we are and how we are connected. While we cannot excuse exclusivity, neither can we always dismiss the need to be with others who are similar to ourselves.

Each of us tends, if only for self-preservation, to think and act within specific limits and boundaries. A healthy respect for the helpful role of such limits created the divisions of labor that mark specialization. But limits, and specialization, can be corrupted. The priest called to minister *with* the people can become instead the minister *for* the people. Physicians assisted by nurses and social workers can lose the gracious thoughtfulness and tender solicitude of the bedside. Assembly-line work can lose its connection with what comes out on the end. Neighborhoods become ghettos. Competition becomes warfare. Somewhere in between lies diplomacy, the struggle to balance extremes.

Charles Henry Brent was the consummate "ambassador of Christ." The ambassador does not just keep the peace among opposites, but rather encourages communication in the midst of differences by nurturing mutuality. For Brent, as for all Christians, the end of ministry is the equipping of all people for the building up of the body of Christ—a body made of many, all deemed integral to the whole, each "given grace according to the measure of Christ's gift" (Ephesians 4:7). His work and ours calls us from the natural impulse to retreat and into the challenge of relationship, away from atomized separateness and toward companionship.

We cannot pursue our vocations and ministries in isolation. Where people are committed to working together the solo yields to the discipline of the ensemble. We begin listening more carefully to one another, sharing separate gifts as singers share unique voices, with an ear to making harmony. We are not competitors, but colleagues. We do not just network, we converse. And it is not just a task, a faith, and a God we hold in common, but each other.

John Keble
Priest, 1866   *March 29*

We need only the first line of each text appointed for the commemoration of John Keble to take the measure of the man. "Let love be genuine" (Romans 12:9) seems simple until we consider how much that passes for love in our own day is manipulation and deception, how much done in the name of love is selfishness and sin. Genuine human need challenges and reveals love's genuineness; need presents the occasion for love's opportunity, or just opportunism. "When Jesus saw the crowds, he went up on the mountain; and after he sat down, his disciples came to him" (Matthew 5:1). Faced with overwhelming need, Jesus in his day, and Keble in his, responded in genuine love's most tangible expression: teaching.

The education and nurture of others is an arduous, tedious task demanding patience and humility. Of the many problems encountered today, few would not be ameliorated or even eliminated by a little more of such genuine love. John Keble's one desire was to be a faithful pastor. He submitted joyfully and with genuine love to the routine of daily worship and teaching, visits to schools and the tedium of a huge correspondence with those seeking his counsel. This learned Oxford don and impassioned leader of one of Anglicanism's most dynamic reforms lived the principles he espoused, committing himself to a humble ministry within which he shared his considerable gifts unstintingly.

The poetic Keble, who could rejoice over something as simple and self-evident as the rising of the sun upon a new day, represents the model of Christian response to God's world. He embodies the call to acknowledge and engage the commonplace, to take time for others, to nurture and care for others, to teach. He challenges our preoccupation with ourselves and our work, our insidious absent-mindedness and our distracting busyness, all of which make us unavailable to and unheeding of the endless opportunities we have to teach and be taught in the simple routines of human relationship. The mark of Keble's greatness was this gift for taking nothing and no one for granted, for offering and giving himself and his learning so freely. It could be our greatness, too.

John Donne

Priest, 1631   *March 31*

It seems an odd irony that one should enter the priesthood and even rise to prominence within it on the heels of public scandal. This is not a customary career trajectory, though we can be grateful for the exception of John Donne who, despite a secret marriage that ruined a political career, became a poet and preacher of great imagination. In this professional turnabout, Donne revealed that, in some events, poets may serve our needs better than politicians. In the face of wrenching change and challenge we are sometimes overwhelmed and cannot see our way out of our plight, not because our problems are unsolvable, but because we cannot *imagine* a new way of living, of being. And while a majority of Americans still profess belief in God, religious life is but a husk of what it was meant to be.

A vague sense of believing is no substitute for a vibrant sense of being; it is not that God no longer lives, nor even that God's church is irrelevant, but rather that we can no longer *imagine* God or the possibilities of a life lived with God in and through the community of God's people in the church. Donne's gifts of imagination and articulation combined to benefit a culture every bit as lacking in imagination as our own.

Yet even while we admire and revere this man of imaginative gifts, there remains a nagging distrust of imagination, and a reluctance to use it. We know that faith is not derived from fact, but in this information age we are skeptical of that which is beyond the quantifiable. Donne imagined the common bond of all humanity in the sound of a tolling church bell; we want DNA results to prove our connection.

Imagination, perhaps as much as expediency, compelled James I to persuade Donne to pursue the priesthood. Imagination filled Donne's priesthood and his preaching, and a people, with the very essence of God. Would that Donne and his resources were accessible to us today. But then again, perhaps they are. Just imagine.

Frederick Denison Maurice

Priest, 1872   *April 1*

A product of the nineteenth century, Frederick Denison Maurice lived in the midst of a great expansion of western culture and technology, a time that gave rise to increasingly complex social systems as western economies shifted from farming to manufacturing. England and America, especially, experienced this shift in a movement toward urbanism and production. These changes created increased poverty in dislocated workers and raised new questions about the rights and roles of women and children, who were often exploited. Much like the situation we find ourselves in today, the very systems by which life was ordered and governed socially and economically were in a state of flux seeking stability.

Maurice was largely critical of our human systems, for our systems move very quickly from being a means to an end to becoming the end itself. Theologians used to call this tendency "idolatry," though we have been somewhat shy of using that word. Maurice held, however, that the task of theology is a rigorous iconoclasm that challenges the human systems that overlay and obscure the truth of God, in order to excavate the truth hidden behind the idol we erect in its place.

For Maurice, the kingdom—or the realm—of God is not a place set apart, but is simultaneous with our human experience. The realm of God is not something to which we aspire, to which we one day retire. The realm of God is here and now, though hidden and distorted by the systems we have erected around and within it. The exchange between Jesus and Pilate in John's gospel captures the tension of this proximity. "Are you the king of the Jews?" Pilate demands of Jesus, who replies, "My kingdom is not from this world" (John 18:33, 36).

The words of Jesus and Pilate do not seem to connect, for each speaks of power and dominion in different terms. The mutual exclusivity of their perspectives is painfully apparent in an exchange that does not bridge the gap. Only later would his own followers, and perhaps even Pilate himself, see that Jesus was the living bridge spanning this yawning chasm between human and divine realms, the one in whom these realms meet and are reconciled, synchronized, and made simultaneous.

Those of us who know the unifying power of Jesus are enlightened and enriched by relationship with the Christ, who reveals the truth behind the idols and ushers us into God's realm. Those of us who share relationship with Jesus, the ultimate iconoclast, are called to strip away all that obscures the truth from us. And we are called to bear that truth to those who do not want our religion half as much as they want the One we are privileged to know, which is to say, the living God.

James Lloyd Breck

Priest, 1876   *April 2*

Our romantic images of the lush vegetation and abundant harvest of rural life obscures the obvious: the cycle of life is not limited to the brief period of green. Seeding itself is a burial; harvest is a death. The "premature" death of James Lloyd Breck, the foremost Episcopal missionary of the nineteenth century, is not a mere footnote to his life; it is the logical outcome of prodigal living, the mark of a life spent in giving.

The simplest farmer knows that a lush plant may produce a stunted fruit, for the energies and resources required to support the life of leaf and stalk are subtracted from those necessary to nurture the fruit to maturity. Indeed, many of Breck's ventures were lean, seeming failures, the original plants long disappeared. It is not the green growth that is the richest contribution; it is the seed, the little seed that dares to die.

In his first letter to the church in Corinth Paul explained to these early Christians, caught in their jealousies and contentions, that it is not they who make growth, but God. "Neither the one who plants nor the one who waters is anything," he reminds them, "but only God who gives the growth" (1 Corinthians 3:7). It is not their efforts, schemes, plans, strategies, or even successes that constitute their greatest contribution to God's mission. It is only their lives, lives from which God creates and from which God brings forth the harvest.

Similarly, Mark likens the kingdom of God to the scattering of seed. The kingdom of God's making is like seed scattered by one who then sleeps and rises daily, one who continues in a pretty mundane routine undistinguished by flamboyant heroics, only to see the seed sprout and grow quite apart from his own activity (Mark 4:26–32). From these texts we appreciate that Breck's contribution was not extraordinary; his resources, tactics, and abilities were in no way superior to our own. He gave himself, nothing more. But he gave himself wholeheartedly. And this is what we least want to hear.

We who fancy ourselves overextended and underappreciated, overwhelmed and under the gun, find this suggestion untenable. God has looked into our hearts and discovered our secret cache, the portion of treasure we have secreted away, the self—the seed—we hoard and protect. Unless that seed dies. . . .

Richard
Bishop of Chichester, 1253   *April 3*

The ministry of restoration is not the same as preservation, for the latter implies stasis, visions of delicate things gently caressed by tissue, arrayed under glass, locked in vaults, or roped off from reach. Restoration implies renewal, recovery from death, destruction, and decay, return to life and service. Richard reversed the downward spiral of the fortunes of his parents' estate and restored it to vigorous life, its fields bearing harvest, its flocks increasing life, its produce bringing profit.

Then Richard turned his energies to his intellect and through education dusted off that portion of himself that hungered to be brought to light and put to use. He caught the glimmerings of a deep faith, perhaps glimpsed in his relationship to his friend and mentor, Archbishop of Canterbury Edmund Rich, and he nurtured that gift in study and service till it brought forth his priestly ministry.

Richard then entered the mire of ecclesiastical politics. Deprived of his diocesan revenues and even his residence by King Henry III, who opposed his election as Bishop of Chichester, Richard brought episcopal ministry back from the dead—and his diocese and church with it. It is little surprise, then, that we remember him best for a simple prayer asking of God the gifts of restoration: the clear apprehension of God within the accretions of our daily living and our human institutions; the discerning affection that comes of discovering anew what is all the more precious for having nearly been lost; and the satisfaction that comes of working association—the prayer to see God, appreciate God, to work with God that guided Richard throughout his life. It is a delicious and holy irony that would no doubt rejoice Richard that in his little prayer he is discovered, restored, and renewed for service.

Martin Luther King, Jr.

Civil Rights Leader, 1968   *April 4 (or January 15)*

History never truly repeats itself, though its themes do recur in seemingly endless variation. The parallels between Moses and Martin Luther King, Jr., are often noted, the experience of any oppressed people and their leaders finding affinities with the archetypal story of the slavery and deliverance of Israel recorded in Hebrew scripture. The dramatic escape of the Israelites from captivity in Egypt and their subsequent exodus is an engaging story. The modern or only occasional reader of these stories may miss, however, less dramatic but equally important realities in the saga. Imagination, like memory, can be selective, editing out those details that are painful or discomfiting.

Escape from oppression is no quick or easy business. There are many oppressors, not all of them as readily recognizable as Pharaoh. Forty years of wandering in the wilderness taught Israel that, important as release from Pharaoh's grip may have been, Pharaoh was in many ways the least of their problems. Pharaoh, after all, was an external foe, a mortal antagonist; he could be defied, even defeated, and one day he would certainly die. The greater oppressors were those that accompanied the Israelites into the desert, carried with them like the ark of the covenant and in many respects as sacred to them. These oppressors were much harder to identify, for they lodged within the heart.

When Martin Luther King, Jr., cried out that he was "free at last," he was not boasting an accomplishment, he was voicing a hope. The freedom he sought, as he well knew, was not a beginning, it was an attainment that comes only at the end, at last. Moses died within sight of the promised land, only a vision on a distant horizon. He probably did not feel any great sadness or anger at being denied entry, for he had been with his people through forty years of wandering. He knew better than any other that the promised land is as unattainable as the rainbow's end. The story of his people continued well beyond his death, documenting what he already knew: that while Egypt was behind them, oppression was not. They would go on to future deprivations and corruptions, some exacted upon them, some imposed by them upon others. Martin Luther King, Jr., knew that civil rights legislation might be a beginning, but it certainly would not be the end of oppressive racism in this land; it was a first step, but true freedom is the last. We may put segregation behind us but racism we carry with us still.

The death of Moses at the threshold of the promised land, the death of Martin Luther King, Jr., within sight of a new era of African-American opportunity, are both cause for sadness. But the real tragedy is the oppression we carry with us still, the racism we guard as sacred, that makes camp in our hearts and souls as we continue our own exodus.

William Augustus Muhlenberg
Priest, 1877   *April 8*

In Paul's letter to the church in Ephesus he tells them they "must no longer be children, tossed to and fro" by the cunning and crafty arguments of competing religious claimants (Ephesians 4:14). If we believe that we must outgrow childhood lightness, that adulthood adds a gravitational corrective, we need only look at Jesus throwing out the moneychangers in the Temple, like a child indulging a freewheeling tantrum as he literally tosses tables and chairs to and fro on the Temple pavement. Children's relative freedom from tradition, blessedly ignorant and innocent, not only exposes them to dangerous ideas, it also opens them to violent acts that chart new, creative paths. Unrestricted by form or convention, children unsettle us by asking "why?" of our world, by forcing us to ask "what is it?" in their freeform crayon renderings of reality as they see it.

It is true, as Paul maintains, that we can be too easily swayed. But it is equally true that we can err in the opposite direction, that we tend toward a gravity preferring the safely familiar. The balance is in wedding free-spirited adventure and thoughtful conservatism. These gifts were abundant in William Augustus Muhlenberg. He was knowledgeable of Christian tradition and drawn to it, especially in its ritual forms. Yet he was not bound by it. He was able to dream big dreams, push back barriers, kick against goads, and just go off and do what everyone else said could not be done. He would be useful to us now.

At one extreme we confuse frenetic activity with creativity, reasoning that doing everything differently is the same as doing it better. At the other extreme, we have passed the point of genuine conservatism, reasoning that doing more of the same is making a difference. Muhlenberg saw God's creative possibility; his prayer for the church was that our eyes might be the eyes of God, eyes that see beyond the closed designs that hold us in thrall. To see what God sees in us, through us, beyond us—what a prayer for the church today!

Dietrich Bonhoeffer

Pastor and Theologian, 1945   *April 9*

The temptation to trust one's own wisdom is particularly acute for us today. "Do not be wise in your own eyes" (Proverbs 3:7) seems patently foolish advice. It flies in the face of all that we know to be best for us. We are widely read, thoughtful and analytical, calculating and careful. And we are fiercely independent. Yet in each of these considerable strengths there resides a profound weakness. In his classic *The Cost of Discipleship*, Dietrich Bonhoeffer wrote, "Only God can take care, for it is [God] who rules the world. Since we *cannot* take care, since we are so completely powerless, we *ought* not to do it either. If we do, we are dethroning God and presuming to rule the world ourselves." In our vain attempts to take care, to be "wise in [our] own eyes," we are actually usurping the role of God in our lives.

It is hard to accept such theological advice from one who died in a Nazi concentration camp, the victim of his own foolishness, a man who had every advantage but failed to take them, whose own decisions led to his untimely death before the age of forty. His example seems so unwise, his actions suspect. Doesn't true wisdom lead to length of days and personal comfort? Only if we equate the care of God with our own personal pleasure and selfish gain.

In taking care of and for this world, God exposes us to risk—calls us to expend our lives for one another, to spend our lives for love. We are to spend our lives, not save them. This comes as news—and unwelcome news at that. It is heresy to those who would have us safeguard our treasures for ourselves, spend our money more wisely and our intimacies not at all. It is foolishness to every right-thinking person whose feet are firmly planted in reality. But this word remains in the scriptural proverbs. And it remains in the life and work of Dietrich Bonhoeffer, true martyr to the cost of discipleship. It remains a word to the wise, and we would be wise to take it.

William Law
Priest, 1761   *April 10*

Despite our best intentions and regular reaffirmation of a single God who created the world, we continue to live and act as though we are in a world of conflicting allegiances and alien origins. It may seem simplistic and foolish to espouse belief in a world that is still united by its origins in that single God, but it is devotion to that tenet that distinguishes us from others, or ought to. There can be no life for the Christian apart from this single foundational principle upon which all the rest of our faith is built.

Once one embraces the unitive kinship of a common life grounded in a single God, and responds seriously to that belief in action, there can be no division. All of life becomes a unity. For his refusal to swear allegiance to the House of Hanover, William Law was denied the exercise and the livelihood of his priesthood. So he became a tutor, founder, and administrator of schools and homes for the poor, finding ample opportunity and a rich ministry in fields others might have cursed as fallow, infertile, frustrating denials of their ability.

Writing to the Philippians, Paul weaves images of loss and gain, law and faith into such a tangle that it is difficult to see that his point is that he has let go of it all (Philippians 3:7-14). He confesses that he does not possess the mind of God, even if he continues to seek it. But the world as we know it, as it is revealed to us, *is* a glimpse into the mind of God. I do sometimes ask myself just what God had in mind the day this person or that one was made, and that is precisely the question to be asked; just what does God have in mind? In that question we take our place with Jesus, for whom this question was central. It would seem that William Law was equally familiar with the question, and explored it as he found himself denied an easy, unquestioning career.

William Law found that ministry is not confined to established structures, that God may have something different in mind for us if we are content to accept that in this unified world of God's making there is no place where God is not, no work that is not ministry, no task that does not serve. Holding fast to his own integrity and to God's, William Law was not denied, he was *delivered into* a ministry that was God's gift to him, and to us.

George Augustus Selwyn
Bishop of New Zealand, and of Lichfield, 1878   *April 11*

Jesus said a good many strange things. On one occasion as the disciples gathered around him, he prepared them to go out to their work; he gave them instructions to preach, heal, instruct. They are to travel lightly and, wherever they visit, they are to remain in one house rather than work their way into ever more comfortable situations. These are straightforward directives. But one is enigmatic: "If the house is worthy, let your peace come upon it; but if it is not worthy, let your peace return to you" (Matthew 10:13).

"Let your peace return to you." That is an interesting instruction, especially to those of us who desire to be reconcilers but find our way impeded by our own shortcomings. In my own case, these shortcomings are the quickly ignited temper, the snap judgment, the word too quickly spoken. At least one meaning of Jesus' strange instruction may be that in losing our temper, we may lose our peace.

Our temper, after all, is our peace, our composure, our frame of mind, the shape of our passion. And when we lose it, when we leave it carelessly behind, we are bereft of that which we need for mediating, reconciling. So Jesus instructs the disciples to take care of that peace—offer it where worthy, where it is valued, praised, accepted. But they are to take it with them when they leave the unworthy places, where their peace is assaulted, devalued, demeaned, or denied. They are not to leave behind the primary tool of their ministry.

We have all lost our peace at some time or other. We carry animosities and grudges, prejudices and angers, often packed in those spaces where our peace once was. We have literally lost our temper, lost our finely-honed edge of peace, our delicately calibrated equanimity, left it behind in the wreckage of some old, ugly argument where it remains. We left it where it is not valued, where it lies out in the rain and wind, growing dull and useless. Is it any surprise that when we need that temper, that peace, we find it missing? We reach for it and find it gone.

George Augustus Selwyn accomplished much because he possessed a peace his difficult times demanded. His career was not an easy one. Yet where he might have harbored resentment, he seems always to have brought a measure of peace, the peace which passes all understanding, the peace to reconcile and heal.

If we leave our peace scattered upon a hundred angry hillsides, it will not be at hand when we need it, as we do so often now. If we find our temper in short supply, perhaps we need to go back and collect it, to undertake the reconciling work of repentance and penitence that turns us around and sends us back to the places we have been and the people we have hurt, to pick up the pieces of our peace—whatever is needed to let our peace return to us. In these times, we cannot afford to be without it.

Alphege
Archbishop of Canterbury, and Martyr, 1012   *April 19*

Anyone who believes terrorism is a modern phenomenon may be surprised to read of an archbishop who was abducted and held for ransom over nine hundred years ago. Alphege, however, did an unusual thing—he forbade the people to cooperate with the demands of his captors. He refused to allow a personal ransom to be collected from his already overburdened people. His action tormented and frustrated his captors, for this refusal made the captive churchman worthless to them. It defused their bomb, disarmed their gun, made them impotent. In their frustration, they did the expected: they tortured and executed Alphege after seven months of captivity.

What, then, is the lesson? What is the point if, in the end, an innocent man lost his life anyway? That is not an easy question to answer, but neither is it any more difficult than the question of why hundreds of men, women, and children must be endangered or killed by responding to terrorism with military force. There is no easy answer, but at least one strand of this Gordian knot is the question of ultimate values. In a jumble of proverbial sayings about hell, sparrows, the hairs on our heads, and blasphemy against the Holy Spirit, Jesus challenges our hierarchy of values—are we to fear the threat of death, or is there an ultimate power transcending even death itself, the power of God?

Alphege realized that there are some witnesses to the power of God that transcend the rhetoric of violent force. A nation at war does not trust God, it trusts only its guns. Alphege realized that paying a ransom places a price, a value, on the threat of death. Some might argue that ransom is paid for the preservation of life, but the weight of experience proves that it is not life, but death that receives the value in the transaction; it is not the promise of life, but the threat of death that motivates the payment. This may seem a subtle distinction, but it is this subtlety that distinguishes faith.

This is the subtle distinction between those who work for peace and those who fight for it, between those for whom faith is a matter of life or a matter of death. The Christian understands and acknowledges that faith is a matter of life *and* death, that these are not choices but inevitabilities, and that our only choice is to submit to the tyranny of death or, like Alphege, embrace the promise of life in God.

Anselm

Archbishop of Canterbury, 1109   *April 21*

Anyone who has ever approached a loan officer at a bank knows the frustrating reality that in order to borrow money, one must have money. Banks insist upon collateral, some tangible backing that gives reasonable assurance that their investment will not be lost. Similarly, neophyte job seekers know the aggravation of being refused employment for lack of experience, when one can hardly get experience until given a job! Never mind that the employer is only trying to maximize the precious investment of money represented in every addition to the payroll.

That is why the gift of Jesus was such an incredible chance on the part of God. Even Paul understood that it would be hard to die for a good and holy person, much less one deemed worthless or troublesome, yet this is what God does daily: "For while we were still weak, at the right time Christ died for the ungodly" (Romans 5:6).

Begin in faith and work toward understanding: this is the heart of the academic enterprise. We begin with a thesis and then work toward proof, toward insight and understanding. Can it be so hard to begin, as Anselm did, with the thesis that God not only exists, but exists in loving relationship with us? It is a thesis that never exhausts our inquiry, does not begin with the manger or end with the cross, but takes us on a journey sufficient to last a lifetime and beyond.

God takes a chance on the lot of us, and on each of us, risking rejection with overture, loss on every investment. From a purely human point of view, God courts despair. I know from my own experience as a rebellious and headstrong young adult who frequently and violently clashed with his father how my dad at times professed in exasperation that he would never really understand me, and how often I abandoned any hope of ever understanding him. I am thankful that he always followed that declaration with an assurance that he would never stop loving me. His assurances were echoes of God. I believed my father; occasionally I understand him.

We are, no doubt, a perplexity and vexation to God. Does God understand us? I doubt it. But God still has faith in us, still loves us. God places love before understanding, mercy before justice, forgiveness before sin. Can we do likewise?

Saint Mark

Evangelist   *April 25*

S peaking the truth in love" (Ephesians 4:15) is not only a matter of enlightening others to some truth of which we have become aware. Our vocations are collaborative and collegial in nature and each part contributes to the whole. So "speaking the truth in love" requires cultivating my own awareness of truth as well.

"Awareness" is derived from an Old English word meaning "watchfulness." Isaiah suggests that news of God's deliverance is transmitted not just by a herald, but by those appointed to watch:

> Your sentinels lift up their voices,
>   together they sing for joy;
> for in plain sight they see
>   the return of the LORD to Zion. (Isaiah 52:8)

In his introduction the evangelist Mark traces the path of God's progressive revelation from the writings of the Hebrew prophet Isaiah, through the ministrations of an itinerant wild man named John, to the person of Jesus, whose message is itself wholly reliant upon God's action and activity. Speaking the truth in love is not something we do alone, but is a shared effort undertaken by many.

In any collaborative and collegial enterprise, all participants must be watchful. Ensemble players in theater, or chamber players in music, or team players in sports can only proceed out of a watchfulness that orders the whole, a watchfulness that knows how and when to encourage and to be sensitive to weakness, when to lend an assist, when to back away or keep silent. Such watchfulness is demanded especially among those who seek such care, concern, and respect from others.

A thoughtful watchfulness reveals that some who seek justice need help to get beyond their own oppression and competitiveness. A thoughtful watchfulness reveals that abiding respect for those who are different is not only something to be sought *from* others, but also something to be extended *to* others. A thoughtful watchfulness reveals that attentive listening to others opens a respectful hearing of our own case, and that standing beside others in their own struggles often makes begging or haranguing others to help us with ours unnecessary. A thoughtful watchfulness reveals that none of us possesses truth in whole, but only in part, and that we must rely upon one another both to perceive and proclaim whatever truth there is.

May we also pray for the grace to be as watchful and aware as we desire others be. May we seek our own conversion as enthusiastically as we labor to convert. And may we yearn for God's truth as passionately as our own.

Catherine of Siena

1380   *April 29*

It is hard to know what the life of the twenty-fifth child of the Benincasa family was like. Doubtless, there are any number of plausible psychological explanations for the fantasies and foibles of Catherine of Siena, yet her visions have been shared by many a spiritual pilgrim whose deepest longing is communion with God. Having found that communion—in Catherine's case in a bizarre spiritual betrothal—such a life finds direction and a vocation, spending itself thereafter on others.

Consider the vast population of those on the margins to whom we are largely oblivious. They are often the most generous with time, talent, and treasure, and they often have the least to spare. I think of the poor women who comprised a congregation with whom I worked in my teen years. These women worked in textile mills long days, tended families through long nights, and were sometimes mistreated or molested by those they trusted in places where they had every right to expect safety and love. Despite their travails they seemed always to have energy to sing and pray, and they never let an offering plate pass without dropping something into it.

I think of a little band of gay men with whom I frequently met when I lived nearby, gentle men who weekly washed ashore at a parish church in a Virginia seaport—of their litany of lost jobs and disapproving families and angry landlords, all translated yearly into food baskets for the forgotten and toys for the children of a depressed shipbuilding economy.

I think of the tired, harassed, and abused who are emptying bedpans and holding the hands of the dying, not because they have to but because they want to. I think of all those who, in our righteousness, we have consigned to darkness, those whom we have written off as lost and confused and crazy, but who live and love despite us.

"God is light and in him there is no darkness at all," the first letter of John tells us (1 John 1:5). The darkness of Catherine's room exists only for those who peer in from outside, for in that darkness she found God. The darkness beyond the reach of our supposedly enlightened vision—the darkness of sin and death and crime and disease, of lepers and cancers and plagues and prisons—was all light to this weird and wonderful woman. She walked in the same world as we do, but she saw it differently. She saw it as God's world, the world of God's making and God's redeeming, the God in whom there is no darkness, only light. It is hard to know what to make of a woman like Catherine Benincasa of Siena, but saint will have to do.

Saint Philip and Saint James

Apostles   *May 1*

They were probably of similar character and personality, and there is no evidence to suggest that either was a towering intellect or distinguished by grace. Philip and James are thoroughly generic saints, people without bravado who toil and suffer in lives unmarked by high drama or deep despair. They are those who, like Isaiah's audience, eat the "bread of adversity" and drink the "water of affliction" while they wait patiently to be taught a better way (Isaiah 30:20). They rely upon the strength of inner conviction, that interior voice Isaiah says will point the way. To those who fancy themselves sophisticated they appear stubborn and dense, these two disciples who can be simultaneously adamant and inarticulate.

Philip was obviously the kind of person upon whom subtlety is totally lost. When at the feeding of the five thousand Jesus asks Philip where they would find food for so many people, he seems to be mildly teasing; Jesus seems to expect Philip's arrow to sail past the target, as it does when he replies, "Six months' wages would not buy enough bread for each of them to get a little" (John 6:7). Some time later, when Philip asks Jesus to "show us the Father, and we will be satisfied," he reveals to a disappointed Jesus just how little he has grasped in their time together

(John 14:8-9). James, on the other hand, is the kind of person totally lost in subtlety, whose imprint upon the Christian story is so slight as to barely register. Commemorating the likes of these two is truly an exercise in humility.

Philip and James reveal how inflated our lives and egos truly are, how quickly we judge the unassuming and discount their abilities. We consign them to oblivion, omitting them from our histories. Yet all ideas and theories find life in them, for they are the ones who carry out the schemes and fulfill the dreams. The architect who forgets the builder, the builder who disdains the maker of steel and dresser of lumber, both stand to learn a profound lesson in respect. But these apostles teach us even more.

When we are honest with ourselves, there is more of Philip and James in us than we care to see; they touch that horrid fear that we shall leave behind as little as these two. James left so little he had to be tethered to Philip to be recognized at all. Philip, living in the shadow of Andrew and Peter, eclipsed by Judas's zeal, blinded by Thomas's inquiring daring, can be forgiven for asking to see what he must have feared he was missing. Like the slow child in the class who painfully admits that he just isn't "getting it," Philip voices the universal fear of being left behind. "Show us the Father," says this same disciple who had only lately witnessed the miraculous feeding of multitudes!

Jesus, looking at his disciples, must either have been delirious or deluded to see in them the capacity for great things. In Philip's bewildered countenance and the uncomprehending quiet of James, in the questioning face of Thomas, the querulous tone of Judas, and the eager stupidity of Peter, Jesus obviously saw something we would have lost. In their common faces, as common as those we pass unheeding and unseeing every day, Jesus saw greater things than even he could accomplish, something that gave him courage, enkindled love, strengthened faith, renewed hope. Perhaps it was the face of God.

Athanasius

Bishop of Alexandria, 373   *May 2*

Arius was partially right; most heretics are. Jesus *was* a man, a mere mortal. To the prostitute who encountered the resurrected Jesus in the garden path, to the skeptical disciple who touched the wounds, to all the fearful then and now, the incredible became credible. That Jesus walked again, talked again, ate again, and probably laughed again, was living testimony that all created by God, including and especially this flesh we inhabit, can never ultimately be severed from God. In the humanity of Jesus, in his ordinary humanness, we see the divinity inherent in all God has made. Jesus, in life, death, and resurrection, bears witness to the radical relatedness between the God who creates and everything that is created. But Arius, who lived two or three hundred years after Jesus, denied the divinity of Jesus.

Arianism breeds a kind of general low self-esteem. To speak of Jesus, or any of us, as "merely human," is to belittle this corporeal existence. I am a little uncomfortable with those who put down the body, simply because it happens to be the only way we have of being, at least for the present. Discomfort, or dis-ease, with the body comes in several guises and extremes.

A narcissism consumed with diet and appearance is a relatively benign expression that can lead to anorexia, bulimia, or dangerously compulsive behaviors. The obsession to run one more mile, lose one more pound, or drop one more size signals unhappiness with what we are. The darkest shadow of such dis-ease is pornography, a literal debasement of the human in the objectification of the body. In either case, the message is the same: a fundamental dislike of what one has been created to be—which is human.

Athanasius believed Arius to be wrong, and he said so. Athanasius asserted that Jesus is the Son of God, fully human and fully divine. The heresy in Arius was not the assertion that Jesus is simply created, but that being a creature separated Jesus—and us—from life in God. To repudiate the divinity of the very human Jesus is to deny the divinity of the very human you and me, to sever our life from God's, to exile us from the only home we know—our very human bodies.

Exiled five times from his native Alexandria, Athanasius no doubt appreciated the sweetness of homecoming. He offers a ready diagnosis for those who are so ill-at-ease, so far adrift from their bodily homes that they must devise ever new ways of decorating, denying, denigrating, or even destroying that which by its very creation is divine. He would point us to this resurrected Jesus who is one with all that we are, there to see the affirmation of this humanness which is our earthly home, a home that allows no doors or walls, not even the fortress of death itself, to exile us from the God who created us. Standing in the midst of us, scarred hands outstretched, yet able to hold the bread and take the cup, this very bodily Jesus greets us, inviting us to touch and feel and eat, welcoming us home.

Monnica

Mother of Augustine of Hippo, 387   *May 4*

A wise friend once pointed out to me that we often give most generously what we most earnestly desire to receive. Fervent in faith and prayer, Monnica possessed the dedication of the new convert—a dedication that seems to have found renewal and encouragement at several points in her life. Monnica pressed her Christian faith relentlessly upon her husband and her children, particularly her eldest child, Augustine. Was her desire entirely motivated by generosity, or could there have been an equal measure of insecurity that sought reinforcement in the converting of others to acceptance and approval? It is a question to be asked not only of Monnica, but of all similar impulses to conversion.

Monnica's insistence seems to have moderated in time. The end of her life suggests a more mature acceptance of life's ambiguities and God's presence as she let go the kind of frantic zeal that animated her fervent concern for others' spiritual welfare. With illness and death drawing near, her assurances to her sons were that they should not worry. "Nothing is far from God, and I have no fear that he will not know where to find me," she told them.

This insight reflects a mature evangelical witness. This sense that nothing is far from God, that God will know where to find each of us, does much to temper any notion that others are lost from God except through our efforts. Respecting each person and honoring God's sovereignty, our task is not to force either upon the other, but rather to encourage each to grow in mutual relationship.

We do not own any other person, that we should present that person before God as the object of our conquest, like the cat who drops the dead mouse at our feet. Neither do we own God, that we should foist God upon another who does not share our own enthusiasms for the Deity. It is enough simply to ask of ourselves if those who have met us today have encountered any greater awareness of God in us, and to go out to those we meet with every expectation of apprehending God in them. Then we, like Monnica, will witness to faith that has every confidence God will know where to find us.

Julian of Norwich
c. 1417   *May 8*

Have we become so materialistic, so literal that we are blind to any truth more subtly expressed? Visions are not rational; they belong to mystery, so we treat all the apparitions of apostles and saints with a reverence that only thinly veils our incredulity, a socially-acceptable condescension toward those whose feet not only march to the beat of a different drummer, but whose eyes see quite another parade than ours. We draw the line between those who have visions and those who do not, between all that is tangible, corporeal, and empirical and the elusive, emotional, and irrational, afraid that we might become like Dame Julian, on the permeable edge of life, where the strict boundaries are freely transgressed.

We confess with Jesus that God is spirit (John 4:24); those who would see God must be able to see the spirit as well as the substance of this world. But do not mistake memory for vision: they are not the same thing. Is it not strange that whenever Jesus appeared to the disciples after the resurrection, he was not as they remembered him? We may treasure memories, revere history and learn from it. We may respect human nature, and suspect it. We may also see the spirit that calls us beyond memories into new learning, toward God's intention for us.

Dame Julian's vision spoke to her in particular tenses, assuring her that all things can be well, will be well, shall be well. Her vision was not a flight into fantasy, from reality. It was, instead, a call to look at the world with the spirit of God, to look beyond the limits of our own weaknesses, our own powers and abilities, to look with an eye for the possibilities and to see that God's possibilities are our realities. We need this vision to counter our despair that we shall never progress beyond the moment, that we shall be overwhelmed by our future or eternally shackled to our past.

It is impossible at this distance to know with any certainty just what Mary Magdalene saw in the garden on Easter morning, or what the assembly of frightened disciples gathered around Thomas saw within their closed room. We can never know what Dame Julian, Catherine of Siena, Teresa of Avila, or Francis of Assisi actually saw. We have only their words, and the spirit of their visions, the indomitable and irrepressible spirit that animated them and generations of faithful people since, filling them with unshakable confidence that all can be well, will be well, shall be well.

Gregory of Nazianzus

Bishop of Constantinople, 389   *May 9*

Cut off from his influential friends and impeded in his rise to prominence, Gregory was bitter. And he was spoiled. Ordained against his will, Gregory was then compelled by his friend Basil of Caesarea to accept the office of Bishop of Sasima as part of his struggle against the Arians. All that intellect exiled to Sasima, all that study and all those influential friends—only to be stuck in some stupid little dog-pen of a place devoid of civilization's blessings. To hell with Basil and their friendship! Then Basil died. Already exiled and in emotional extremis, Gregory (like the legendary Alice) fell down his own rabbit hole, lost with all his prodigious promise and imperious intellect in his own wonderland of grief and despair.

Somewhere in that far-off land described as "near death" and what we might call today a total emotional breakdown, Gregory learned humility as he learned to see the world in wonder. Answering a summons to Constantinople, he emerged into daylight anew, arrayed in wisdom. When a ray of sunlight sought him out in the midst of a crowd, Gregory was drawn into the power and position that gave him tremendous influence over Christian theology and the shape of the church.

I cannot believe that power and position meant nothing to a man who had once had the arrogant temerity to dismiss a whole region and everyone in it as beneath his talents and his time. On the contrary, power and position meant everything to Gregory; that was his tragic and sinful flaw. Until exile shattered his dreams, and the best friend he had ever had died, denying him any hope of reconciliation. Then, in the shadow of loss he learned the true value of power, the privilege of position. Only then was he fit to hold either.

[Florence Nightingale]

[Nominated but not yet approved for inclusion in the calendar]   *May 12*
Ezekiel 34:11-16; Matthew 25:31-40

Florence Nightingale is probably best remembered for her service in the Crimean War where, with thirty-eight nurses, she reordered the military hospitals in less than three years. Under her leadership a Medical Staff Corps and a Sanitary Commission were organized, and during the same period she established the Nightingale Fund for the training of nurses. Only four years into her work, at age thirty-seven, her own health caved in and she remained for the next fifty years a semi-invalid.

Hers was a brief career, by our reckoning, and yet it is the image of a gentle woman in the midst of battlefield fire that is seared in our collective consciousness at the mention of her name. We remember Florence Nightingale for the heroic and romantic image, but the substance of her contribution was not in the particular care she rendered, important as those individual acts of mercy were. Florence Nightingale was an administrative genius—something we do not often recognize as heroic.

The righteous are not commended by Jesus for what they do *to* the hungry, the thirsty, the naked, the homeless, and the imprisoned, but rather for what they do *for* them (Matthew 25:37-40). While the disciples are thinking in very particular terms, Jesus is urging them to a more widely connected system of life. They had never given him food or water, yet he indicates that the connectedness of life is such that care extends through a whole network of relationship, arcs across the connections of God's making. Unlike service rendered *to* others for the relief of our own discomfort or for the satisfaction of our own egos, service rendered *for* others seeks always to provide or point the way toward what is truly best for the other.

We talk much of ministry in the church, but we seem to choke on the word "administration." Many in ordained service wrinkle their noses in disgust or drop their shoulders in despair over the mention of administration, disdaining it as interference with ministries deemed of greater importance, like spiritual direction and pastoral counsel. But administration and ministry are inseparable. They share the same root and are, arguably, the same work. Florence Nightingale, in the reorganization of the London sanitorium, changed health care in England. It was not nursing that the sanitorium lacked, it was sufficient order to allow what nursing there was to be most efficiently and effectively deployed and delivered. Before Florence Nightingale came along there were military hospitals, so it was not lack of medical care that made them so miserable, but lack of organization. In her several works, it was not what she did as a nurse but what she made possible for all nurses that distinguished her.

The lesson is that our ministries may be too small, our perspectives upon those ministries too narrow. While we cannot cease to help the individual who comes to us in need, our ministry is not limited to what we can do alone. Our priesthood, whether ordained or lay, is not measured in how many good deeds we can rack up in a day's time, or how many prayers. It is not measured in how many individuals we personally counseled or fed. It is measured in what we have made possible, how much ministry we have encouraged and supported, how much service we have rendered for the unleashing of the varied ministries of the servants of God. There is no lack of ministry in the church; the ministries of God's people are infinite in variety and sufficient to meet even the most compelling needs. What we lack is not ministry, but administration—the ability and vision to move us beyond the personal and institutional bottlenecks that prevent a more just and efficient deployment of our many talents and gifts.

Florence Nightingale had to be both innovative and creative in her administration; in her time as in ours, the old patterns and the accustomed ways will hardly serve our stewardship. No doubt the fire she knew on the Crimean battlefield was as nothing compared to the strafing she took within those human institutions who resisted with all their might the reform she advocated. She calls us to reconsider what it means to minister in that holy calling which is administration, reminding us, as Jesus reminded the disciples, that it is not simply what we do *to* others but what we desire and do *for* others that touches his life and extends his work in the world.

Dunstan
Archbishop of Canterbury, 988   *May 19*

People are sometimes rattled (or annoyed) that I do not often wear my clerical collar. It is not that they need the symbol, but that they resent a religious person who goes stalking their world in plain clothes. Collaring the priest is rather like belling the cat so the birds will hear it coming: clerical collars warn the unsuspecting of a dangerous intrusion of religion into those spheres of life they prefer to keep separate from the church.

Dunstan believed that such separations are false, even contrary, to God's reality. There is no place in this world where God is not, and no place where we should not be. For him, politics and government were as much a part of life in God as his monasticism.

Jesus cautioned that the day of the Lord's coming would be sudden and unheralded, and those found doing what God has given them to do will be blessed. Jesus does not say those blessed will be at prayer, or worship, or the study of sacred scripture. In fact, he offered the example of a servant charged with responsibility for household meals, a menial chore hardly associated with deep religious significance (despite attempts to make this a eucharistic reference). Meal preparation is of the ordinary work of life, part of the endless cycle of necessary but mundane labor. Those who are doing what God has given them to do will find blessedness.

For some this will mean prayer, worship, and study, but for the larger majority God has given other work, for this world requires many talents and labors. God formed the earth and made us keepers of the chaos, co-creators. Dunstan brought this conviction to everything he did, closing the gap between religion and government, between religion and the arts, between religion and labor. He believed that the work of reconciliation entrusted to us is more than bringing affections together, uniting sentiments; it is also bringing the physical world back into union with its Maker. Doing just that, nothing more nor less than doing the work God has given us to do, here and now, is as sure a recipe for blessedness—happiness—as any.

Alcuin

Deacon, and Abbot of Tours, 804　　　　　　　　　　　　　　　　　*May 20*

Much of what we treasure in the realm of classical learning we owe to Alcuin, who preserved the library of western civilization by encouraging its use in dialogical instruction. Alcuin was, literally, a conservative—a true conservative. Yet his conservatism seems counterintuitive to our modern impulses to "save" the world, to protect our heritage by not admitting new ways of being and behaviors into our established patterns. Indeed, we can be obsessed with the urge to purify and conserve, to lock our lives away in safety, as though our lives, like bottles of precious wine, are in danger of emptying. The greater danger is that the wine turns to vinegar.

"A disciple…is like a homeowner," Jesus told his followers (Matthew 13:52, TEV). Nothing ages a house faster than vacancy; the empty house declines rapidly without the lively and watchful care of occupants. The homeowner knows that a house demands constant attention. It takes our little nips and tucks, and occasional hard labor and extensive investment. It demands a vast storehouse of knowledge and odds and ends, old things and new. So, too, does discipleship demand daily use, sometimes in small measures and sometimes in vast and exhausting expenditures. But above all, it demands full-time, committed occupancy. The life of the disciple, like the valued text or sheltering house, is lived in, worn to a warm patina, bearing the marks of constant coming and going. It is not always tidy or neatly ordered, but it is often open and always welcoming.

Jackson Kemper
First Missionary Bishop in the United States, 1870   *May 24*

Doomsayers remind us with annoying regularity that membership in the mainline churches is declining. Public opinion polls cite widespread dissatisfaction with all institutions in American society, including the church. If we are diminishing or even dying, however, it is not for the superficial reasons that make the headlines but more likely for lack of vision, courage, and perseverance—all qualities ascribed to Jackson Kemper. In many respects our mission field is similar to Kemper's. We are still met by a social climate indifferent or even hostile to our message and mission. Our ancestors feared freezing to death and we fear being frozen out; they feared the sizzling heat of summer and we fear the withering heat of controversy.

We seem to have vision, courage, and perseverance in abundance when serving our own ends; we have proven quite adept at creatively meeting challenges, courageously undertaking new tasks, working diligently to build better lives for ourselves. We have shown considerable vision in our personal lives, often literally seeing ourselves to a far different and distant end than our origins would suggest or allow. We have proven courageous in the face of oppression and opposition, overcoming profound addictions and defying crippling prejudices. We have persevered in enhancing the quality and the quantity of our life. But we have yet to prove that we are people of God, a people willing to deploy all those virtues in service to God as skillfully as we employ them for ourselves.

The prayer for today does not ask God for gifts of vision, courage, and perseverance; it assumes that these gifts are present, and acknowledges that God has given them to us. We have, it seems, everything we need—incredible vision, ineffable courage, inscrutable perseverance. All we need now is to turn them to God's service as enthusiastically as we employ them in our own.

Bede the Venerable

Priest, and Monk of Jarrow, 735   *May 25*

A dmitted to monastic education at age seven and ordained at nineteen, Bede seems to have been always a little precocious. It is appropriate that he should be remembered for his pioneering scholarship, embracing disciplines that gradually became the standard for historians. Certainly, early talent is admirable, but to venerate Bede's surpassing gifts does little to encourage those of us who are more modestly endowed. There were, we can be sure, other women and men of Bede's day who were his equal. We revere his courage as much as his excellence.

Separated from his peers and playmates at an early age, there is no evidence that he indulged homesickness or whined to be set free from the monastery's rigors. In adulthood, when he might have filled his hours with the uncritical copying of manuscripts, he undertook the analysis of earlier documents. Instead of simply copying histories, he made history.

It is lonely and risky to be ahead of one's time. It is so much easier to "hang back," to underachieve lest we distance ourselves too much from the pack. Heaven forbid that we should take the lead—or worse, that we might fail. Stick to the safe and tried path, the middle way, we tell ourselves, and make no waves. It is not prudent to be too far ahead of one's time. It can lead to vilification or, as in Bede's case, to veneration.

Augustine

First Archbishop of Canterbury, 605   *May 26*

The "middle way" is not always mediocrity. As the sixth century slipped to the seventh, Augustine, the first Archbishop of Canterbury, exchanged letters with Pope Gregory. Augustine's concern? Diversity in the English church. Gregory gave Augustine good advice: mediate between custom and conversion, chart a course through human diversity that tolerates a broad middle way. Thus, from its inception Anglicanism chose a course for the middle of the road; for that choice Anglicans are called wishy-washy, noncommittal, even "chicken." Yet even the chicken would tell you, if she could, that it is the side-ditch, the extreme edge of the road's path, that promises safe haven; the middle of the way is most dangerous, exposing one to injury and death. The middle of a struggle between warring factions is the place of greatest danger.

Paul tells us we are to be ambassadors of Christ, entrusted with the message of reconciliation and the work of mediation (2 Corinthians 5:18). In that ambassadorial ministry we are thrust into the midst of conflict, not delivered from it. Our ministry, as Gregory counseled Augustine, demands a nonpartisan position. Our work is not to win our own point, not to secure our own way, but to bring all into full dialogue with God. To achieve this end we must be in the midst of things, sticking our necks out.

To shift metaphors, like the disciples to whom Jesus said, "Put out into the deep water and let down your nets for a catch" (Luke 5:4), we shall fish in deep waters. The shallows indulge our caution, for we can see there, even before we drop the net, what kind of fish we might expect and how many. In the deep, farther from shore, where the catch is not visible, our nets may fill with only God knows what, our boat fill to the gunwales and sink. No wonder Peter fell to his knees and begged Jesus to depart from them.

"Success" broke their nets and was sinking their boats. Even Jesus' reassurance that in future they would be fishing for a different catch—for people—was of little comfort. Peter's instincts were sound. The implications of this metaphor was a discipleship in the deepest, most dangerous ocean; a heart filled beyond capacity and broken with the haul; a life swamped by the strain, drowned far from shore. It was a fearsome prospect for Peter and remains equally so for the church that succeeds him.

If we undertake to be like Augustine of Canterbury, we shall find ourselves in the midst of the church's diversity. Our church will be overrun with new customs and strange practices, our old habits will be broken, our familiar and trusty vessel swamped and drowned. We will be out in the middle of that vast sea of God's creativity, in that place where all the differences meet, that storm-tossed, dangerous ocean. We will be in chaos, where God calls forth new and abundant life.

Visitation of the Blessed Virgin Mary

May 31

The miraculous is inseparable from the mundane; the walls between the human and the divine are permeable. This we learn from the story of the cousins, Mary and Elizabeth. Elizabeth was old and barren, well past the age of conception, nearing the end of a life of sad frustration in a community and culture for whom children meant everything. Her faithful husband was a priest, a man whose faith was no doubt daily tested in the question of his cursed childlessness. Mary was still a child by our standards, possibly still a teenager. Even setting aside the biological questions of her conception, the disparity between her youth and the aged man to whom she was betrothed—this marriage arranged not by romantic liberty but bald practicality—was enough to cause her embarrassment and sadness multiplied many times over by the burden of a child.

Each of these women, beset with socially problematic pregnancies, reveals to us the paradigm of the faithful life. For these two women who ought to be burdened and depressed instead express real joy; they praise God for their respective predicaments. Their attitudes are unrealistic, even absurd.

Elizabeth's child was a delayed joy, a child she would have to care for in her old age, a child she would likely not see to adulthood. And at her advanced age, she probably encountered derision—and more attention than any of us would desire under the circumstances. Mary's child, on the other hand, was a premature burden. She was catapulted into adulthood and harnessed to responsibility as the beast is put to the plow. Hardly the stuff of blessedness, then or now.

Yet Elizabeth and Mary believed God had given them cause for joy. They found divine meaning and personal fulfillment in their predicaments. And they reared their sons with that same singularity of purpose, reared them to see God at work in their lives, God at work in them every day. These women and their sons believed themselves to be of God, to be partners with God.

God is in the midst of our predicaments, too. We need not merely settle for the hand that is dealt; God invites us to examine the cards carefully, to weigh them strategically, and to play them skillfully. We may reflect upon our experience, see through the walls that divide the sacred from the mundane and thus see ourselves, like Mary and Elizabeth, Jesus and John, as incarnate partners in God's creative activity.

Out of that intentional, disciplined, and reflective presumption we bring our joy to God's table. Out of that presumption we offer back to God what God so freely offers us as presents and predicaments, finding joy in all.

The First Book of Common Prayer

This feast is appropriately observed on a weekday following the Day of Pentecost.

As a Christian people, we Anglicans are distinctive. Other traditions within the body of Christ possess and make confessional statements and creeds inherited from history, derived from distant times and places. From our inception, our common prayer and worship have been the articulation of our faith. Worship is our central act of being together, our most consistent and convincing witness.

Perhaps because we were born to a shamelessly political cradle and our childhood nurtured at English royal courts, our youth spoiled by empire, our coming of age marked by a revolution, and our present maturity lived within a worldwide Anglican communion of staggering diversity, we are loathe to draw sharp distinctions between world and worship, between what we say and what we do. We have never known "good old days." We have burned and beheaded one another over theology and politics in our English origins and shot one another over prayers for monarchy in the midst of a revolutionary bid for democracy in America. We have depleted our resources to build churches that will burn incense across the street from ones that will not. We have marched for civil rights while supporting segregated churches and celebrated the eucharist on the steps of the Pentagon in protest of a war while consecrating a bishop to serve the armed combatants of the same. We are thoroughly inconsistent because our worship is the way we work at living with and loving God, neighbor, and self.

That is why I love this church. In its struggles, its strife, and its silliness, it negotiates that nearly untenable tension that John's gospel describes as "true worship" (John 4:21–24). True worship is engagement in spirit and in truth. This unseemly combination of spirit and truth sometimes stretches us to our limits but, as frequently, allows us to resonate with the fullness of God, like a taut string plucked.

The Book of Common Prayer is now and ever shall be central to that life. But no prayer book ever written is immutable. I have stood within the walls of one of the oldest shrines of the Episcopal Church, at the very heart of our nation's history, and read the intercessions from a prayer book whose pages are blotched with ink, forceful and angry lines crossing out the name of a monarch to make way for the first prayers of a fledgling democracy. Our words of worship are living words, subject to the fullness of life, including the death from which all new life springs. Our words are not truth, nor can they capture the spirit; they are only our faltering and fragile attempts to give expression to both. Neither our first prayer book nor our last is perfect or eternal. If it occasionally gives us glimpses of truth, if it is sometimes animated with the Spirit of the living God, that is enough.

Justin

Martyr at Rome, c. 167   *June 1*

For us education can be a palliative to restlessness, since the object of much modern learning is to secure answers and solve problems. But Justin, like many before and since, was stimulated by knowledge and hungered to use and add to his learning. Such restlessness for knowledge needs the focus of relationship and commitment.

Emotional and sexual restlessness, if not grounded by commitment, can dissolve into promiscuity. Spiritual restlessness, if not grounded by commitment, can dissolve into vague and vapid aimlessness that masquerades as faith. Academic and intellectual restlessness, if not grounded by disciplined commitment, can dissolve into incomplete courses, unfinished degrees, or even complete mental breakdown. Justin encountered in Christ the commitment to harness the power of his restlessness for knowledge.

Jesus himself evidences commitment in a strong sense of calling that focused his energies and directed his ministry. He believed he was personally called, that his life and his gifts were related to someone and something beyond himself. His own restlessness was committed to Israel's God and therein was its power. Similarly, Justin found meaning for his life in his relationship to God, and more specifically, to Jesus. Thus Justin died, like many an early Christian martyr, not for an ideal or an idea, but for relationship, for love of another; his commitment was steadfast to death.

Martyrs like Justin always astonish their tormentors, who assume that what they demand of the martyr is the mere capitulation of an idea, the recantation of a principle or premise. What tormentors do not understand is that to ask the genuine believer to deny their faith is asking the believer to deny the primary relationship in his or her life. Justin might well have recanted his teachings, refuted his ideas, or rephrased his premises, but he could not and would not renounce his relationship with God in Christ Jesus.

The gospel assures us that restlessness need not be aimless; in relationship to God we find our lives, our intellect, and our abilities called to specific service in specific relationship. God provides purpose, direction, and meaning to our restless urges. For God is committed to a particular relationship with each of us in and through Jesus Christ. God is committed to us in a relationship that has never wavered, never compromised, and never denied us—that would rather die first, and did. That is what Justin had—a relationship to die for.

The Martyrs of Lyons
177   *June 2*

Christianity was still a young religion in the year 177. Scattered congregations throughout the Roman Empire who gathered in the name of Jesus were largely ignored, even tolerated. But sometimes one was singled out for cruel and unusual punishment. Such was the fate of a community of Christians centered around the cities of Lyons and Vienne, in Gaul.

Their persecution began quietly. At first they were simply ostracized socially, snubbed in public places and intentionally dropped from the guest lists of Roman hostesses. Then they were denied access to basic amenities, much as certain neighborhoods today get short shrift from city services. Gradually, the Christians became the butt of jokes, then the brunt of pagan insults, then of stones and blows. Their homes were vandalized, and they were rounded up as suspects.

Slaves became a popular target, especially if they worked in Christian households. Extracting confessions—even for wildly fabricated charges—was particularly easy. Informing on their Christian bosses was common; it mattered little that the charges were false if lying spared their own lives and occasionally evened the imbalance between slave and owner. It took as little then as now to arouse the anger of the poor—especially the working poor—to violence. Given opportunity, unbridled pain can inflict brutal wounds.

The description of Blandina's tortures, recorded by Eusebius, is graphic, her endurance legendary. Her repeated confession was as simple as it was pathetic: "I am a Christian: we do nothing to be ashamed of." It would be more difficult for us to make that confession, for in the intervening centuries the church has done much of which to be ashamed.

This theme of shame is echoed in Jesus' warning that "those who are ashamed of me and of my words in this adulterous and sinful generation, of them the Son of Man will also be ashamed when he comes in the glory of his Father with the holy angels" (Mark 8:38). When we measure our life against Blandina's confession, asking ourselves how, why, and where we have compromised her witness—and Christ's—in words and deeds, we *ought* to be ashamed. We have too often been ashamed of Jesus and his words in this "adulterous generation."

Yes, adultery extends beyond the marriage vow. Compromising the baptismal vow to honor and respect every human being is as harmful an adultery as any extramarital sexual liaison; the distinction between these adulteries is not degree, but kind. Adultery is a form of idolatry, a corruption of the covenant promise to have no other gods, neither to fashion nor worship images of the one God.

Consider all those instances in which we place anything else above the priorities of our baptismal promises. We compromise our promise to be faithful in worship when other priorities that seem more important take us away from the life of the community. Our pride so easily allows us to compromise our promise to be repentant of our sins and to work for reconciliation. And our insecurity and lack of charity tragically urge us to compromise our promise to respect the dignity of every person.

Blandina would not be able to make her confession of the church's blamelessness today as she did in 177. We cannot undo our history, but we can examine our lives and our community. We may profit from this examination, even if we cannot pass it.

The Martyrs of Uganda

1886   *June 3*

The writer of the letter to the Hebrews reminds them that once they were under heavy siege and severe persecution. They "endured a hard struggle with sufferings, sometimes being publicly exposed to abuse and persecution, and sometimes being partners with those so treated" (Hebrews 10:32-33). Yet by the time of this letter their ardor has cooled, life is no longer so difficult, and faith is being eroded by ease. Jesus foresees the very predicament this letter addresses when he ventures that in the aftermath of predicted persecutions "many will fall away, and betray one another and hate one another. And many false prophets will arise and lead many astray. And because of the increase of lawlessness, the love of many will grow cold" (Matthew 24:10-12). The description sounds sadly modern.

The martyrs of Uganda were burned to death in 1886 by a king who was jealous of their fidelity to Christ. His anger and their executions are the more remarkable since the defiant Christians were not rebel peasants; they were members of the royal court. Instead of containing the king's problem, their deaths only amplified it. To the consternation of the jealous and controlling, the gospel will not be confined. It will grow despite efforts to contain it. It has the power to draw together and to blow apart. Maybe we have emphasized the former to the detriment of the latter; perhaps the explosive power of the gospel is God's corrective to our cold, calculating, controlling hearts. The gospel planted by white missionaries among royal Ugandans ultimately detonated, scattering the Good News; white missionaries were replaced by black, an elite royal Christianity supplanted by a common, universal one.

Sadly, modern witness continues to inflame the anger of those who would keep Jesus and the gospel to themselves and their kind. The gay or lesbian couple making vows of fidelity and seeking God's grace for their life together infuriate as many as they inspire. Women or people of color with professional standing, lay or ordained, are still as often denigrated as admired. The poor, struggling against great odds to achieve neighborhoods long ago abandoned by any with the resources to move on, are castigated and categorically denounced as welfare cheats, social parasites.

The point is that those of us who enjoy social and material privilege and comfort are too often closed to those who do not. Perhaps it is our desire to put behind us our own difficult memories and embarrassments, to distance ourselves from our own pasts. We fear that partnership with those in the midst of struggle will upset our own fragile security. Our fears are not groundless; solidarity with those in danger *does* make us vulnerable. The martyrs of Uganda were remarkable not for daring, but for caring. They were, for the most part, privileged people. But they were openhearted. That was their undoing, and their salvation.

Boniface

Archbishop of Mainz, Missionary to Germany, and Martyr, 754   *June 5*

After a lifetime of accomplishment, it could not have been easy for Boniface to go back to Frisia, to a place associated with early frustration and failure. Failure is something we want behind us. It is a relief to write off the things we no longer want to deal with, the old responsibilities. When we fail in school, we are loathe to go back to learn what we did not know; drop the course, change our major, take an incomplete, move to another school. When we fail at love or friendship, it is so much easier to write the person off, erase the phone number, let him drop. When we fail at commitment, move on; when we fail at work, move on; when we fail at community, move on; when we fail ourselves, move on. And do not look back.

In the midst of his travels Paul returned to Jerusalem, not knowing what awaited him there. He was going back to a place he had been earlier to face possible trouble, unresolved tensions over allowing Gentiles to become Christians. Even as he urged the Ephesians to turn back to recover the unity and confidence they were in danger of losing entirely, he faced the painful prospects of going back either to be ruined or redeemed by what awaited him.

Redemption demands a return; our redemption demanded that God return to a disappointing people, to Israel, to us. Our eucharistic prayers render thanks that when we had turned away from God, God did not abandon us to sin and death, but returned to deliver us. How much easier it would have been to have walked away, to have stayed away. Jesus, too, when tempted to abandon his own vocation, to save himself from certain danger and probable death, resolved to return to Jerusalem, the beginning of his ministry and his mistakes—for surely, being human, he made them.

So Boniface returned to take up the work he had begun so many years before. While waiting for a group of confirmands, he was murdered. Denied the satisfaction of confirming the few converts he had instructed and nurtured in the faith, he died in Frisia, where his faith had first and finally called him.

Columba

Abbot of Iona, 597   *June 9*

A halo surrounds Columba, this irenic figure whose life was so charmed (and charming) that legend says he died peacefully, at prayer before the altar, rested and with a smile on his face. There is a breeziness about his biography that stands in stark contrast to the tragic stories of so many who toiled and were tormented in faith's name and cause. In contrast to the opposition experienced by so many missionaries of the gospel, Columba was received graciously by the Picts and among them he launched an extensive ministry.

Success is often characterized as conquest, the road to achievement a battlefield. We scheme, plot, threaten, demand, bully, and batter one another, and sometimes even for noble purpose. Anything of value demands work; the higher the value of the prize, the more demanding the work to obtain it—no pain, no gain. Moreover, we have become as cynical and suspicious of the gracious reception as of a free lunch; somewhere there will be an accounting.

When a group of excited disciples came to Jesus filled with the enthusiasm and wonder of their own works, he advised them to be wary of reliance upon advanced pyrotechnics; after all, he told them, he had "watched Satan fall from heaven like a flash of lightning" (Luke 10:18). They were to represent the gospel not in displays of power, but rather in their own names and upon the strength of their own character. Decades later, Paul would counsel the Corinthians not to rely upon rival claims of authority based upon exploits or achievements—theirs or their heroes'. Instead, he admonished them to live and act out of their own integrity, an integrity based upon their birthright as God's own progeny and heirs. They were, in short, their own foundation, for Christ had made them so.

Columba and the Picts enjoyed rare trust. Columba must have been possessed of a rare integrity, and the Picts likewise, for they seem to have met like lovers made for each other in heaven's workrooms. Each found in the other the basis for long, lasting, and fruitful relationship. How it was achieved, we are not allowed to know. Perhaps it was reward merited by long and patient growth; perhaps it was sheer grace. But God smiled on Columba; Columba smiled upon the Picts and they upon him with a radiance that even death could not erase.

Ephrem of Edessa

Deacon, 373   *June 10*

The story of Christianity is a fine story, but it is a family story. Much that is good and even holy has grown from the sharing of this story among the members of this family, but our greatest failing and our greatest challenge is moving from this important but isolated monologue to engage in dialogue with those beyond ourselves. When we do have opportunity to share with those who do not espouse our faith, who are outside our family, we launch defensively (and offensively) into our story. We use the esoteric vocabulary we have developed within the family for talking about these things, further excluding others with the arrogant assumption of our superiority. Moreover, we who have heard the story many times have not always listened attentively and we sometimes garble and distort the story when we pass it along.

A growing number of people in the world around us, and next door to us, do not know our story. Nor do we know theirs. The challenges ahead of us are to learn our story well, to learn new ways of telling our story, ways that communicate beyond the limits of our specialized jargon and our insider assumptions, and to listen to others' stories and learn their languages—not with the intent to change, correct, or convert their story into ours, but with an honest appreciation for the truth of their experience, honoring their family. Our shared challenge—theirs and ours—is to understand.

When we set about "building community" and "working for inclusivity," we act as though there is no family save our own and our sole mission is to make everyone like us. But we espouse a creed that affirms we all originate from one God. If we truly believe this, we are already surrounded by community; we do not have to make it. We do not have to work for inclusivity; God includes us all in the family, a community. We need only discover—uncover—that reality and free it from all that we have done to obscure and hide it.

In Ephrem we find a companion in labor. He wrestled with words, struggled with syllables, measuring meters and multiplying metaphors—all to tell the story. In dialogue with his predecessors in the written record of scripture, in conversation with his contemporaries through his teaching and preaching, Ephrem left a legacy of poetry and music. Through him, generations have literally sung themselves to faith.

Our most daunting and demanding assignment may not then be to make our song in unison, but rather to find our place in the human choir, to decide whether it is more important to grow larger churches or to nurture greater respect, whether to sing our own song louder, or to welcome new harmony and counterpoint to the mix. Whether to sing ourselves to sleep, or to life.

Saint Barnabas

Apostle   *June 11*

It is strange to conceive of anyone outstripping Peter and Paul or the immodest evangelist, John. But Barnabas was a prodigious apostle. It was Barnabas who was sent first to a man named Saul who had been struck down by blindness in the Damascus road. It was Barnabas who nurtured the faith of Paul, introduced the former zealot and persecutor to the wary community of early believers, among whom he had no standing until Barnabas established it for him. And it was Barnabas who, in his senior capacity as apostle to Antioch, called Paul to be his assistant. From that point onward, the two worked side by side cultivating what would become the church, a federation of believers made of Jewish sectarians and non-Jewish converts forged in the furnaces of conflict. Observers of their work in Antioch attached the name "Christian" to their community, naming and shaping this community and its successors with a distinctive identity. But of the things we know about Barnabas, his highest achievement was this: "he was a good man, full of the Holy Spirit and of faith" (Acts 11:24).

There is no catalog of his many accomplishments or his deeds; Barnabas is remarkable for what he enabled and encouraged in others. His goodness was the result of his being a person full of the Holy Spirit, a person filled with faith, animated by relationship with God. He sought no reward or gain; he never received any wage from the church but served and lived off his own labor apart from his ministry. He undertook his ministry because it was something he loved doing, a way of giving tangible expression to the pleasure he derived from his relationship to God.

Like Jesus, whom he followed, there was nothing more important to Barnabas than God and God's family. When embroiled in controversy he was more concerned that the right and good thing be done than whether a thing be judged right and good. Wherever truth could be realized and practiced, Barnabas acted, even if it meant violating propriety and religious law, even if it meant making the rest of the church angry with him. He did what he deemed best and accepted the consequences—the mark of a good person, full of the Holy Spirit, and of faith.

Basil the Great

Bishop of Caesarea, 379   *June 14*

He was pushy, he was slick, and he was the consummate politician; in short, Basil was the kind of churchman few of us admire today. Born to privilege and given every advantage, he was aggressive and ambitious. Battling heretical controversy, which is always as much a matter of personal taste and partisan politics as it is theology, became his central work. His legacy is a strange mixture; he made profound contributions to the theological doctrines of the church and equally impressive contributions to the practical relief and pastoral care of his people. The ironic complexities of his life are happily preserved, a wonderful mass of contradictions.

The life and ministry of Basil remind us of the paradoxical nature of faith, the balance of opposites that gives life its dynamism. Separate the work of the Holy Spirit from the hardball politics of human interaction within the institutional church, and spirituality becomes a pale and passive thing. Basil's life and example reveal that the power of the Holy Spirit is manifest in the human arena and incarnate in human action.

I do not admire those who, like Basil, blatantly campaign for ordination to the episcopate. But I confess a begrudging respect for those who perceive their ministerial vocation so clearly and with such conviction that they risk the slings and arrows of politics, and worse, in its cause. Basil possessed a particularly hardheaded devotion, a constellation of intellectual gifts afforded him by his advantage, and a towering self-confidence, all of which he harnessed in service to the church. While his example and the hierarchical structures of his time may not accord with our present sensibilities of right order in the church, they served their purpose and contributed to our inheritance.

Oscar Wilde created Dorian Gray, a fictional rake whose polish and seemingly eternal youth won him admiration and even envy; meanwhile in a dark closet the portrait of Dorian Gray eerily aged, bearing in its withered, rotting visage every evidence of his corruption and vanity. Basil's life was nearly the opposite: while Dorian Gray's closet hid a portrait literally going to hell, Basil's contained a portrait yearning for heaven. At Basil's death, he willed to Caesarea an entirely new town, built on his estate with adequate housing, health care, and welfare facilities. Thus even as he argued and politicked on behalf of the Holy Spirit's place and role in the doctrine of the Trinity, he was actively incarnating in very material ways the ministry shared with Jesus. Neither his theology nor his spirituality were divorced from the necessary work of the human community.

Basil's complex life challenges every tendency to divide and dilute theory and action, to substitute a vague spirituality for an active faith, to substitute arguments about theology for practical ministry. It challenges economics separated from the common good, law from justice, medical research from human healing, literary theory from words that communicate, learning from wisdom, head from heart.

Pray for grace to continue Basil's example, but take seriously to heart those things for which we ask. For such grace will draw us into the contradictions, to that busy crossroads where faith and action, theory and practice, creed and ministry all meet in integrity.

Evelyn Underhill

June 15

Someone has cautioned that mysticism begins in "mist," centers in the personal pronoun "I," and ends in "schism." It is a helpful and handy reminder of the power of mysticism, defined by *The Oxford Dictionary of the Christian Church* as "an immediate knowledge of God attained in this present life through personal religious experience."

Evelyn Underhill found within the Anglican tradition an abiding appreciation for the doctrine of the Incarnation: human living and human experience are hallowed by God's participation in this life in Jesus and in us. But she also found in Anglicanism a profound respect for transcendence, a clear distinction between our experience and God's, an insistence that God is wholly other; without this independence and transcendence we could have no real relationship with God. While Anglicans have no corner on these Christian precepts, we have emphasized their theological prominence in a life and witness unafraid—even eager—to engage this world.

The balance of these two fundamentals—incarnation and transcendence—is the safeguard against the extremes of mysticism, preventing our fanciful flight into a denial of our humanity. God's transcendence—and ours—guards against a spirituality that sees God as one of many human psychodynamics (making God something within us) or sees us as microbial bacteria coursing through God's bloodstream (making us something within God). It puts the lie to many of the sundry images that have either of us absorbed into the other, including the popular notion that God is somehow distributed in nature, thus denying all that is distinctive in our being and distinctive in God's being and essential to our relationship with one another. This balance is expressed in Underhill's conviction that mystical life is simultaneously open to and woven into everyday experience.

These qualities are essential to spirituality. For while one can have an intensely personal experience or apprehension of God, such experience must also be open to critique, open to validation and repudiation, for the sake of witness. To hold such experience strictly in private deprives others of a larger vision of God; this is irresponsible stewardship of experience. Our God is a giving God; our personal knowledge of God belongs not only to us, but to all who share our human experience and hunger for a deeper knowledge of what it means to be truly human. Indeed, we ought to be suspicious of any evangel that does not address our human being.

Spirituality, woven with our experience, is the fabric of our human being. Woven threads are essentially cruciform, warp and woof intersecting in the vertical and horizontal planes of the cross. Spirituality divorced from human experience has nothing to hold it up; human experience without the Spirit has nothing to bind it together. The tight entwining of the two is essential to the integrity of life's fabric. Evelyn Underhill recovered the gifts of mysticism that allow us to see with imagination what has been and what can be, without closing or diverting our eyes from what is.

Joseph Butler

Bishop of Durham, 1752   *June 16*

What must I do to inherit eternal life?" The lawyer already knew the answer to his question. When Jesus responded with his own questions, "What is written in the law? What do you read there?", the lawyer was quick to offer the ancient summary of the law: "You shall love the Lord your God with all your heart, and with all your soul, and with all your strength, and with all your mind; and your neighbor as yourself." And Jesus said to him, "You have given the right answer; do this, and you will live" (Luke 10:25-28).

What is it about us that keeps asking the question as though the answer is today somehow different, as though the fundamental principles changed while we were asleep last night? Are we really that forgetful? Or that hopeful? Or is it just our nature to resist the answer, that particular answer, an answer that was already ancient when the lawyer reached back into Judaism's earliest writings and dragged it forward to his own time?

Joseph Butler challenged the Deism of his own day, a theology that characterized God as a divine watchmaker who had set the creation in order, wound its mainspring taut, and then left it to run by itself. This belief supports human independence and self-sufficiency, and offers a neat solution to the nagging problem of why bad things continue to happen to good people. But it also underestimates the frustration of human nature untethered from God.

One major difficulty of the ancient summary of the law is that it does not tell us precisely *what* we are to do, and that is worrisome. The summary's "answers" are insufficient for us and for the lawyer because they are so inexplicit; though it tells us we are to love, and even whom we are to love, it never tells us *how* we are to love. For those who want a clear set of instructions, a checklist of duties and obligations, rules and regulations, trying to live by this almost skeletal summary is madness.

But Jesus answers us as he answered the lawyer; you know the right answer, just do it and live. But loving God is so abstract, so diffuse. What does it mean? Figure it out, says Jesus, in the only way love is ever figured out—in the loving. Love one another, love yourself. The way to love God is to engage relationship with God, and at least one way to engage relationship with God is to engage relationship with one another.

We claim not to know what to do about the difficult questions besetting the church: what to do about crime and injustice, hatred and inequalities, the yawning gap between poverty and wealth, hope and despair. So we keep asking the question. But we know the answer. We even know it by heart. All that remains is to do it, and live.

Bernard Mizeki
Catechist and Martyr in Rhodesia, 1896   *June 18*

The word "friend" recurs frequently in the story of Bernard Mizeki's life, ministry, and martyrdom. Fleeing oppression in Portuguese East Africa, Mizeki was befriended by Anglican missionaries and became a Christian. He, in turn, befriended the people of Central Africa, and they likewise came to Christianity. In Mashonaland he was caught in conflict between the natives and the Europeans who lived there—both of whom he loved as friends—and was killed. Bernard's experience is a story of deadly friendship.

We have domesticated friendship too much. Merest acquaintances are called friends; friendships are useful to professional life and enhancements to social status. We seek as friends those who share our perspectives and reinforce our egos. Where are the robust friendships, the dangerous friendships, the life-changing friendships like Mizeki's?

Jesus said that the greatest love is evidenced in fearless confession; speaking to those he called friends, he said that "everyone who acknowledges me before others" will also be acknowledged "before the angels of God," suggesting that these words were intended for an audience hesitant to claim friendship with Jesus (Luke 12:8). In both Jesus' time and Luke's such hesitancy would have been understandable, for to be the friend of Jesus was potentially deadly.

Even when they are not fatal, friendships can be life-changing, introducing death in another guise. Friendship can change us, profoundly convert us, challenge and confront us. Friendship can bring death to old ideas, set us in opposition to prevailing norms, bind us in loyalty to the undesirable or despised. Deadly friendship can cost us our jobs, our securities, our lives. White students from Princeton Seminary were felled by bullets in the South because they befriended blacks; physicians and nurses have lost their own lives caring for persons with AIDS and other deadly diseases; congregations have died because they befriended the unlovely, the untouchable, the unfortunate. Bernard Mizeki reminds us that the measure of ministry is sometimes taken in friendships—deadly friendships.

Alban

First Martyr of Britain, c. 304   *June 22*

When a frightened priest struggled through the gate of the Roman fort at Verulamium, he could have hidden his faith; maybe he did, initially. Maybe that is how he got into the fortress in the first place. But something about Alban, the Roman soldier who befriended and sheltered him, encouraged him to open up and share his faith. Do we really appreciate that when that priest "came out," telling Alban who he was and what office he held in the Christian community, he was giving Alban considerable power? Alban could have killed him on the spot. Or, since the priest was the leader of a community, Alban could have taken him prisoner and tortured him to extract the names and whereabouts of his flock. That is the tremendous risk the priest took. But Alban took some risks, too.

Alban did not have to defend the priest, did not have to don the priest's clothes, to suffer the torture intended for him, and he certainly did not have to die for him. The only thing more amazing than Alban's story is that we are surrounded by so many like him today, people who are different from us, strangers to us, even frightening to us. We are not always sure how we should act toward them, what we are supposed to say to these people who see the world so differently than we do. Maybe all we are to do is trust them—share our story with them, tell them who we are, where we are from and how we got here, by God's grace, with Jesus' help. That unnamed priest survived. Maybe we will, too.

The Nativity of Saint John the Baptist

June 24

Not one family but two knew a miraculous birth's herald and the weight of God's choice, each family given the other, the better to bear the burden of blessing. When Mary came to visit Elizabeth with news of her untimely pregnancy and Joseph's reticence, she found in Elizabeth's girth and Zechariah's muteness both confirmation and comfort. And surely Mary's unswerving faith offered some steadying ballast for Zechariah's conflicted spirit, spinning within him like a tornado in a bottle.

Of the two children, Jesus fills our center stage. John gets a walk-on part in Advent, the wild-eyed, locust-eating prophet of the desert who baptizes and preaches repentance in preparation for a messiah. Apart from Jesus' baptism, however, we seldom find the two in proximity and therefore do not often think of them together. As men, they were polar opposites—John harsh and wild, ascetic and solitary, Jesus quiet and subdued, familiar at table and social to the point of scandal. As Luke described them, John "became strong in spirit" (Luke 1:80), while Jesus "increased in wisdom" (Luke 2:52). John lived in the wilds, says the gospeler; Jesus enjoyed public favor.

It must have been difficult for John, the elder cousin who was miraculously conceived and born first. John rose to public notice well before Jesus, a phenomenon in his own right. His notoriety brought him to the government's attention and eventually into their custody. Great crowds flocked to hear him and even years beyond his death refused to be deterred from their loyalty; in their eyes he was the true prophet, the one foretold of God. His head on Salome's silver charger seems the ultimate sacrifice, but John had made his most impressive gift long before.

It could not have been easy for John to take the lower place. His charism and his daring opened the way for Jesus; by sheer force of personality the path had been cleared. The bold cousin, unafraid to speak out against injustice, was the first to risk and the first to die. Why should he not have the higher status? He earned the right to claim it, but he took a different tack. He stepped aside, not of modesty, but of will, for this was his ministry, the work he believed God demanded of him.

In this me-first, give-me-my-rights world, John proves that blessedness and virtue do not always mean the highest place, that vocation does not always lead to the top of the heap. God also calls to supporting roles. What we initially experience as a setback or loss may be a new call, a vocational urging to understand our role as John understood his.

We make much of Jesus' humility, marvel at his strength in turning aside flattery and the expectations of those who sought to make him king. We admire the poise with which he met both rich and poor and yearn for the kind of spiritual gyroscope that kept him balanced and sane and so secure in himself. But his cousin, John, was ahead of him there, too, preparing the way.

There can be no doubt that Jesus learned from John. For as his own end neared, when Jesus might have diverted from his course and saved his own skin, even profited from his charisma, Jesus determined that it was not for himself but for someone else that he was called. Giving up his life, he fulfilled his own vocation by following the example of the cousin he joined in death. With steadfast faith and awful symmetry, Jesus, like his cousin John before him, confirmed the pattern of discipleship: he decreased that we might increase.

Irenaeus

Bishop of Lyons, c. 202   *June 28*

Seriousness is our besetting sin. Ponderousness weighs down our churches, universities, corporations, and governments. We are intense about the least things, able to work ourselves into a lather over tabloid headlines, the market for plastic toys, or some trivial fashion accessory. We are particularly inclined to take our intellect seriously, to assume a superiority for what we know. It is, therefore, hard to distinguish between early Christian gnostics who despised the flesh and exalted the spirit, and communities of modern Americans who deny or sacrifice basic human relationships for the pursuit of the "life of the mind," or its fruits. Most of us with experience in student mental health, corporate stress management, professional burnout, or the like could probably write our own treatise on *The Refutation and Overthrow of the Life of the Mind, Falsely So-Called.* But Irenaeus beat us to it.

Irenaeus chafed not simply at the idea of heresy, but its tyranny. The sin of heresy is not just what it says, but the vehement insistence of how it says it. Orthodoxy, at its best, accepts a kind of blessed ambiguity, forfeits hard claims to certainty. Faith, being faith, can never be anything but a hunch. And truth, being truth, needs no armed defense to sustain it. And both faith and truth welcome the challenge of open conversation, even of the lighthearted variety.

To be a person of faith does not require that we take ourselves seriously all the time; as G. K. Chesterton reminds us, "Satan fell by force of gravity." Paul says as much to Timothy when he admonishes the young disciple not to waste time and energy in stupid, senseless controversies. He is, instead, to be kindly to everyone, and to be prepared to learn as much or more as he has to impart (2 Timothy 2:22-24).

Be careful, Jesus admonishes wryly, lest the light in us be hidden in darkness. The eye is the lamp of the body; it not only admits light, but is equally capable of emitting light, reflecting it back with the sparkle one can almost see in Jesus' eye as he uses the funny image of a candle huddled under a bushel basket to teach about discipleship (Luke 11:33-36). The light of the gospel is evidenced in the spark of divinity caught in the human eye, the momentary insight into God as fleeting as the twinkle in the delighted eye.

That is what we remember of Irenaeus—not just his theology, but his sparkle. One can see it in the humor with which he refutes and deflates the deadly damper of heresy, whether in his day or ours, in the twinkling of an eye.

Saint Peter and Saint Paul

Apostles   *June 29*

They are an unlikely duo, Peter and Paul; their paths often separate one from the other and their opinions more than once have divided the church. One of the things Peter and Paul held in common, however, was the difficulty of their ministry. I do not mean the darkness of their times, the malevolent oppressions that occasioned their struggles, but a greater difficulty: the battle of competing lights. This is what Paul tried to convey to Timothy and Jesus to Peter.

For the youthful Timothy, animated by the zeal of the new convert, ministry and mission were still relatively uncomplicated. It would be years, if ever, before he came to see, as had Paul, that the most demanding discipleship is not the battle with darkness. The far greater threat to the gospel, and to our faith in God, is not evil cloaked in darkness, but evil decked in light.

Paul's ministry was conducted in a world of dazzling brilliance. The Roman Empire was near its apex; the religions of Athens and Rome, Israel and Egypt had been around long enough to build firm foundations and impressive cults. Learning was alive and exciting, world trade and communication brought peoples into vibrant contact. Set against the powerful forces of these venerable empires of commerce and culture, Christianity was a small potato, indeed. How could a gospel of self-denial and service to others long survive in a world of creature comforts and entrepreneurialism? Christianity was not nearly so likely to be swallowed up in darkness as it was to be eclipsed by the overwhelming vigor of its competition.

That, at least in part, seems to be Jesus' message to Peter as well. Their strange interchange about feeding sheep as an expression of love and service is set within an odd context: it happens right after Jesus and Peter have eaten breakfast. Is it not strange that Jesus would instruct Peter to feed the sheep when both of them had just satisfied their own appetites? Is Jesus reminding Peter, and us, that ministry is always more difficult when we are satisfied?

A single star hovering above Bethlehem does not stand a chance in the galaxy of twinkling competitors; the hardest work of ministry is not in that obvious place of deepest, darkest contrast, but in that dazzling firmament of power that threatens to charm us out of our convictions. The light shines in darkness and the darkness has never overcome it, but lost among the lights the star is hard to see. Those who would follow must look with care, or be lost.

Independence Day

The spirit of every courageous adventurer, every great pioneer, is summarized in a single sentence from the letter to the Hebrews: "They did not keep thinking about the country they had left" (Hebrews 11:15, TEV). Most of us are descended from people who were so desperate, whose circumstances were so dire, they were compelled to leave everything that they held precious—family, homeland, friends, language, and culture—and strike out for the unknown. Poverty, war, famine, and oppression literally propelled them across the seas to find sanctuary in another place. Their survival depended not only upon their ability to embrace this new and challenging wilderness; their survival depended, as well, upon their disciplined letting go of all that was behind them. They had to let go of the warm memories of love and comfort, of home and security, of loyalty and patriotism. But they also had to let go of the despair, the anger, and the fear that had driven them to leave.

Our frontiers and wilderness places are less tangible. Our frontiers are not bounded by oceans, not charted on maps. Our places of wilderness, barren of the familiar and secure, are less geographical than spiritual, emotional, and social. Yet our new frontiers and the challenges they present require as much courage, daring, and faith of us as any frontiers opened by our ancestors. Many of us, like our ancestor pioneers Abraham and Sarah, find ourselves facing the unknown in a dim and indistinct future.

"They did not keep thinking about the country they had left." It seems salient advice to us now, an encouragement to declare again our independence from old securities in order to take the bold steps forward into the new frontier God has prepared for us. And it is a timely encouragement to those who profess belief in and relationship with a truly living God, a God who is not revered as some figment or fragment of the past, but a living God whose presence is with us here and now.

Our God is present, accompanies us in each step, walks with us into that unknown.

Like our Hebrew forebears, we could return and settle in our past. But God has promised us a new land, a brighter country where all people dwell in love and mutual respect. Our God accompanies us, yet always with the leading step. God is the great pioneer, walking with us as a bush blazing in the desert, as a cloud of smoke by day and a pillar of fire by night, in the transfigured Christ ascending victorious over death, as the fresh and liberating spirit present whenever and wherever we venture beyond our past to embrace one another. God is leading us into our unknown future, where we will find new depths of compassion, new heights of understanding, and a greater breadth of affection.

Benedict of Nursia

Abbot of Monte Cassino, c. 540   *July 11*

As Benedict of Nursia became aware of the world in which he lived, he was moved to disgust by the barbarism he witnessed in the political instability and general dissolution of society around him. Benedict did what many of us would very much like to do: he checked out. He found a nice hillside cave overlooking Lake Subiaco, about forty miles outside Rome, where he set up a household with a monk who had prior claims to this hole in the ground—probably another malcontent seized by a longing for higher moral ground. Gradually a community grew up around Benedict, a development about which he was none too happy, but which he seems to have indulged, if begrudgingly. There is no evidence that Benedict ever contemplated establishing a formal order, and it is particularly noteworthy that he was not ordained.

That an order grew up around Benedict and became the abundant stream that eventually gave life to nearly all western monasticism may be due, in part, to these factors, and to Benedict's faith. By the latter I mean not his pious devotion, but rather his quiet and very practical confidence that God will care for and make order of our lives. This quiet confidence does not rely upon its own designs, but is content to approach each day openly. In short, Benedict seems to have approached discipleship content to make it up as he went along.

Along the way, Benedict came to the realization that the incarnate Christ visits as the guest, that the attention of others is less intrusion than it is gift. That he insinuated himself into the life of the monk who had already staked out that hermitage on Lake Subiaco reveals a rude selfishness in the young Benedict. As others came to intrude upon his life, however, Benedict was challenged to make room in his life for them, was forced to give as much as he had demanded from his unnamed host.

This is one of Christianity's hardest demands on the modern person, whose propensities tend toward self-protection and privacy, toward suspicion and isolation—all the ingredients of the barbarism we claim to deplore. When Jesus speaks of the builder who must calculate the whole cost of the tower before breaking ground, of the ruler who assesses the enemy's strength before sending troops to battle, or of every disciple's inevitable encounter with the cross (Luke 14:27-33), he is simply reminding us that participation in the life of God means anticipation and acceptance of its full cost. For Benedict, the cost was a solitude invaded by God incarnate in others, a life prized open to the world.

In our modern affection for and affectations of the spirituality of the monastics, and of Benedict in particular, we neglect this component to our detriment. We have emulated monastic retreat and envied monastic solitude. We have imitated monastic prayer and yearned for monastic community. But if we desire a closer relationship with God, what we need most is the monastery's open door.

William White

Bishop of Pennsylvania, 1836   *July 17*

In 1772 William White became assistant minister and later rector of Christ and St. Peter's Church in Philadelphia. Despite holding a number of other offices during his lifetime—including chaplain of the Continental Congress and the United States Senate, the first Bishop of Pennsylvania, and the first Presiding Bishop—Bishop White remained the rector of Christ and St. Peter's Church until his death. Sixty-four years of service in one place, among one community. The secret to his longevity is no miracle; the collect for his day describes him as a man endowed with "wisdom, patience, and a reconciling temper" whose ministry and example led his church, in both its local and national manifestations, "into ways of stability and peace."

The virtues of wisdom, patience, and a reconciling temper are rarely evident in a culture where it is no longer laudable to be wise, only to be smart; where patience is sacrificed to action; and where a reconciling temper is no match for an intransigent conviction. It is not so much that we have abandoned these virtues, we just lost them in one of the moves of our highly mobile culture. Only the dead stay anywhere for sixty-four years anymore. The secret to Bishop White's virtues is probably his sixty-four-year pastorate; when you settle in for the long haul, you need different equipment.

The prophet Jeremiah, lamenting his lack of qualifications for the task of prophecy, cried that his youth was insufficient to the task. But God chastises the boyish prophet: "Before I formed you in the womb I knew you, and before you were born I consecrated you; I appointed you a prophet to the nations" (Jeremiah 1:4-5). Jeremiah's call, his vocation, is not a sudden impulse on the part of God, neither is their relationship a thing only come lately. They have a history. God has been part of Jeremiah's life from eternity and knows full well the capabilities of this messenger.

After his resurrection Jesus appears to Peter and, having shared breakfast with the disciple, issues the call to discipleship. Three times Jesus asks Peter of his love, and three times Jesus issues the command to feed his sheep (John 21:15-17). The repetition reinforces the single-minded focus this disciple will need to stay the course. For this is Peter, the unstable rock, the one whose uneven temper drew the sword in the garden and cut off the servant's ear, the one whose loyalty caved under the questioning of a servant girl and who woke to his own perfidy only at the sound of the cock's crow. His vocation is made very simple and very clear: Stick to it; stay with it.

Sixty-four years in the same place with the same people. It takes a tremendous amount of wisdom, unfathomable patience, unwavering commitment to reconciliation, and a love as limitless as eternity—a love so profound, it could only be of God. Sixty-four years in the same place with the same people seems so foreign and far away, but it actually is very current and increasingly common, for this small planet is becoming a very small place; we are a lifetime in the same place with the same people. We are, if our creeds prove true, for all eternity in the same place with the same people. God bless William White, and keep him ever present to us who need him now as much as ever.

Macrina

Monastic and Teacher, 379   *July 19*

The lives of Basil the Great, Gregory of Nyssa, and their sister, Macrina, are central to the vibrant life of the church in the fourth century. Macrina persuaded Basil to leave a promising secular career for the priesthood and Gregory was sufficiently appreciative of her talents to write a biography of her that is far more than the expression of brotherly affection: it is a rare historical account of a remarkable woman.

Macrina, Basil, and Gregory could have enriched themselves enormously had they turned their considerable gifts to worldly commerce. They might have increased the world's store of knowledge had they unleashed their intellects to empirical studies. Instead, they took off on the great intellectual snipe hunt that is religion, tramping through the thick underbrush of rumination in search not of answers but of wisdom.

The pursuit of wisdom is not an undertaking so much as an inclination; "I inclined my ear a little and received [wisdom], and I found for myself much instruction" (Ecclesiasticus 51:16). Such an inclination is far different from the intense pursuit of truth, as though truth can be secured and tamed, brought under our control and made our servant. It is the difference between journey and destination; for those whose only concern is the destination, the journey is but an inconvenience, a hindrance and aggravation, a blur of white lines on miles of pavement or sleep aided by the hum of a plane's jet engines. But the journey itself is filled with riches—the journey is the "getting there" as well.

Macrina, as monastic and teacher, understood this difference and set her sights upon wisdom. With her brothers she pursued not an empirical knowledge of Jesus, but rather a closer relationship with one another and with life itself based on the principles evident in the life and gospel of Jesus. They reflected upon the ministry of Jesus, savoring and enriching their lives along the way; they knew the joy of the journey without ever reaching their destination. This is what wisdom teaches and imparts to those who attend her ways.

In this task-oriented, product-driven world, it is a point worth pondering—that it is the vocation of the Christian in this world ever to seek and yet never to attain. It is our joy and our glory never to possess truth absolutely, yet ever to know the companionship of wisdom. It is resurrection wisdom to know that there is no goal, no glory worth more than the road that takes us there.

Elizabeth Cady Stanton, Amelia Bloomer, Sojourner Truth, and Harriet Ross Tubman

Liberators and Prophets   *July 20*

Four amazing women, of two different races, whose lives touched three centuries are the subject of a single commemoration. They gave themselves to the cause of justice in a variety of realms, and through their energies and imaginative leadership, they made significant and lasting contributions to the rights of all people, but most particularly of women.

Elizabeth Cady Stanton challenged the church's oppressive limiting of women to subordinate roles in marriage and in church life. Amelia Bloomer took on the fashion mavens of the day, advocating for less restrictive clothing for women, whose health was endangered by the corsets worn even by pregnant women. Sojourner Truth found affinity with the abolitionists and the advocates of women's rights, both groups benefiting from her considerable gifts for preaching and oratory. Harriet Ross Tubman was a literal liberator, personally responsible for freeing over three hundred African Americans by securing refuge for them in Canada, where she had gone to escape slavery herself.

These four women, whose biographies offer many examples of heroism and virtue, are united not only in their commitment to justice, but in a principle of faith—that God does not intrude, but rather invites and awaits our asking. The presumption that God orchestrates human affairs is challenged in Jesus' own instruction that we are to ask for what we need and desire: "Ask, and it will be given you," he tells his disciples. "Search, and you will find; knock, and the door will be opened to you. For everyone who asks receives, and everyone who searches finds" (Luke 11:9-10).

Each of these women believed that God called them to the struggles they engaged. But they were not passive agents; they were formidable, forceful women. They had a lively, energetic faith attuned to their energetic lives. They did not blame God for the conditions of the world they inhabited; the sources of evil and oppression were—in their cases literally—man-made. Thus, as they sought to redress the wrongs, they took responsibility and called others to accountability. And when they needed something of God, they asked for it.

The tragic flaw in many a would-be hero is the pride that seeks to go it alone. The single-handed liberator, the lone ranger, sets out to achieve great things independently. Life's highway is littered with the tragic *momenti mori*, the sun-bleached remains of the burned-out, used-up messiahs who could not or would not ask God or anyone else for assistance. Ask, says Jesus, and it shall be given. But ask we must. Ask these four amazing women; they will tell you.

Saint Mary Magdalene

July 22

According to Byzantine tradition, Mary of Magdala was a wealthy and influential woman. She is reputed to have visited Tiberias Caesar, to whom she brought news of Jesus' resurrection from the dead—and a pointed complaint against Pilate. Explaining the resurrection, she picked up an egg from a table to make her point, but before she could proceed, Caesar interjected that a human being could no more rise from the dead than the egg in her hand turn red. The egg immediately turned a deep crimson, the color of the eggs exchanged at Orthodox Easter celebrations.

Another tradition in the church links Mary with the more sordid life of prostitution, making her story particularly compelling in the midst of this age, wherein the whole nature of Christian faith, life, and witness debates the ministries of the divorced, of women, of gay men and lesbian women, of those without educational credentials, or of any who do not meet whatever standards we set for exemplary humanity. Paul urged the Corinthians to "regard no one from a human point of view" (2 Corinthians 5:16); they must now set aside human standards of judgment—standards by which Mary Magdalene would be excluded from the apostolic order to which she rightfully belongs. Similarly, Judith, the beautiful and wealthy Israelite widow who risks her life to slay the enemy of her people, undertook her mission with a prayer that acknowledged, as her actions vindicated, that God relies not upon the power of numbers, nor upon the strength of men, but upon the lowly, the oppressed, the forlorn, and those so devoid of hope as to need a savior even to draw breath (Judith 9:11-14).

From the moment Jesus first met Mary Magdalene in the garden after the resurrection, a faint familiarity is aroused in anyone who knows the biblical stories and a symmetry emerges. He identified himself, calling her by name as if to jog her recognition. He warned her not to touch him, perhaps because she had no need to make contact with the wound in his side so reminiscent of the legendary source of woman's genesis in Adam's rib. This time it was the new Adam who proffered the gift of knowledge, entrusting her with the news of resurrection. It was she who would go to the others and share the first witness of the gospel, not as some act of atonement for original sin, but as a sign of the new world order—a reversal that rendered a woman the first apostle, the first post-resurrection witness, the one who would set all others in motion. But it was more than that; in her person she was, as much as Jesus himself, an incarnation of resurrection life.

Witnesses to and ministers of the resurrection have much in common with the Magdalene, or they should. We do not have all the answers; we do not even have the right questions. We come to this work bearing no qualifications other than a tenacious hunger to know and be close to God. But the greatest gift of all ministers, lay and ordained, is that gift of Mary Magdalene to be in the places where others will not go. Whether of ignorance or intention, Mary Magdalene dared to venture into that dark predawn cemetery that is the very epitome of hopelessness.

What brought Mary to the garden and compelled her to find the others who, in fear and hiding, were waiting for some hope to guide them to the light? We do not know what brought her to that place or took her beyond it, but I wonder if it was a new confidence, akin to the nerve that caused Abraham and Sarah to make that first step away from the safety of camp and head into an unknown wilderness. I wonder if it was determination, not just grim but graceful; courage, not fearless but faithful; a new sense of herself, not meek but mature. I do not wonder *about* these things so much as I wonder *at* them. For in Mary Magdalene I gradually discern the qualities and characteristics that distinguish a truly resurrected life.

Thomas à Kempis

Priest, 1471   *July 24*

My own copy of Thomas's *The Imitation of Christ*, not opened for many years, bears the inscription of a seminary classmate who gave me the book over twenty years ago, on my birthday. I first read it as one seeking a way out of the frustrations of my own life, in prayer and meditation that would settle for nothing less than the sweet refuge of perfect virtue. My notion of imitation was based on a simplistic understanding of Jesus. I appreciated too little the very human nature and qualities of the Christ; my eyes searched only for ladders into heaven.

After choosing his twelve apostles, Jesus went with them to meet a great multitude of people seeking to be healed of their diseases. "And all in the crowd were trying to touch him," Luke tells us, "for power came out from him and he healed all of them. Then he looked up at his disciples and said: 'Blessed are you...'" (Luke 6:19-20). It was not to the multitude that Jesus addressed the beatitudes, but to the disciples—to those who were there in order to learn and to follow.

What Jesus taught them was strange, indeed. What he offered was not a ladder out of this world, nor even a list of virtues to be imitated. Instead, he spoke to them of poverty, especially poverty of the spirit, and of hunger. He told them that in their poverty and hunger, in their tears and troubles, they possessed the kingdom of God, the very realm of heaven. The tears, the hunger, the poverty, and the pain themselves are of the kingdom of God, of God's realm and subject to God's sovereignty.

We do not find heaven up a ladder, nor God in flights of fantasy. We find heaven with our feet firmly planted on the ground, and God in the midst of our gravest difficulties. The imitation of Christ, then, is not some blueprint for virtue, not some pattern of behavior to which we are to conform our lives. The imitation of Christ is an invitation to see the world, and life, anew. It is to see the world and human experience as Christ sees them. Not as subdivided into exclusive territories where the good and pleasurable belong to God and the devil take the hindmost, not as something to be subdued or escaped, but as the very substance of God whose hand has made everything that is.

To see God we must look into the places we would sooner flee—the hard labor of loving, the difficult business of sharing, the frustrating experience of failing, the heart-rending pain of loss. There, in the difficulty of living, we follow Jesus. That is imitation of Christ—not some vain seeking after haloed perfection, but the stubborn insistence that life is to be lived, even if it leads to the cross. That is imitation of Christ: the patient determination to live into the mystery that defies our sense. For, as Thomas reminds us in his conclusion to *The Imitation of Christ*, "Whatsoever thou canst not understand, commit it faithfully to God; for God will not deceive thee."

Saint James

Apostle   *July 25*

M ore than anything else, they wanted to be first. James and John—sons of Zebedee—seem always to have sought the premier place. They may have been twins, always the center of attention as children. Even if their mother exhibited all the worst attributes of the pushy parent when she came to Jesus and, in the presence of the sons, begged that Jesus give them preference in his kingdom, there is no indication that either of them was the least embarrassed by the brazen request. They clearly were headstrong. "Sons of thunder," they were called—probably for their zeal, but perhaps also for personalities given to loud and obnoxious behavior; that would certainly explain their affinity with Peter. The three of them must have been quite a handful.

Judging from the biblical narrative, James and John were nearly inseparable from one another and from Jesus. They are often mentioned as a pair and frequently appear in notable episodes of Jesus' life and ministry. Was their presence a response to the specific invitation of Jesus? Or did they insinuate themselves into the front row? They were present with Peter at the Transfiguration; they saw Jesus raise Jairus's daughter from the dead; and they were among the handful present for Jesus' agony in Gethsemane. They held a privileged place.

When we learn that James was the first of the disciples to be martyred, it is difficult to see anything but the irony. Here was the boisterous, pushy, selfish bully who wanted to be first, achieving his goal not as he had intended, but by being the first of the lot to lose his life for his associations with and loyalties to Jesus.

Moreover, Jesus may actually have liked and admired, encouraged and nurtured James in his zealous determination. James probably invited Herod Agrippa's fury. What is most discomfiting about James is not that he was so demanding, but rather that we know somewhere in ourselves we should really be more like him. All those qualities we deem detriments or deficits in his character were actually the energies and gifts that led the post-resurrection community out of its grief and mourning and put them back into the world.

What the example of James suggests is that some of the very qualities we disdain in ourselves and in the world around us are of use to God. It is true that our selfishness and our determination can be our undoing. Our arrogance and pushiness can be hurtful to us and to others. But these same qualities are also useful to the proclamation of the gospel. We do not need to throw over our sensitivity to others, or abandon our skills in diplomacy and politics, or neglect our gifts of hospitality. But we do need to rethink our standard operating procedures.

James certainly was not reluctant to assert himself, either on his own or through his mother. When the disciples sat at table with Jesus in the upper room and argued among themselves about their future status, we can be sure that James and John were in the thick of that pitched battle—they very likely started it. When their mother sought preferential position for them, Jesus said they did not understand what they were asking, but quickly followed their request for privilege with a question of his own: are you ready to share my life; are you ready to share my fate?

James was prepared, his life the first to be paid. But it is no longer James, but *we*, who must answer. At the heart of our baptism are the same questions Jesus poses of us: are you ready to share my life; are you ready to share my fate? For the Christian, in the beginning and at the end, it all comes down to this.

Parents of the Blessed Virgin Mary

July 26

Little is known of the parents of Mary, and the gospels add nothing except to suggest that she was of Davidic descent and nurtured in Judaism. All the evidence is fragmentary, and legendary—stories giving Mary's mother and father the names Anne and Joachim, and childhood tales so obviously derived from other, older Hebrew stories they seem no more than a clumsy attempt to manufacture an ancestry.

The second century—when these legends of Mary's family seem to have emerged and multiplied—was a time of tender vulnerability for the young Christian church. From its inception it was divided, factionalized around the charismatic personalities of Paul, Peter, Apollos, John the Baptizer, and others. Beyond these divided but nonetheless loyal followers of Jesus stood the detractors, those who refuted any and all of the claims made about Jesus. His loyalty to Judaism and the claims of his messiahship went head to head with growing controversies over the perplexing business of his divinity and his humanity. Life among the religionists was complicated; it helped matters not one whit that their internal conflict was matched and even surpassed by assaults of persecution from a surrounding imperial culture invested in emperor worship, and more.

If one were to have any rootedness, one had to search it out. Genealogy is actually a very important undertaking, most important when we are disjointed and fractured. The storytellers and authors of the second century who gave us legends of Mary's parents were reaching for a foothold, attempting to ground the faith of a family. They would appreciate our plight today, assailed as we are by a glut of information purporting to free us from ignorance, but also heightening awareness of our differences and, thus, separating and dividing us—not only from one another, but from our very selves. So much information has the capacity not only to educate, but to obfuscate; not only to enlighten, but also to confuse. I must know who I am, where I am coming from, what I am made of, if I am to have any sense of who I am and how I am related to all that I encounter every day.

I know who I am, at least in part, because I have studied the stories of the members of my family as far back as documentation will carry me. And where the documentation ends, I dare to wander into imagination. But I also know who I am as a child of God, because of Jesus. I know that this person, Jesus, was bone of my bone and flesh of my flesh, because he was born as I was born, of a mother. And that mother, whose person has at various times in history threatened to vaporize in mists of theological theorization, was herself born of humankind. We are grounded in Jesus and the mystery of the Incarnation by these wonderful holy grandparents, the parents of Mary.

Whether Anne and Joachim were as the myths made them makes little difference. That they lived at all, we accept in faith, upon reason. In such times as these, we accept with gratitude the insights and impulses of second-century imagination that reached out to find them and, with us, found comfort and strength in the faith that they were there.

William Reed Huntington

Priest, 1909 *July 27*

The Civil War only temporarily interrupted a growing conflict within the Episcopal Church between the Anglo-Catholic proponents of the Oxford Movement on the one hand and the low-church adherents of Evangelicalism on the other. While William Reed Huntington was not able to avert the departure of those who formed the Reformed Episcopal Church, his leadership in the House of Deputies in this period was a key component in preserving the remainder of the church. Huntington's passionate commitment to unity extended beyond his own communion to dreams of a national church, dreams easily forgiven one who had lived through the bloodshed of civil war and the spiritual hurricane that battered his church in his own lifetime.

Paul cautioned the church in Ephesus to contend against a certain "flightiness" within the church—a tendency of the membership to be "tossed to and fro and blown about by every wind of doctrine" (Ephesians 4:14). But while we are subject to a certain amount of rudderless buoyancy, the greater danger presently seems just the opposite: that we Christians have lost any lightness, any agility. Far from being tossed to and fro, we are so solidly hunkered down as to be immovable.

For those of us within the churches themselves, there is less a sense among us of being tossed than of angry weariness, a kind of heavy exhaustion. At the least we are like children kept up past their bedtime, cranky and tantrum-prone as we struggle to remain alert beneath the burden of too much intense conflict carried on too long. As if that were not enough to depress, we fractured Christians stand beneath the accusing specter of Huntington's lofty ambitions for unity. Yet there is another side to Huntington.

Strange as it may seem in this proponent of unity, it was Huntington who boldly proposed one of the earliest revisions of the American *Book of Common Prayer.* This man who subscribed to fundamentally unyielding principles for unity set in motion a revision of the prayer book that would render it far more flexible. In fact, his proposals for the prayer book were considered too radical and only a moderate revision was passed. No person who desires the peace and unity of the Episcopal Church today could seriously suggest prayer book revision as the path to achieve those ends!

Yet this dynamic tension between foundational principles and necessary change lies at the heart of all life. When Jesus offers prayer for unity, his embrace is inclusive: "I ask not only on behalf of these, but also on behalf of those who will believe in me through their word" (John 17:20). Jesus prays for everyone on all sides of every issue. The oneness for which Jesus prays is not a unity to be achieved, but a unity already established. Not our ending place, but our beginning place; not what we work for, but what we already are. In the acknowledgment of our essential oneness, we are freed to move into our respective differences.

The loving unity for which Jesus prays is the loving unity of siblings who grow up in the profound knowledge of their essential union with one another, a union that does not confine, but rather encourages and allows them to be the very different people they are. In my own family that means five siblings whose births span over a decade and whose experiences and opinions are as varied as any five people can be. We fight, we argue, and we increasingly appreciate the differences that have stretched us. Our conflict has been shared openly, has even verged on violence, especially when we reached our teens. We were ruled by passions and unbridled in our expressions of opinion. There was only one place where conflict was not allowed to intrude, and that was at table. When conflict did arise there, the discipline was excommunication—the offender and sometimes the offended, too, were either sent from the table or (as we grew older) voluntarily left, until we made peace.

This may not be the unity Huntington dreamed of, but one he would settle for, the unity Jesus prays for: unity not as the place we end, but where we begin.

Mary and Martha of Bethany

July 29

Jesus had friends. Mary, Martha, and their brother Lazarus enjoyed a relationship to him different from that of the disciples. In his relationship to Martha and Mary, we see a man who claims two women as intimate friends, a most unusual reality in Jesus' day and culture, and hardly commonplace in our own.

The story of Jesus' visit with Mary and Martha recorded in the tenth chapter of Luke's gospel—Martha bustling over the meal and Mary entertaining Jesus—is familiar to most of us. Jesus seems to chastise Martha for her preoccupation with her busyness while extolling Mary for her leisurely hospitality. But it does not seem likely that any friend would impose such a divisive judgment between those he loved; whatever words passed between them were words of friendship, honest and sincere. Lacking his tone of delivery and the history of their long relationship, the words we have are out of context. I am inclined to hear them as a kind of good-natured kidding exchanged among friends, not a rigid moral distinction between the virtues of one sister over another.

We know nothing of how Jesus happened to come to this friendship, but my hunch is that it just happened. Mary, Martha, and Lazarus were a gift to Jesus; this has certainly been the case of the best and dearest friendships of my life. The dearest friends—like Mary and Martha—have been the unlikely ones, the ones I would not have chosen for myself, the ones who in some cases proved as awkward, even embarrassing, as they were enriching and lasting. The dearest of my friends have been people who have chanced into my life, people I have met on the way.

Our frustrated attempts at fashioning friendships often come to naught. Friendships would be easier if we *could* exert more control over them, could pick and choose and shape to our own liking those who would share our lives so intimately. Jesus might certainly have chosen more wisely and impressively than Mary and Martha, whose friendship probably did little to enhance his career or advance his agenda. These things are important to remember, however, for the friends we need and in some instances deeply desire are likely very near at hand. God has planted them in our way—and has placed us in theirs.

If we are lacking in friends, it does not mean that we are unlovable, or that we are unworthy; it may mean nothing more than that we have difficulty accepting the gifts God holds out to us in others. Our prayer is that God might give us a will to love, might open our hearts to hear and strengthen our hands to serve those who come to us. These friends are a reminder that the dominion of God is, as we have been assured, very near at hand—and that those prepared to love us are even now among us.

William Wilberforce

1833   *July 30*

Well-educated, sincere in his faith, generous, kind, and a gifted speaker, William Wilberforce might have been a fierce and formidable Evangelical priest, but friends and mentors encouraged him into the world of politics. Those were insightful friends who realized that William Wilberforce was particularly gifted and that the influence, charm, status, zeal, sincerity, and ability that Wilberforce possessed were needed for unusually high purpose, even dangerous service. For though his name is virtually unknown in this country, it ought not be; William Wilberforce was the single most dedicated opponent to the slave trade. He gave himself to a lifelong campaign to eradicate slavery and the slave trade in England. Slave trafficking was abolished in 1807, fully twenty-seven years after the young Wilberforce was elected into Parliament; twenty-six years later, in 1833, Parliament abolished slavery in all the British dominions, one month after his death.

To root out so invidious a system as slavery required an intimate and politically skilled relationship within the very system itself. The difficulties we face today are no less hideous. The drug trade, which makes more slaves than all the chains ever forged, is simply a trade deeply rooted in our own systems of economics, the military, and the government. The imbalances of wealth that keep more locked in filth and hopelessness than were ever sealed below decks of trading ships are deeply rooted in our systems of theology, philosophy, sociology, economics, and politics. The inequities and iniquities of racism, sexism, nationalism, and the host of jealousies that separate this human family as viciously as those who tore husbands from wives and sold children for a price are deeply rooted in every fiber of our lives. The system is vast; its reformation will demand everything of all of us. And we need friends and mentors with the insight to direct our gifts and clarify our discernment, that we might be servants like William Wilberforce, wholly and skillfully dedicated to God's service.

Ignatius of Loyola

Priest, Monastic, and Founder of the Society of Jesus, 1556   *July 31*

How did the restlessness of a wounded soldier named Ignatius lead to a renunciation of the military life and noble entitlement, and a voluntary surrender to poverty? How did the experience of poverty lead that same searching soldier to take as his model the very disciplines of the military life, adopting the language and images of warfare for spiritual purposes? How did a rigorous and disciplined spiritual exploration lead him to alliance with the very institution—the church—he sought to reform? How did Ignatius leave the structures of wealth, nobility, and the military, only to end his life as the Superior General of an order that is distinguished by wealth, nobility, and military structure?

It is one of God's ironies that reformers like Ignatius seem to end up pretty much as they begin; spiritual pilgrimage often leads us back home, takes us back to old places by new ways. This pattern suggests that we ought to be more thoughtful about our renunciations in this life.

Leaving home for college, I was thrilled to get some distance between me and everything I had known at home. I was never very happy living in the midst of rural farms, surrounded by people I believed hopelessly backward, woefully ignorant, politically mean-spirited, and religiously hypocritical. Away at school, I was excited to be among peers who shared my enthusiasm for art and literature, who soaked up the variety of life's experiences like parched sponges. I turned away from all that was familiar, including the church. In the end, however, I find myself not far from where I began.

I am caught up in an all-too-human institution with all its petty and aggravating frustrations, living my life among people not at all different from the people I knew in my youth, in the midst of a city whose neighborhoods are often as insular as the farms that dotted my childhood's landscape. While all my reforming impulses were directed outward, toward the institutions and structures of life, and while my attention was diverted, God reformed me. The same seems to have been true for Ignatius.

It was not Ignatius's wealth that needed reforming so much as his attitude toward all wealth and its proper deployment in God's service. It was not his privilege that needed reforming so much as the purposes to which he put such privileges as education and position. It was not military discipline and structure that needed reforming so much as the ends to which these disciplines and structures were devoted. All of which suggests that the world's salvation, and ours, depends not upon the reform of human institutions but the reform of humans, the radical reorientation of each of us—what our Hebrew ancestors identified as the exchange of hearts of stone for living, loving hearts inclined toward God and one another.

If, as Ignatius's experience indicates, the pilgrimage tends to bring us back to where we begin, then perhaps we should look a little more appreciatively at where we have come from, where we are, what we have been, and what we have done. In these people, places, and experiences we divine the seeds of vocation. They are not to be denied, but claimed; not to be regretted, but celebrated; not to be repudiated, but redeemed. They are the road that takes us to God, and leads us back home, never to be the same again.

Joseph of Arimathaea

August 1

It is difficult to guess the motive of Joseph of Arimathaea, who went to Pilate and secured possession of the body of the crucified Jesus, which he then took down from the cross, prepared for burial and wrapped in a shroud, and laid in the rock-hewn tomb this man of means had purchased as his own final resting place. He may only have been a fastidious man who believed that form should be observed, if only for form's sake.

As one who looked for the kingdom of God, as a good and righteous person, he may simply have done what he felt goodness and righteousness demanded, without any particular affection for the person of Jesus. He was careful to do everything with the precision demanded of the Jewish law, removing the body before the beginning of the sabbath, the women completing their preparations in time to observe the commandment to rest. But there is something interesting about Joseph of Arimathaea.

We might call it his *chutzpah*, the Yiddish word for that kind of courage we sometimes call sheer nerve. For all his fastidiousness and care, there is an audacity in Joseph of Arimathaea. He was obviously a person of standing in the council and yet the narrative makes it clear that he stood alone against the rest. He had not consented to the motive or the means by which the council had dealt with Jesus; he did not see how these actions could possibly serve the coming of God in righteousness. His subsequent actions constitute the "minority report" to their deliberations and decision.

Furthermore, in the midst of those turbulent hours when many shied away, Joseph of Arimathaea had the effrontery to go face to face with Pilate and ask for the body of Jesus. Pilate was, we can be sure, quite touchy at that point, having been exhausted and exasperated by the council, in particular. One can well imagine just how difficult it had to have been for a member of that council to step forward with one more request.

Literally taking matters into his own hands, Joseph of Arimathaea, probably with the help of Nicodemus, removed the body from the cross. It was a dirty job and an act that exposed him to the censure and ridicule of his peers. But this man of dignity and standing handled the corpse, and literally gave up his own final bed that Jesus might receive honorable burial.

The man of Arimathaea seems not to have bothered much with what others would think. He drew heavily against his balance of reputation and risked a lifetime investment in status just to care for the dead Jesus. We need the nerve of Joseph of Arimathaea to stand against the self-righteousness of our own councils and to challenge all presumptions that make justice subservient to pacification. We need the nerve of Joseph of Arimathaea to stand before Pilate. We need the nerve of Joseph of Arimathaea to receive gently into our own arms the broken body of the Christ, which is the church, and to tend it with dignity and grace as it suffers the death of all human institutions. We need the nerve of Joseph of Arimathaea to risk for the sake of the gospel the opulence we have reserved for the entombment and memorialization of our own righteousness. We need the nerve of Joseph of Arimathaea that waited not for others, but waited boldly and faithfully for God.

History does not record the reaction of Joseph of Arimathaea on the day of the resurrection. Probably just as well. No words could ever express what he must have felt when what he had been waiting for suddenly and unexpectedly arrived. But one with nerve to stand steadfast against the opinions and actions of peers, to stand unafraid in the presence of Pilate, to stand under the weight of the crumpled Christ, and to stand humbly in his own tomb over the body of a condemned criminal surely had the nerve to welcome with joy the surprise of God.

The Transfiguration of Our Lord

August 6

People who demand a literally glowing Jesus on a mountaintop with phantasms of Moses and Elijah on either side have no sense of poetry; the story of the Transfiguration is an artistic struggle to give voice to an intangible insight. In the accounts of Matthew, Mark, and Luke the story falls near the center of each evangelist's record; in Luke, the Transfiguration is pointedly positioned between two incidents.

Just before the Transfiguration, Jesus asks his followers, "Who do the crowds say that I am?" and receives varied replies: "John the Baptist; but others, Elijah; and still others, that one of the ancient prophets has arisen." Jesus then asks them, "But who do you say that I am?" Peter answers, "The Messiah of God" (Luke 9:18-20). Jesus then recounts the expectations of the messianic mission, speaking to them of duty and of death.

About a week after this exchange, Jesus goes up a hill to pray, taking Peter, James, and John with him. While in prayer, Jesus' face takes on a new radiance and Moses and Elijah appear on either side of him, and they talk *to* him—not *with* him. Jesus presumably learns from them the manner of God's purposes for him and is perhaps encouraged to meet the suffering and death ahead of him. The vision ends with a thundering voice from the cloud repeating the acclamation heard at Jesus' baptism in the River Jordan, "This is my Son, my Chosen," adding the instruction, "Listen to him!" (Luke 9:35).

But there follows immediately another story. The very next day Jesus encounters a man who begs Jesus to come look at his son. The distraught man is concerned that his boy is possessed by a destructive spirit that "convulses him until he foams at the mouth; it mauls him and will scarcely leave him." The desperate father has come to Jesus because, he says, "I begged your disciples to cast it out, but they could not." Jesus is provoked to an unusual outburst: "You faithless and perverse generation," he charges, "how much longer must I be with you and bear with you?" (Luke 9:37–41).

The Transfiguration is an ordination. It is not a formal priestly ordination, but it is certainly the feast affirming the particular vocation of Jesus. Before he goes up the hill, he reveals his own doubts and his need for greater clarity of discernment in his little poll, asking "Who do they say..., who do you say that I am?" He ascends the hill with their answers still resounding in his head. Peter's response confirms that at least some of the people understand him to be the Messiah. Once on the hill he is told exactly who he is, presumably by Moses and Elijah, and emphatically in the voice that proclaims from the cloud, "This is my Son, my Chosen."

Upon descending from the mountain, Jesus experiences the first test of his new ordination as he is confronted by the faithlessness of his own disciples. He encounters their poverty of trust and assumes the full burden of his vocation. He expresses so poignantly his frustration when he demands to know how long he must put up with them. But even in expressing this exasperation, he has obviously accepted what God has demanded of him. His question is rhetorical; he knows as well as we do that the answer is "for all eternity."

After that strange experience on the hill Jesus possessed something he had not known or evidenced before. He bore within and expressed without the unmistakable assurance of one who knew his place and what was demanded of him; he knew he was loved and chosen by God. That knowledge was his authority and the core of his integrity; he knew it so surely he could never relinquish it, even to the power of death. He was changed, and everyone who saw him saw that change. He was transfigured. The brooding shadow of doubt—doubt over his own place in God's order and affections—was replaced by the clear light of assurance.

That transfiguring light, that blinding flash of insight, opens any person as it opened Jesus. That unassailable assurance in God, in one's place within God's household, of one's worth as a child of God, illuminates life. Such transfiguration begets transfiguration in others, as the light is passed from person to person, until the whole world is ablaze with glory and God's voice resounds, "This is my world, my Creation, my Chosen."

John Mason Neale

Priest, 1866   *August 7*

Only when one adds up the dates does one comprehend the shape of John Mason Neale's ministry. Though ordained in 1852, Neale's health was so poor he was prevented from being instituted in his first pastoral assignment. Four years later, his health still less than robust, he was posted to the wardenship of Sackville College, where he carried on a prodigious career as a writer, translator, and compiler and found sufficient energy to found the Sisterhood of St. Margaret for the education and relief of women and girls. Still, his activity was severely limited by a lifetime of ill health, and the burdens of his convictions.

An adherent of the Oxford Movement, Neale's fondness for ritual was somewhat problematic in his time. In 1847, five years after his ordination, he was (as euphemistic nomenclature so deftly puts it) "inhibited" by his bishop, denied the exercise of his liturgical and sacramental ministry. When he set about to found the Sisterhood of St. Margaret, his efforts were met with violence. The Protestant quarters of the community rose up in anger and mounted ugly protest over his attempts to be of service. His ministerial office was restored to him in 1863, only three years prior to his death at the age of forty-six. Thus, John Mason Neale conducted his incredibly prolific and powerful ministry while deprived of health and the celebration of the sacraments.

Against these realities, it is all the more surprising that he was described by contemporaries as a man of "unbounded charity." Was he a fool? Where was his anger, his righteous indignation? Why do we not see his bitterness? Few of us would have stood for the kind of treatment Neale received at the hands of the church. At the very least, we would have argued with the bishop, or made a stink in the community; we would have transferred to another communion, one more amenable to our preferences. Or we would have left altogether, washing our hands of such a thankless institution and abandoning our faith completely.

But Neale continued to write and translate, giving the Anglican communion and the wider Christian community some of our sunniest and most popular hymn texts, and he gave himself unstintingly to his work with the Sisterhood of St. Margaret. Only a sincere and somewhat single-minded devotion to one's vocation can survive such severe buffeting. Small comfort that we remember John Mason Neale today; he knew no such recognition in his own time, but went to his grave at a relatively young age, spent by the burdens of disease—the disease in his own body, and the dis-ease of those who struck out against him.

If the kingdom of heaven is, as the parables suggest, invested with an integrity marked by singular devotion, then we must acknowledge that John Mason Neale achieved union with the realm in life and in death. His tenacious, patient, and charitable dedication to his ministry prevailed over all else and he was never deterred from his labors. He gave us much about which to sing, and the words with which to sing it.

Dominic
Priest and Friar, 1221   *August 8*

The popular and widely-emulated example of Francis of Assisi has all but eclipsed his Spanish contemporary, Dominic. Dominic, like Francis, advocated the abandonment of all possessions, with one exception—learning. Dominic was devoted to solid, learned preaching and, in the controversy with the Albigensians, his devotion was much tested.

The Albigensians embraced rigorous asceticism. Believing that all matter is inherently evil, they developed a severe code of behavior and insisted upon rigid compliance to it. They were, to put it mildly, obnoxious in their insistent attempts to impose their values on everyone else. They posed a menace not only to the church, which they viewed with hatred, but for the whole society, which they judged irredeemably fallen. Convinced of their own inerrancy, they attempted to force their rigidity upon everyone, provoking a vicious response that not infrequently ended in execution—which they interpreted as persecution and their opponents interpreted as self-defense.

Dominic realized that the Albigensians were only a symptom of a much deeper and more subtle disease, an abiding hunger. That they were hungry was obvious; their desire to dominate and the imposition of their point of view made them rabid bigots convicted of their own righteousness and virulent in their imperialistic pursuit of their particular brand of holiness. They were perceived as a dangerous lunatic fringe; the quickest response to a mad Albigensian was a sound thrashing, preferably till all breathing stopped.

But Dominic thought about the Albigensians long and hard, and likely concluded that the antidote to Albigensian extremes was a heavy dose of prudent balance. No doubt he listened to them; it is inconceivable that he could have taught them any other way. Ultimately the Albigensian conflict was resolved not by those with cudgels and canons, but by those Dominicans who persuaded the Albigensians that they, in their simple fleshly humanity, were worth loving and that life itself is worth living. The genuine hunger of the Albigensians was a hunger for the word of God that affirms our humanity and redeems our otherwise meaningless earthly life.

In serving others, we must sit with them in their pain and think long and hard with them about its possible meanings. As we grow more aware of the systemic nature of the problems and pains that beset us, we appreciate how much more we need to know. It was probably no great comfort to Dominic that in order to reach the Albigensians with the gospel, he would have to open himself to their life. Neither he nor we can indulge the presumption that we know what others want or need; we have to live, listen, and learn together. In so devoting our intellects to this enterprise, we may find ourselves not prescribing so much as listening, not speaking so much as hearing, not feeding so much as being fed, not preaching so much as apprehending the very Word of God. Then, in the paradoxical and parabolical manner of Jesus, we may be taught. And we may actually learn enough to teach.

Laurence

Deacon, and Martyr at Rome, 258   *August 10*

By the third century the Christian church had gained some influential friends in the upper classes. Jealous of the church's gains (and worried about the consequences of a sincere Christianity), the emperor Valerian targeted the clergy and laity of means. He seized all properties used by the church and forbade all assemblies for Christian worship. Pope Sixtus and his staff of seven deacons were tracked to the catacombs, arrested, and executed, with the exception of Laurence, the archdeacon.

Laurence was held for questioning and interrogated at length. Valerian wanted to plunder the church's riches, so Laurence was commanded to reveal their whereabouts. The archdeacon assembled all the sick and poor among whom he had distributed the church's assets in relief funds. He presented them to the emperor's prefect saying, "These are the treasures of the church." For his impertinence, he was roasted alive on a gridiron, a legend disputed by some who maintain he was beheaded along with his compatriots, which hardly seems an improvement.

Laurence's witness is indicative of the paradoxical nature of Christian living. The point he attempted to impress upon the prefect is that the hallmark of our life in faith is that we do not see or measure things as others do. We do not measure riches by how much we can amass for ourselves, but by how much we are able to invest in others. This unusual form of bookkeeping presents a considerable challenge to those who oversee the church's finances, but any honest accounting of the church's true wealth vindicates Laurence: our riches are measured in human lives. The bounty of the Christian table is measured in grain broadcast far and wide, in life freely given and abundantly returned.

It is not of our nature, however, to scatter so generously. We grow more constrained every day, more eager to gather in than to give away. We worry that our resources are diminishing and conservation is our only hope of survival, our overriding fear that what we have might be taken away—or worse, that we might be surpassed by someone else. We are afraid of dying, of being done to death by the many demands and the complexities of our living, afraid that we shall not be adequate to all that is asked of us. We may not know the threat of the gridiron, but we do know martyrdom.

For the word "martyr" does not mean death; the word "martyr" means "witness." In our case, as Christians, martyrdom is evidenced in the whole of our lives, in the giving of self in fullness that holds back nothing. As we live, and when we leave, our treasure and the church's will not be measured by how much we take away, but by how much we have spent, our legacy measured in the lives of others.

Clare

Abbess at Assisi, 1253   *August 11*

Like her friend and companion, Francesco Bernardone, Clare was the child of wealth and privilege. Both lived in thirteenth-century Assisi, a town few of us today would have heard of but for them. Francis was the first to abandon his inheritance, renouncing his father and all the excesses of his age. In their place, he embraced the opposite extreme in a radical poverty. Clare was among those whose attention and imagination were captivated by Francis. Once assured of her sincerity and devotion, Francis assisted her in establishing a sister order to his own fraternity of mendicants.

Separated only by gender, the orders represented a rare expression of equality in every other way. And Clare's evenhandedness was evidenced in her care for her nuns, a reminder that we ought always to extend our pastoral sensitivities as generously to those who serve besides us as to those placed in front of us.

As she lay dying, she said to those gathered around her, "Go forth in peace, for you have followed the good road. Go forth without fear, for he that created you has sanctified you, has always protected you, and loves you as a mother." But the most distinctive word was yet to come. Having pronounced blessing upon the others, she added, "Blessed be God, for having created me." Without the evidence of her life, and the generosity of her blessing upon others, the final utterance would sound self-centered and arrogant. Within that context, however, the words take on a luminous and profound beauty.

Too many of us believe that to follow Jesus we must cultivate a hatred of ourselves, that genuine enjoyment of ourselves is a departure from the path of righteousness. For Clare, the service of others was a self-serving. Her commitment to the gospel, to the disciplines of godly service, restored her to the fullness of life she rightly considered lost in her former life of wealth and privilege. Commitment to the gospel, by Jesus' own word and promise, is always rewarded with personal gain; in losing our very selves, we find our very selves. In serving others, Clare served herself to a full life.

She found her self at death, at the end of a life filled with such meaning and purpose it gave rise to thanksgiving. She had given it all away to serve the same endless round of mortality's demands—tending to the poor who would always be poor, caring for the sick who would never be well, coaxing life out of those who would, like all of us, eventually die. At the end, when she might have been bitter and resentful, when she might have lamented her leaving or fretted about who would carry on after her, she gave the most profound benediction any believer can utter: "Blessed be God, for having created me."

Jeremy Taylor

Bishop of Down, Connor, and Dromore, 1667   *August 13*

The Caroline Divines were a group of seventeenth-century scholars and churchmen whose ministries spanned the reigns of Charles I and Charles II, and whose proclivities tended toward high church theology and royalist politics. Among them we count Jeremy Taylor, a Cambridge-educated scholar and priest who, enjoying the support of the powerful archbishop William Laud, was appointed to a fellowship at Oxford and served as chaplain to Charles I. The turbulent life of England in this period, created by the struggles with Cromwell, resulted in several periods of imprisonment for Taylor, whose sympathies were unswervingly loyal to the crown.

It was a time of strong opinion. Jeremy Taylor knew the value of tolerance and moderation, for these themes are prominent in his writing. His moderation is evidenced in his stabilization of Dublin University and his considerable contribution to religious toleration in his own day. But Jeremy Taylor, as Bishop of Down and Connor, was also harsh in his treatment of those Presbyterians of his land who refused submission, and his condemnations of Roman Catholicism are scathing. Thus we find that Jeremy Taylor, whose most prominent legacy is a collection of devotional writings espousing moderation and toleration, was also an angry and somewhat mean-spirited man capable of treating others quite badly in the name of pure religion. He would find plenty of company today.

There is no easy antidote to this poison, but there is an ironic suggestion in the collect derived from one of Taylor's own prayers: "Make us," the prayer asks, "deeply aware of the shortness and uncertainty of human life." There is nothing like the breathtaking awareness of life's brevity and precariousness to focus our minds and hearts on the most important truths.

What could be more important than learning to distinguish between those things that are worthy of our tempers, and those that are ephemeral or inconsequential? This distinction is an economic one, touching the matter of precious human resources of time and energy as well as of life and limb; it is a matter of stewardship.

In his stories of the owner of the house who must be watchful for the thief in the night and the slave in charge of the household while the master is away, Jesus urges us to a readiness that is more than right judgment (Matthew 24:42-47). It is a readiness of being found in the right posture, of doing the right things at the moment of ultimate accounting. This readiness is a prerequisite of Christian living and its absence is evidenced in our nattering over petty concerns about which the world cares not a whit. We persist in our divisive arguments with no sense of time, no awareness of what they take from us—or what they ultimately withhold from others.

Paul reminded the Roman Christians that "we do not live to ourselves, and we do not die to ourselves" (Romans 14:7). Our lives are connected in God; to isolate ourselves from one another, to shut ourselves off from the world's contamination, seems a luxury, but it is an illusion. The prayer for Jeremy Taylor cuts right to the bottom line: this life is short and uncertain, and thus, all the more precious. It is wasteful to give so much of our lives to worthless and pointless pursuits when there is so great a need for Life in the world.

Jonathan Myrick Daniels
Seminarian and Witness for Civil Rights, 1965   *August 14*

This day belongs to two men: Jonathan Daniels and Thomas Coleman. By the spring of 1965 Jonathan was in his mid-twenties and a second-year seminary student. Thomas Coleman was the deputy sheriff in Selma, Alabama. That spring Martin Luther King, Jr., made his first attempt to march from Selma to Montgomery, Alabama. The march was viciously opposed and there was much bloodshed. King made a public plea for justice and invited others into the struggle.

Along with several classmates and hundreds of other students from all over the country, Jonathan flew to Selma, and took up residence with the black families among whom he worked as they struggled for the privilege to vote. On August 14, Jonathan and his companions were arrested for participating in a picket line and were unexpectedly released six days later. The party of four—black and white—needed transportation and refuge from possible violence. They approached a small store where they had shopped before without trouble; Ruby Sales was the first to reach the door. As the black teenager stepped toward the entry she was met by Thomas Coleman, armed with a shotgun, who cursed her. Jonathan intervened and took the shotgun blast pointblank to the chest; another person was shot in the back as the others fled. Thomas Coleman was eventually acquitted on a plea of self-defense.

The outrageous and tragic story of Jonathan Daniels and Thomas Coleman is a saga of instincts; intelligence fails to make rational sense out of this story. It was instinct that caused Jonathan to shove Ruby out of the way and Thomas Coleman to pull the trigger. Instinct informed and framed the decision of every person in the hearings that followed. Instinct impels us from within. It is, quite literally, that something that sticks deeply in us and, on certain occasions, that sticks us in our deepest places, prompting us to act in a certain way.

I want not to be too hard on Thomas Coleman; I know too many people like him. I am related to some of them and have even loved a few of them. But the instincts that caused Thomas Coleman to pull that trigger were fear, greed, and hatred. Thomas Coleman and many more like him fear that to grant someone else—especially a black someone else—any entitlement is to in some way diminish one's own share. Thomas Coleman learned to fear and thus to hate those who were different, fearing the consequences of equality with them that might lead to his own disenfranchisement. If we understand the words of Paul to the Galatians, we know that the whole world is prisoner to these same instincts: "Before faith came, we were imprisoned and guarded under the law until faith would be revealed" (Galatians 3:23). All we need do is look around us and watch the daily news to see this bondage.

Nor do I want to romanticize Jonathan's death; he did not ponder the consequences of his act. Something within Thomas Coleman compelled him to fear; something within Jonathan Daniels compelled him to faith.

It serves no purpose to demonize Thomas Coleman, and there is little to be gained from beatifying Jonathan Daniels. We need each of them to see that what met on the top step of that little store in Selma was more than Thomas and Jonathan: fear met faith, greed met hope, hatred met love. The outcome could have been predicted.

It is that meeting of fear and faith, greed and hope, hatred and love that made the occasion we commemorate in the eucharist the cause of our life together. We must not shrink from that difficult conversation, but rather invite it. We need to make a place for it daily within ourselves—and in all the places of our lives we need to encourage and even incite that meeting, bringing those opposing instincts into conversation. We must work and pray for their conversion to the instinct of Christ revealed in Jonathan Daniels: fear become faith, hatred become love, greed become a prodigal hope.

Saint Mary the Virgin

Mother of Our Lord Jesus Christ   *August 15*

In his letter to the church in Galatia Paul cuts through romantic nonsense to say that Mary's ministry, like her son's, was above all else to be the incarnation of a fundamental gospel message. The two of them, this mother and her son, are our hereditary links to kinship with God. To prove that we are sons and daughters of God, says Paul, this child was born of this woman, "so that we might receive adoption as children" (Galatians 4:5).

The primary images of our human relationship one to another and of our relationship to God are not images of husband and wife, nor even of father and son, for these relationships are known only to some of us. The inclusive and archetypal image of mother and child affirms our common humanity and, in this particular birth, affirms our common inheritance. The fact that that child happens to be male does not represent male hierarchy or superiority; it represents gender symmetry. Arguments over which is the greater—mother or son, male or female—are as inconsequential and as circular as the argument of whether the egg precedes the chicken; madonna and child, like chicken and egg, are inseparable.

In them we have an icon of our relationship to God and of our kinship with one another. In the reality of something so simple, so fundamental, and so common as a human birth, our relationship to God is affirmed and our status as children of God's own making is confirmed. But such relationship challenges our autonomy and independence. It is not "modern."

In the popular television series "Northern Exposure," Dr. Joel Fleischman is a young Jewish doctor from New York transplanted to a remote little town in Alaska to work off his medical school loans. His character is a good representative of the secularized religious persons who make up an enormous percentage of our population. In one episode, Dr. Fleischman learns of his possible ties to a dissident Jew in the former Soviet Union.

As he reads the story of Evgeny Fleischman's flight from oppression, the young Jewish doctor recalls the stories of the Soviet Jews shared around the family table in his childhood and youth. As he reads on, Evgeny Fleischman becomes more and more real, an incarnation of things he has only lightly apprehended in imagination. Joel is fascinated and moved.

Though a part of him repudiates the relationship and objects that it means nothing to him, he is drawn by the story and the images it evokes. Finally, Joel picks up the telephone at his crude desk in Cicely, Alaska, and dials Israel. For long, pregnant moments, all he can do is recite the name, "Evgeny?...Evgeny Fleischman?" When he realizes that they are connected, in the literal and the figurative senses, Joel is overcome with tears. The scene ends with this young, thoroughly modern, secularized Jew asking tearfully, but with sincerity, warmth, and noticeable reverence, "Evgeny, how are things in Israel?"

In the person and the image of Mary we are invited to be reunited with that radical connectedness we share in our common birth and life. This was and continues to be the "greatness of the Lord" proclaimed in her song: that God is firm in the promise to our ancestors, that God has not forgotten to show mercy to Abraham and Abraham's children's children, from generation to generation, even to our own day. This is the greatness that rejoices her spirit and ours: that in God's greatness we are all embraced as one family. This is her eternal mission and ministry—that we might look upon these elemental images, ponder them in our own imaginations until they become incarnate in our own lives—reunion with God, with neighbor, and with self as whole, and as holy, as the union of mother and child.

William Porcher DuBose

Priest, 1918 *August 18*

Born in South Carolina in 1836, William Porcher DuBose was unusually modern in his thought, one of those persons born seemingly ahead of his time. Oxford tractarianism, the liberalism of F. D. Maurice, German biblical scholarship, and the evangelical spirit of fervent revivalism all found haven in this man of prodigious intellect and imagination. At the heart of his faith DuBose held a tenacious and fundamental belief in the Incarnation, the premise that in Jesus Christ God places before us not just the image of what it means to be human, but the very person who fulfills God's intention for humankind. DuBose would have had little patience for our spiritualizations of Jesus that make him an oddity, the exception rather than the rule of what we are to be.

We are reductionists by habit; we whittle away at the many demands thrown at us, attempting to break them into manageable bits. Breadth of scholarship is sacrificed for narrow specialization, breadth of thought is sacrificed for narrow literalism, breadth of affection is sacrificed for narrow privatism, breadth of tolerance is sacrificed for narrow judgmentalism—all with the excuse that this narrowness is the necessity of our limitations. But there is a difference between narrowness and focus; narrowness confines us to a single path, while focus regards breadth itself as a prerequisite to intense attention to the particular.

The Incarnation offers an antidote to this painful and life-threatening constriction; it reveals the tremendous expanse of the human frame. When we say that God became incarnate in Jesus we are acknowledging that human substance, human life and being, is capable of containing and sustaining the vast complexities of God. As DuBose reminds us, Jesus is not just the image of God—not a mere pencil drawing or poetic metaphor; Jesus is the wholeness of God in human frame.

There is a liberating word in that presumption. To those of us who feel we simply cannot take in one more thing, cannot deal with one more idea, cannot possibly entertain one more request or sustain one more relationship, the Incarnation assures us otherwise. Our fears that we shall disintegrate or explode if we let one more conflicting element into the mix of our crazy lives is put to rest in the reminder that human flesh was sufficient to hold the enormousness of God.

As Jesus walked the road to Emmaus with the two disciples, he was astounded by their dullness. They were so confined, had so withdrawn into their grief and self-absorption that they failed to recognize him. Very much like modern pilgrims, they were so narrowly confined to their private concerns that they had actually forgotten all they had been taught, had completely lost their history. So Jesus spent his time with them retelling the story. In something so small as a loaf of bread, the whole story was contained; in its breaking their eyes were opened and they saw as if for the first time.

The daily demands of personal evangelism, of sharing the gospel, consists in breaking open our self-absorption and admitting others to our lives. William Porcher DuBose, and the gospel itself, assure us that there will be sufficient room.

Bernard

Abbot of Clairvaux, 1153   *August 20*

Today Bernard would not be canonized; he would be regarded as an addicted person and remanded to a recovery program. His life was a prescription for personal and professional burnout: he denied himself sleep in order to read and write. His preaching is credited with the foundation of sixty new Cistercian abbeys as affiliates of the abbey at Clairvaux, making his an administrative and pastoral organization that was larger than some modern dioceses—all without the benefits of phone and fax. His writings were, by 1140, quite well-known and gave him tremendous influence. He is said to have been involved actively in every controversy that threatened the church of his time, certainly setting him apart from the models of monasticism that we associate with retreat, quiet, and the avoidance of conflict.

The willingness to devote long hours to the relatively thankless task of bringing diverse people together to form a community, whether it be in twelfth-century France or modern-day America, is an affront to those of us who want nothing to do with anyone except our own kind, or more frequently, want little more than to be left alone. Such devotion is commendable, especially among the professional compulsives in our society whom we pay to bear responsibility for us.

I emphasize the pejorative dimensions of compulsiveness since many active believers are members of that class of paid compulsives in the "helping professions" of ministry, counseling, and teaching. The word compulsion has become a dirty word, a disorder to be treated, not a quality of character to be emulated. Yet this is a misuse of an important word in the sacred vocabulary.

Compulsion can be destructive for individuals and for institutions, but compulsion, in its most positive dimensions, is the heart of our faith. The word "compulsion," at its root, means to drive together. Jesus left his disciples with the commandment to love "that my joy may be in you, and that your joy may be complete" (John 15:7-11). The life we are commanded—compelled—to live in God is a life of love, a life that brings complete joy, brimful and running over. This is the positive dimension of compulsion. We are driven to love, that our joy may be complete.

I am well aware that some of my own compulsiveness comes of deep-seated, even destructive, forces. But I am also aware, happily, of compulsiveness that is the product of sheer joy, of a love for God and for my life and work that is sometimes so full it cannot be contained. It is good for us to contemplate the example of Bernard and be reminded in our paranoid fear of professional or personal exhaustion. We need to remember that our lives were given to be spent, that as Christians we pray that our lives may be consumed in the passionate flame of devotion to the Spirit. Burnout is one thing; the unselfish offering of one's self and gifts to the consuming fire of life is quite another. It is good to be reminded when tempted to save ourselves for some indeterminate end that our lives are already safe in the God who gives that life back to us in the abundant commerce of service.

Poor Bernard never knew his Meyers-Briggs profile, never knew the salutary therapy of a recovery group. Poor Bernard did not just burn out, he burned up—with a light casting illumination that can still guide us in the way.

Saint Bartholomew

Apostle   *August 24*

The remarkable characteristic of Bartholomew is his low profile. We cannot even be sure who he was. Early sources suggest his full name was Nathanael bar (son of) Tolmai—later, Bartholomew—the Nathanael who was the friend of Philip and who questioned, "Can anything good come out of Nazareth?" (John 1:46). Even though he is reputed to have written a gospel, it did not survive. Neither do we know for certain of his ending. While not the only one of the twelve to live in relative obscurity, Bartholomew represents a quiet alternative to the more visible and vocal public witnesses so frequently associated with the apostles.

Is it purely by accident that Bartholomew is overshadowed? Is it merely that his signal contributions, like so many, were lost for lack of archival care or scattered in subsequent upheavals? Were his contributions intentionally destroyed by jealous or rival factions of the kind that divided the post-resurrection community into separate cohorts of loyalty to Peter or Paul or Apollos? Was Bartholomew one of those persons who actually did very little, who only went along for the ride, so to speak? Or was Bartholomew the thoughtful one, prone to process his faith internally and intellectually, without a big fuss?

Paul reminds the Christians of Corinth that the practice of Christianity is not always comfortable, especially for apostles, who are hungry and thirsty, held in disrepute, weary and reviled (1 Corinthians 4:9-13). But he also reminded those who obviously enjoyed some visible and vocal prominence in their community that faith and witness take many forms; evangelism and its expressions are as different as the followers of Jesus. Similarly, Jesus told those among the disciples who disputed their relative ranking that they had missed the point. All witnesses are necessary—the oldest and the youngest, the leader and the servant—and each is blessed, in the telling of God's story among us (Luke 22:24-30).

We are never to excuse cowardice or demur from opportunity, but neither can we look down on those whose genuine gifts manifest themselves quietly. The meditative and thoughtful, the quiet and unassuming, also serve. That we have a written witness of Jesus' life and teachings at all we owe probably not to the flamboyant but to the cloistered imaginations that shaped the narratives and hands that recorded them. That we have a faith at all we owe to the multitude of anonymous scholars and scribes who wrote, tended, and translated the story.

"Here is truly an Israelite in whom there is no deceit!" Jesus greets Nathanael bar Tolmai (John 1:47). Behold, a man from Israel, a simple and artless person. It was his only qualification, and his gift. And he was called.

Louis

King of France, 1270   *August 25*

The juxtaposition of a French monarch and the founder of Franciscan monasticism seems unreconcilable, but Louis IX of France and Francis of Assisi shared the thirteenth century, and a common commitment. Both were born to wealth and position, both willingly deferred the prerogatives of privilege; the difference between the monarch and mendicant lies only in the manner of their witness and devotion. This is where the dissonance is pronounced, for while Francis embraced poverty, Louis wore the crown. Yet strange as it may seem, Louis may be for us the more applicable and the more admirable exemplar.

Francis certainly enjoys the greater popularity, but, for many of us, an uncritical embrace of his single-minded devotion to poverty is fundamentally flawed. While Francis rightly taught by word and example that we do not need nearly so much as we think we do, his radical mendicant life presumes a culture with the means and the will to support him.

Ironically, Louis of France provides a way more appropriate to our circumstances. Louis, it is said, wore a hairshirt beneath his royal dress; Francis dealt with wealth and privilege by retreat and denial, Louis by fearless engagement of stewardship and responsibility. Francis gave us only half the equation; Louis finished working the problem.

Were Francis alive today, he would no doubt be doing what his contemporary equivalents are doing: running soup kitchens, rehabbing single-room occupancy hotels as affordable housing, and generally challenging the presumptions of our greedy society. But Louis shows us that while the immediate relief of Franciscan service is admirable, it is no substitute for the systemic relief that challenges and alters the conditions that make soup kitchens and single-room occupancy hotels a necessity. Hard as it is to set up and maintain a soup kitchen or rehab a building, it is nothing compared to identifying and eliminating the forces that make such services mandatory.

None of us will be monarchs of France, but we probably already have access to more wealth and actual power than Louis ever knew as king. The ears that listen to us, the eyes that watch us, the people who consult us, the media that give us voice and visibility and accord us place in print endow us with authority. We can deny that authority and shrink from its demands, or we can struggle, like Louis, to wear the crown with grace and compassion.

Louis's crown went not to his head, but to his heart; he was one of those rare rulers who understood the responsibility of birth and office, the authority of gifts. Louis understood that his power and his gifts were not of his own making, a lesson obviously lost to his heirs, who literally lost their heads for lack of it. Power and authority is ours by virtue of God's gracious gift and by the indulgence of our contemporaries.

We are what we are, and we have what we have, because God has given us abilities and because our contemporaries and culture have afforded us opportunity and advantage to cultivate and use those abilities. We are only stewards; our feet on the ground and our heads bared and bowed to the heavens, we are the place wherein God's work is done. When we mediate all that God has given us in abilities with all whom God has given us as companions and colleagues, sisters and brothers, our ministry is made.

Thomas Gallaudet with Henry Winter Syle

August 27

Is it not a biting irony that we should commemorate Thomas Gallaudet (and his wife, Elizabeth Budd) and Henry Winter Syle—all of whom were deaf—with a reading from Mark's gospel recounting the healing of a deaf-mute (Mark 7:32-37)? Does it not seem insensitively cruel to juxtapose the story of one who was healed miraculously and instantaneously with the realities of those who were not given so speedy a remedy? And is that cruelty not compounded by our easy assumption—an assumption shared with the author of the gospel account—that to be healed of deafness means to hear as we hear, to be cured of muteness means to speak as we are able to speak? What distinguishes the deaf-mute of the gospel account—and excites the enthusiasm of his contemporaries—is that he became, at the touch of Jesus, just like everyone else. What impresses us about this account is not what it says of deafness and muteness or of their remedy; it is the deaf, unheeding crowd that fills the frame of that picture.

The story takes place in the region of the Decapolis—the territory of the Ten Towns, a place made legendary by Jesus himself. Here Jesus had earlier cast the demons out of the Gerasene demoniac; the unseated demons suddenly entered a herd of pigs, driving them over a cliff to their death. Now the people have brought him another hopeless case. It is curious and ironic that when Jesus casts the curse of deafness from the man they have brought to him, that deafness finds a new residence in the people; despite all his protestations and defying his orders, they carry on about what Jesus has done. "Jesus ordered them to tell no one"—the frustration is palpable in the words—"but the more he ordered them, the more zealously they proclaimed it." They are obviously interested neither in what the deaf-mute has to share, nor in what Jesus has to say. They are excited only that Jesus has made the one who was different just like themselves.

This commemoration omits a portion of the cast. We need, additionally, to remember Thomas Gallaudet the senior, and his wife, Sophia; Elizabeth Budd, the wife of Thomas Gallaudet the younger; and we need not only Henry Winter Syle, but Bishop William B. Stevens of Philadelphia, who prevailed over opposition and ordained Syle. Together they constitute an impressive memorial to the power of communion.

What they accomplished is, frankly, a greater miracle than the simple healing recounted in the gospel; Jesus himself insisted that his ministry was more than miracle-working and faith-healing. What was accomplished in the lives of the Gallaudets and their colleagues was the power of communion. They bore one another's burdens and shared one another's joys. Of sheer love for one another, the Gallaudets (senior and junior) expanded the sacramental respect and affection of their marital relationships to encompass the world beyond themselves. They exemplify in an extraordinary manner the petition of the marriage service which prays that all those united in such commitment "make their life together a sign of Christ's love to this sinful and broken world, that unity may overcome estrangement, forgiveness heal guilt, and joy conquer despair" (BCP 429). It seems a far better collect for this occasion than the one appointed, extolling the opening of deaf ears; it more accurately expresses the genuine power wrought in the lives of those we commemorate and more adequately conveys the purpose of our remembering.

The Gallaudet wives and husbands found in communion ways of being with one another in the world despite the barriers nature had imposed. Commitment to the gospel and its vision of the church united Henry Winter Syle and William Stevens in communion that opened to them ways of being in the church despite the barriers imposed by human nature. Thus we see in these six, and their legacy, the miracle and power of the gospel. Lay and ordained, women and men, all differently-abled—their legacy to the church is far more than the sum of the institutions they built or the institutions they challenged and overcame.

It is not the healing of hearing but the healing of hearts that is the miracle. It is not the leveling of all to a common hearing or uniform speech, but the building up of all into a respectful and affectionate communion of different gifts and diverse perceptions that truly bears the image and likeness of Christ. Irony is redressed in irony when we consider that this gift is communicated to us not in any word they spoke, nor in any word we may hear, but in the silent image projected across time—the image of Thomas and Sophia, Thomas and Elizabeth, Henry and William—in communion.

Augustine
Bishop of Hippo, 430   *August 28*

He was restless and flirted with the trendy religions of his time. He had a mistress with whom he lived faithfully for fifteen years. He had a decidedly dominant mother. Augustine's life was as conflicted, and as modern, as any today. Perhaps from the complexities of his own life he saw that all life is similarly entwined; Augustine was intolerant of easy solutions.

When the disciple Philip turned to Jesus and asked, "Lord, show us the Father, and we will be satisfied" (John 14:8), he must have been surprised by the evident shock and irritation in Jesus' reply. Jesus seems more than a little edgy when he asks in return, "Have I been with you all this time, Philip, and you still do not know me?"—or in the contemporary idiom, "Where have you been?"

Knowledge of God's truth is found in relationship, in the companionship and the conflict that comes of sharing life with others. What Philip seeks, he cannot have. He wants someone to give him God, or to give him a theology, if you will. Yet even Jesus refuses to comply, refuses to do for Philip what Philip must do for himself.

Augustine's theology, his knowledge of God and God's truth, was derived from dynamic confrontation and human relationship. Nearly every great treatise Augustine wrote was a refutation or disputation, a response. He worked out his knowledge and love of God in human experience. The inner struggles, and the outer ones, became the sources of his knowing and the places of his loving God. A convert several times over to differing philosophies and theologies, he apparently knew well the role of debate and dialogue in the matter of growth, those successive conversions that move us from one stage in life to another. He became a Christian largely because someone—usually his mother, Monnica—argued theology with him.

In the give and take of relationship, Augustine formed a theology. It was not handed to him, but came of looking for and living with God in all the contradictions and confrontations. When we turn aside from conversation and confrontation, turn away from others, from the difficult questions, we turn away from God. As we grow ever more aware of the diversity of our human race, it becomes the more difficult to embrace the demands of relationship, ever more tempting to let those who are different go their own way and to simplify our lives by admitting as little controversy as possible. Still, in Augustine, we see the blessing and promise inherent in our present opportunities and our future possibilities.

Augustine died on August 28, 430, as the Vandals were besieging his beloved city of Hippo, threatening its destruction. For Augustine, the greater tragedy of his dying was that it precluded confrontation with the invaders and the lively conversation that might have ensued; such questions as Augustine had for the Vandals would have to be put to God, and I have every conviction that that is exactly what he did.

Aidan
Bishop of Lindisfarne, 651   *August 31*

We fancy ourselves a long way from northern England in the seventh century; while "pagan" seems an antiquated designation, it is a pretty apt description of many of our colleagues and contemporaries. For in truth, a pagan is only someone who is not a Christian, a Jew, or a Moslem. Early Christians applied the term to any idol worshiper; the word can also be applied to any irreligious person.

We too live in the midst of a pagan reaction, a blip on history's graph that finds many people unbelieving, wary, cynical, or downright hostile toward anything or anyone confessing faith in God. Profound distrust of the church is as much a part of our experience as it was of Aidan's.

Aidan may have derived some comfort, as I have, from reading of Paul's experiences among the sophisticates of Rome and Corinth, whose intellectual and social defenses must have been as hard to crack as any we encounter today. It is always restorative to hear Paul say again that his greatest reward as an apostle is that in his preaching he can offer the gospel as a gift: "What then is my reward? Just this: that in my proclamation I may make the gospel free of charge" (1 Corinthians 9:18). It confirms that our primary ministry—and our hardest one—is giving away the incredible gift we have been given.

The difficulty is in giving this gospel away in a culture remarkably like the one described by Matthew, a culture in which even the apostles themselves attach a price to ministry. Peter asks Jesus, "Look, we have left everything and followed you. What then will we have?" (Matthew 19:27). They wanted to know what was in it for them, and so long as they held fast to that kind of attitude they would convey to everyone else around them this cynical bottom-line attitude. Milton Friedman is economically and even theologically correct in his assertion that there is no such thing as a free lunch; what he does not seem to acknowledge is that there is such a thing as a free gift. That someone else might pay the price, that someone else might actually give us something free and unencumbered, is fast receding from our consciousness and our experience. This point was vividly made to me when a student apologized because he had shared dinner with us, but had to excuse himself from the conversational program that followed saying, "I fear I have taken advantage of your hospitality." Funny, I thought that was why we are here—so people can take advantage of us, all the time.

Neither sadness, nor frustration, nor anger, nor exasperation will serve our gospel; we must accept, as Aidan apparently did, that at the heart of his country's so-called paganism was a profound distrust. Perhaps it was nothing more complicated than the loss of their king: maybe they thought that faith was a talisman that would protect him and them from harm, and their faith crumbled when they saw him struck down in battle. But whatever the cause, they retreated to paganism, which is to say only that they retreated to unbelief, to a cynicism grounded in the hard simplicities of human experience.

Aidan did not win them back by force, but by gentleness. One by one, a little at a time, he loved them back to wholeness. It is an important lesson. In a culture where we are all, including the churches, so afraid someone will take advantage of us or overlook our needs, the way back will be long, hard, and slow. God grant us the gentle perseverance of Aidan.

David Pendleton Oakerhater

Deacon and Missionary of the Cheyenne, 1931   *September 1*

The story of David Pendleton Oakerhater combines several American stories. The chief character, David Oakerhater, was a zealous Cheyenne warrior who fought the United States government in the bloody disputes over Indian land rights, rising to distinction among an elite corps of Cheyenne warriors and to legendary status among his antagonists. In 1875 he and twenty-seven other warrior leaders were taken prisoner by the U. S. Army, charged with inciting rebellion, and imprisoned in a Florida prison.

While in prison, Oakerhater came under the influence of an unnamed and unusually compassionate Army captain who worked to educate the prisoners. The Army captain, enlisting assistance from concerned Christians, secured financial aid from a Mrs. Pendleton of Cincinnati, whose benefaction made it possible for four of the prisoners, David Oakerhater among them, to go north to study for the ministry. Oakerhater was baptized in Syracuse and, in honor of Mrs. Pendleton, took her name as part of his own. Ordained to the diaconate in 1881, he returned to Oklahoma, where he founded and operated schools and missions and ministered as a deacon among the Cheyenne until his death in 1931. The story has all the makings of a good mini-series.

David Pendleton Oakerhater's story would be greatly enhanced were it enlarged to include his companions in ministry. What of the Army captain's wars? Even in the nineteenth century it was inconceivable that a disciplinary officer, not an ordained chaplain, could find support within the military for his campaign of compassionate care. He did not have to educate those prisoners; more likely he bucked many a bureaucrat to secure the necessary permissions and resources to establish that program and impart that education. And, racism being what it is, one can be sure that this Army captain took his share of disdain and hatred for his efforts on behalf of those native American prisoners.

And what of Mrs. Pendleton? All she did was write a check. That is probably what most would say. But what role does philanthropy have in this story? Americans are reputedly among the most generous people on earth; our extensive system of social welfare depends upon private generosity and public support for taxation. Where it is failing, it is for lack of this generosity. Yet David Pendleton Oakerhater was obviously influenced by more than Mrs. Pendleton's money.

What was their relationship, and what mutual respect does it encompass in a Native American who would compromise his precious warriorhood in tribute to a woman of privilege and status who willingly shared her name and identity so publicly and so sacramentally?

David Oakerhater conducted his ministry at great personal sacrifice, in the face of apathy from the church hierarchy and resistance from the government. This story is not the achievement of institutions; this story is remarkable, at least in part, for what it says of the power of relational ministry, that ministry evidenced in Jesus' own deployment of his disciples. Jesus sends them out two by two—but notice that he charged none of them to establish congregations. They are dispatched in modest number. They are told to confine themselves to single households along the way and to take nothing with them (Luke 10:1-9). This latter detail supports the image and necessity of traveling light, but it is also an assurance that they would need no special equipment or ability for their ministry, that everything they needed was possessed in the fullness of their person.

Taking all of that into consideration, the life and ministry of David Pendleton Oakerhater and his companions becomes a paradigm for modern ministry. It is the story of ministry carried out not because of hierarchical, institutional supports, but more often despite them; there is a relentless horizontality to this story as it struggles not to take the hierarchical path of institutionalization.

Had the story taken place in a different time—like our own—the Army captain might have taken early retirement, gone to seminary himself, and become a priest. Mrs. Pendleton might have used her money to put herself through seminary and ordination and moved to Oklahoma to work side-by-side with Oakerhater on the reservation. And Oakerhater might have spent less time educating and more time climbing the ecclesiastical ladder. Instead, the Army captain remains an Army captain, Mrs. Pendleton remains a Cincinnati matron, and David Oakerhater remains a deacon among the Cheyenne. Each remains committed to the place to which each has been called.

The Army captain took responsibility for the welfare of his prisoners. The Cincinnati matron took responsibility for the financial resources entrusted to her care. David Pendleton Oakerhater took responsibility for his considerable leadership abilities among his own people. They stayed put, but in and through their ministries and stewardship the kingdom of God was advanced.

The Martyrs of New Guinea
1942   *September 2*

There are many kinds of war and there are many ways of killing; even those of us who have hands clean from blood are still capable of killing the spirit of another human being and walking away from the crime unhindered. Indeed, we reward with honor those who are most skillful at personal achievement, with little or no regard to the reality that the winning of the honor may have cost others dearly along the way.

Whenever we step outside our own self-interest, diverting time and energy away from our own accomplishment, we are risking a substantive portion of our lives. Whenever we take time from our own concerns, or give assistance to someone else, we run the risk that we may diminish or jeopardize our own standing. There is precious little incentive in a capitalist economy or a competitive classroom to look beyond one's own welfare.

Yet as Christians we live beneath a standard that holds the sparrow in equal regard with the eagle, that holds every person precious in the eyes of God: "Are not five sparrows sold for two pennies? Yet not one of them is forgotten in God's sight. But even the hairs of your head are all counted" (Luke 12:6-7). It is a value system that is easily forgotten in the fray. And it is a ministry that calls us to a certain kind of martyrdom every day. For the most part, we and our colleagues are constantly concerned with our own survival and the successful completion of our own goals; diversion from that course is to invite a bloodless martyrdom, but martyrdom nonetheless.

As Christians, we are called to risk ourselves, our own fortunes, for the sake of others. Daily we live with wounded people, people who are bleeding from their own failures and mistakes, as well as those innocents caught in the crossfire of dueling egos and sniping self-promoters. If we intervene or get involved, making ourselves available to those who are hurting, we may find ourselves endangered, in the midst of controversy or injustice. Risking ourselves for others, we are called to bring care to the wounded. More often than we would like to acknowledge, we may even literally save the lives of those who might otherwise perish, for there are those who have perished, some in body and probably many more in soul.

When our own day is done and the toll is taken, will we be remembered for the honors and benefits we gained for ourselves? Will we be remembered for the victories we won, and the lives we took? Or, like the martyrs of New Guinea—eight missionaries, two Papuan martyrs, and their compatriots who risked death in the Japanese invasion of 1942 to save the many more who might have died—will we be remembered for our care, for the risks we ventured, and the life we gave?

Paul Jones

Bishop and Peace Advocate, 1941   *September 4*

Ordination to the episcopate is normally considered an ennobling act, and resignation from such an office a disgrace, especially when the resignation is pressured by controversy. Paul Jones upended that assumption when he resigned his position as Bishop of Utah in 1918 in response to a commission of the House of Bishops that found his opposition to World War I untenable; his contention that "war is unchristian" was denied by his own Christian colleagues.

Bishop Jones's most enduring legacy, however, is his theology of ministry. Literally driven from his office under circumstances that most would consider defeat, he did not abandon his life in the church. For nearly a quarter-century after his resignation, he continued a ministry remarkable for its calm and care within the church. In his own words, "Where I serve the church is of small importance, so long as I can make my life count in the cause of Christ."

The importance we place upon where and how we serve the church is particularly acute; ordination has become less an ordering of the church's human resources than a means of self-affirmation, to the end that many of the church's most capable ministers go unrecognized. This is a small matter of concern to the humble, but the church needs their model as antidote to a disorder of ministry in ordeals, ordinals, and ordinations that serve the wrong ends.

Service to the church is not bounded by office, and making one's life count in the cause of Christ sometimes demands standing against and outside the structures of the church that bears his name. Important as his contributions to the cause of peace were, Bishop Jones served us, and Christ, best in gracefully reordering his ministry, and ours.

Constance and her Companions

Commonly called "The Martyrs of Memphis," 1878   *September 9*

What would these Martyrs of Memphis think of their church today? Would they be embarrassed and angry, sad and scandalized that the spirit of their witness and the manner of their ministry are not much in evidence? While it is true that some have rallied behind crises like AIDS and abuse, the majority of churches and individual believers have retired to higher ground, or vanished altogether. Yet who can argue that we too live in the midst of epidemic despair and destruction, where over half of all marriages end in divorce and far too many children are killed by random violence and abuse?

The principle that kept the Martyrs of Memphis faithful to their mission and ministry is not limited to the catastrophic occasion; it is only the more clearly revealed under such pressure. The principle of the shared life forms the core of what it means to be a faithful Christian. It is essential to what it means to be an Anglican Christian, for we of all Christians confess a profound fidelity to the belief that Jesus is the profoundly human manifestation of God's truth—not an idea, but incarnate in living flesh. Godliness and righteousness are not principles; they are practices.

Yet we seem fearful of contamination, fearful that if we embrace the incarnate realities we shall die, and the truth is, we probably shall. Yet, as Jesus reminds us, that is precisely where our ministry begins. "Very truly, I tell you, unless a grain of wheat falls into the earth and dies, it remains just a single grain; but if it dies, it bears much fruit" (John 12:24). Indeed, like the grain of wheat to which we are likened, unless we die we shall never give life to the gospel we confess. Our fear ought not to be of getting dirty; our fear ought instead to be that we shall not get dirty enough, that we shall lie useless upon the surface of the ground and never be plunged into it, to the depths where we might be changed from seed to living plant.

Alexander Crummell

Priest, Missionary, and Educator, 1898   *September 10*

To transform society is a daunting task. How does one change hearts and minds, alter long-standing practices and notions? We change as a people only by changing as persons; we achieve social change in the main by converting society one person at a time. The most effective transformation is the result of personal experience and equally personal witness. It is one thing to say that we should end our racism in principle; it is another thing entirely to advocate and even fight for greater love and respect out of our own love for a friend.

Alexander Crummell fought to keep black and white Episcopalians together in a single body, even though it might have been more comfortable for everyone to have a little more breathing room. He worked hard to keep us at the same communion table, because if we were ever going to have any unity it was not going to be earned on principle, it was going to be the product of our practice. The most effective way to defeat the walls of segregation is to keep them from being erected in the first place, to keep our differences up front and visible, and to keep working at our relationships with one another. Out of our personal knowledge of and affection for one another will we overcome our estrangement.

The personal experience of friendship with another is like the seed that falls into good soil and brings forth grain; the seed that falls on rocky ground or among thorns cannot grow. The ground we are, the ground we provide for others, matters deeply. I cannot separate incidents of racism from friends who are dear to me and whose lives are touched by such hate. I cannot tolerate the jokes made at their expense, nor can I stand by and allow them to be put down. Thus the important work of social ministry is, as the name might imply, cultivating our social life.

Bringing people together, working at our relationships with one another, is the most effective way to usher in the kingdom of God's love and justice. It is as simple as that, yet not even that is simple in a culture and an age that constantly urge us inward, drive us into isolation, and provide us every encouragement to stay apart. Closed up tight in our self-contained, self-sufficient worlds, and preoccupied with activities that keep us constantly moving to and fro without ever stopping to connect, we are as impregnable as the rocks, as impervious as the path. Only when we stop actually to be with one another, to invest ourselves in relationships, can the seed take root and grow. And when it does, what it yields is abundant, filling not only our own lives but spilling over into many other lives around us.

What the parable of the sower neglects to tell us is that the sower must do preliminary work, that good soil is only made good by cultivation. The soil must be plowed, rocks must be removed and hard paths plowed up, the soil turned to receive the seed. Alexander Crummell labored hard to keep us together during some very difficult times. His work was arduous, and so is ours. It means that we and our church will always be in something of an uproar; walking a freshly-plowed field is difficult going. The newly turned earth is constantly changing under your feet. Put your foot on a clod of earth and it rolls to the side or gives way. Dirt mires the foot and slows the pace; ridges and valleys in the earth must be navigated.

Be thankful for Alexander Crummell. Continue doggedly in his footsteps, combating at every turn the age-old tendencies to revert to stone and path, where the going is easier but the growth is not.

John Henry Hobart

Bishop of New York, 1830   *September 12*

The Episcopal Church was born out of the Revolutionary War, rising from the vestiges of the Anglicanism that had preceded it in the colonies. That time, like our own, was one of tremendous and fast-paced change. It was also a time of confusion and internal conflict, as institutions long dependent upon foreign rule came to grips with the novel demands of taking responsibility for themselves. In the first two decades of its life the Episcopal Church, like the nation itself, struggled to find its way. The first twenty years of our life in this new country must have been dazzling, dizzying, and dazing—the kind of times that leave one breathless, longing for respite and retreat.

One of the shapers of that time, John Henry Hobart, in his first four years as Bishop of New York, doubled the number of his clergy and quadrupled the number of missionaries in his charge. By the time of his death he had planted a church in almost every major town of New York state and had begun a missionary work among the Oneida Indians. He was instrumental in the founding of The General Theological Seminary and revived Geneva (now named Hobart) College.

Lately, we are much concerned with a perceived scarcity of resources. More congregations are resorting to part-time clergy, merging with other congregations, or closing altogether. Campus ministries, which have for many years been an important bridge for bringing newcomers across the difficult waters of personal faith development and religious options into the Episcopal Church, are in danger of disappearing. New congregations are begun only infrequently, and often without the active moral or monetary support of neighboring parishes or dioceses. Robust Christian education and youth programs intended to lay and nurture the foundations of faith have all but vanished.

Where is the spirit and the mind of a John Henry Hobart? Where are the ones who call us back to Jesus, who, in a moment when he might well have capitulated to despair and defeat, or at the least might have counseled conservatism, instead sent his disciples out, knowing that the world they faced would do much to discourage them, even to destroy them? "I am not asking you to take them out of the world," Jesus told his Father, "but I ask you to protect them from the evil one" (John 17:15). In the early life of the church, a disheartened congregation received a letter of encouragement reminding them that discipleship is a process of building up the faith—not simply maintaining what we have or preserving what used to be, but actively building, continually reaching out (Jude 20-21). That letter also commended the struggling to Jesus who, said the letter's author, would keep them from falling—and would keep them from failing, as well.

We tend to measure everything in very meager portions and to see the coffers as only half-full and draining fast. We have lost any sense of giftedness, have blinded ourselves to our considerable resources. We seem never to speak of what we have to share with others, but only of how much more we need from others. We are concerned lest we ordain too many clergy, when Hobart before us dared to double their ranks despite there being no parishes to send them into. We are stretching our existing clergy and lay leadership to unreasonable thinness, when Hobart before us quadrupled his missionary forces and dispatched them throughout his diocese.

The collect for the commemoration of John Henry Hobart is a prayer for the revival of the church, a prayer to rouse us from "complacency and sloth," words we do not like to associate with ourselves. Yet we are complacent; if we did like things the way we have them, we would make bolder moves to change them. And we are slothful; we do not exert ourselves in behalf of our faith with anything like the energy we can put forth for the things in our lives we deem worthwhile.

Perhaps we ought to pray this collect more frequently, even daily, beseeching God to restore us to "faith and vigor of mind," that we might become again the living body of Christ on the move, in the world.

Cyprian

Bishop and Martyr of Carthage, 258   *September 13*

Carthage in the third century was not a felicitous home to Christians, if Cyprian's eventual beheading is any indication. The pressing matter before him was more than misery's love of company; then as now the truth is that a community united is stronger in the face of oppression than a community divided. The greatest investment we can make in our own safety and well-being, and the foundation of the greatest gains we make in all aspects of our life together, is profound commitment to a commonweal. For the early community of the baptized, that meant dedicated loyalty to the church. If Cyprian's insistence that the fate of our souls, our salvation, depends upon unswerving loyalty to the church seems overbearing, it was only because the threat to the very life of Christian believers was overwhelming.

From this side of Constantinian privilege, surrounded as we are by religious and political freedoms, his position seems exaggerated. But we could use a little of his rigid insistence applied to our own common life. For we, too, are overwhelmed by the enormity of evil; we lament the incursions of violence and corruption into our lives. In some ways, our times are even more frightening than third-century Carthage; at least Cyprian could go into hiding. Today even within the supposed safety and security of home the random bullets of gang violence and ignorance claim innocent lives. Those to whom we entrust our confidence and treasures too often turn out to be frauds.

In Cyprian's day, the choices were death, hiding, or abandoning the faith. Many took the last option; they have much company today. Most of us choose not to stand up to violence, nor hide from it; we simply ignore it and withdraw from the social and political commitment that is our only hope for reversing its tyranny. Cyprian's proposition that "you cannot have God for your Father unless you have the church for your Mother" seems archaic and authoritarian until we consider its secular equivalent—that we cannot claim liberty's benefits unless we shoulder liberty's burdens. We cannot be patriots, cannot claim the patrimony of a homeland, unless we revere the country and its society as a mother. In our complacency and evasion, we turn our backs on our motherland even as she is being raped and abused. A brutal image, yes. But I suspect Cyprian, who lived under house arrest until his beheading, would understand.

Holy Cross Day

September 14

What does it mean that our faces and fates have been sealed with the cross in baptism and confirmation, that our foreheads are marked with the cross in yearly ashes, that our hands are marked with the cross in ordination, that our hearts are signed with the cross in absolution? What does it mean that the centerpiece of nearly every place of Christian worship is a cross?

Why do we concentrate our considerations of the cross in Lent and Easter, see this symbol as most appropriate to times oriented toward sin and suffering, penitence, pitifulness, and death? The cross is just as appropriate to the birthplace of Jesus as to his death. No doubt it supported the roof above the baby's head, for every building, no matter how humble, is made of crossed supports. The cross very likely supported the infant, too, for the manger might well have been constructed of crosspieces. The cross is the sign of mortality, the intersection—and tension—of horizontal relationship with one another and vertical relationship with God; it is the intersection of life here in this earthly plane and life with God.

When we pray that we "may have grace to take up our cross and follow him," we are wrong to see within that prayer a petition for grace to shoulder our burdens and to suffer willingly the pains of this life. Our bearing toward one another, says Paul to the Philippians, is to arise out of our life in Christ Jesus, a life which is not characterized by hierarchy or authority, but rather by mortality. For this Jesus, "though he was in the form of God, did not regard equality with God as something to be exploited, but emptied himself, taking the form of a slave, being born in human likeness" (Philippians 2:6-7). The greatness of God, and the holiness of Jesus, says Paul, is manifest in mortality and thus in humanness.

Bishop William Wiedrich tells a wonderful story of a conductor who, while directing a large group of percussionists, raised his arms and signaled a huge corps of timpanists to sound their instruments. The din lasted a moment, then he raised his hands again and waved them to silence. Addressing the percussionists, he reminded them of a principle they had obviously overlooked: "The music," he said, "is in the drum, not in the mallet. One does not beat the music into the drum; one coaxes the music out of the drum." Then, taking a mallet, he struck the drum and gently let the mallet rise off the skin, as if the mallet were pulling sound from the kettle. The resulting sound was musical, full and resonant.

The cross is like the music of the timpani; it is not something one puts on, but rather something that is coaxed out of us. The wearing of the cross is not an accessory to life, but rather is the embrace of life itself. Indeed, Christians do not wear the cross as an emblem of exclusivity or a talisman of spirituality; Christians bear the cross within, in the daily embrace of all that it means to be human. To be a Christian is not to take the cross upon oneself, but rather to have the fullness of life coaxed out of oneself. For life was not imposed upon Jesus. Life was not beaten into Jesus; nor is life beaten into us. The life is in him, and he is in us, even as the music is in the drum.

Ninian

Bishop in Galloway, c. 430   *September 16*

In the collect today we pray to express our thanksgiving for Ninian's life and labors by following the example of his zeal and his patience. That is an odd combination: zeal and patience. Indeed, they seem almost to cancel one another out. It is of the nature of zeal to be headstrong and impetuous, while it is characteristic of patience to be humble and measured. Yet it is these gifts that are most needed in time of transition, needed in balanced and equal measure.

Today we are caught up in the painful realities of institutional change of far-reaching consequence. The church and the world with it are moving toward God's design. It may be that our own contribution will be small, like Ninian's. Our role may only be to stand faithfully between times, in the midst of change, bridging the span from one era to another. The small connecting roles are important and demanding.

Zeal means literally "to boil," while patience means literally "to suffer." We are not sufficiently engaged in faith to boil with either rage or enthusiasm. We are not sufficiently committed in faith to suffer its joys or its failings. This could be because the church holds so little power, and because it is power that holds us in such thrall that all else pales by comparison. It is difficult to feel either zeal or patience for any but the most consequential things—like our own careers and accomplishments, our own influence and wealth, our own authority and security.

The church, the people of God, will survive this time and this generation. It will make its way from what it has been to what it shall be. But what of us? Where and what shall we be in this time of transition? As we remember the example and assess the small ministry of Ninian, we offer thanksgiving for Ninian, the link—and we ponder the ministry of the link, remembering that the strongest chain is no stronger than its weakest link.

Hildegard

Abbess of Bingen and Mystic, 1179   *September 17*

The twelfth-century abbess of Rupertsberg was given to visions of the supernatural, visions that shaped her theology and the communities she established and guided. Confusing the supernatural with the fantastic, we may dismiss visions and those who confess them as mental deficients. Fantasy need have no basis in reality; fantasy can be entirely imaginary, unconstrained by fact. But the supernatural is always grounded in reality. In order for a thing to be supernatural, it must at least be natural at the core. Thus an experience of the supernatural is not a flight into impossibility or unreality, but is rather an encounter with nature surpassing our common experience.

As Christians, as people of God, we are invited—even commanded—to embrace the supernatural as the gift of God. We are invited to experience the world and everything in the world not only for what it is, but for what it reveals beyond itself. But I tend to charge through each day, moving from task to task and place to place with a determined and narrow focus. As I rush through the day I take the sky above for granted, find Lake Michigan little more than a navigational aid orienting my forays in the city, and see people either as obstacles to or instruments of larger designs and activities.

Sad to say, such behavior is natural. It is natural if one accepts—as most Christians do—that human nature is essentially flawed. As the gospel reminds us, it is our natural tendency to prefer the darkness, or in this case, to constrain our living to this shadow world wherein the skies, the waters, the people, and everything else given to us by God are experienced only opaquely.

To experience the sky, the waters, and even other people as transparent, light-bearing gifts is to have a supernatural experience, an experience well beyond the common experience of our basest nature. Looking into faces of friends, new and old, I can see far more than I had ever noticed before; gazing at the sky, the lake, the city and those who inhabit its streets, I see them as though for the first time. It is then that I appreciate the experience of Hildegard, whose clarity of vision makes her an exception in her own age and in ours. Her supernatural visions were grounded in a life of scientific exploration, for she studied nature and wrote of it.

Her scientific and theological writings exhibit a degree of skill and intellect unusual to her time. She gazed into nature and saw the evidences of God.

Our busyness is our best excuse for ignoring the world. It is easier to rush through the days, to focus narrowly on the task, to retreat into the confines of our material world, safely bounded by flat, familiar planes. Perhaps that is why we recoil from the supernatural and disdain it, for an encounter with the supernatural is risky. In the open depth of the sky and the lake—or another person's eyes—we risk engagement with the living God.

It is of God's nature to be clear, illuminating light. And we, being created of God, are also created in light. We are created as open, light-bearing, light-giving vessels for and to one another. Hildegard's visions opened her to this reality and she, in turn, invites us to follow. She understood and expounded a profound ecology that saw us and the world as both varied and related, and all bound in union with God. And in that union she found joy.

Edward Bouverie Pusey

Priest, 1882 *September 18*

The name of Edward Bouverie Pusey, eminent Oxford scholar and Victorian high churchman, is synonymous with the Oxford Movement. The Oxford Movement itself was a wondrous thing: a vast and momentous ferment of intellect and activity centered on the doctrines and disciplines of the church. For those of us who live in its wake, only ripples remain. To most, the Oxford Movement conjures visions of liturgical pageantry and incredible debates over vestments, candles, and acts of devotion. Mention of the Tractarians suggests pamphleteers whose jottings chronicled the arcane arguments of the principles engaged in this struggle. For most of us, the whole affair has a long-ago and far-away quality.

But the Oxford Movement was more than a mud fight over liturgy; it was a serious attempt to grapple with the heart and soul of Anglican Christianity's theological foundations. And far from being pamphlets, at least some of the tracts—such as Pusey's own four-hundred pages on baptism—amounted to a *summa* of Anglican theology and doctrine.

In one respect the Oxford Movement belongs to a series of upheavals unique to its time; this same period gave rise to the First Vatican Council. And both phenomena were a response to tremendous changes, especially the difficult transition from agrarianism to industrialization that affected all the western cultures to considerable degree. The world was a new and challenging place and our relationship to the land and to one another was profoundly affected by machines and mechanization—as were our relationships to God and to the institutions of education and religion. In such times all notions and institutions of authority come into question, and some are radically altered.

Religionists of the time retreated into their past to find secure moorings for authority. Pusey was unswervingly convinced of the truth of his Anglican heritage, believing that Anglicanism did indeed possess the genuine balance of Catholicity and the remedies of the Reformers. A student of the new biblical criticism emerging from Germany, yet thoroughly grounded in the teachings of the early church, Pusey—like the scribe portrayed in Matthew's gospel who "brings out of his treasure what is new and what is old" (13:52)—knew that there was merit in both tradition and reform.

John Henry Newman arose early in the Oxford Movement to become its most visible proponent. Newman enjoyed a close friendship with Pusey. They were well-matched, and Pusey's generous spirit warmed easily to Newman's enthusiasm. Newman's decision to quit Anglicanism for Rome marks the measure of these men. Surely, Pusey must have felt some sadness, even betrayal, to see so close a friend, so promising a scholar, so prominent a leader in the debate decide for what Pusey himself believed the inferior course. Pusey might well have retreated in disappointment, yet in his utter dedication to Anglicanism, he was unflinching. He became even bolder and moved with greater determination into the cause.

There is no evidence that either of these men undercut the other. Profoundly convinced of their own positions, and equally profound in the erudition and skill they brought to their defense, they did not stoop to the backbiting and hatefulness that so frequently overtake such struggles. Thus when we pray for the "integrity and courage" of Edward Pusey, we make no light request.

Pusey himself was subjected to mean-spirited academic politics when he was condemned for a sermon he delivered at Oxford and, without a proper hearing, was banned from the pulpit for two years. Yet he never succumbed to bitterness or vengeance. He seemed only to grow more generous and more dignified as his involvement with the movement progressed. Through Pusey's influence, few followed Newman into the Roman Catholic Church, but remained by Pusey's side in the Church of England.

Pusey is credited with bringing "stability" to the Oxford Movement. In the end, however, it was not his erudition but his example that proved stabilizing. We remember the life and ministry of Edward Pusey, his friendship with Newman, and the spirit of dignity and peace that prevailed in his dealings with those who most differed from him. When the dust clears on our own generation, whatever stability remains will not be attributed to the arguments we won, but the examples we set.

Theodore of Tarsus
Archbishop of Canterbury, 690 *September 19*

Born in the city of Tarsus in Asia Minor, the birthplace of the apostle Paul, in the early years of the seventh century, Theodore, a learned monk steeped in the traditions of Eastern Christianity, made his way to Rome. When word came to Rome that the English church was in a shambles, ruined by plague and internal strife over the clash of Celtic and Roman customs, Pope Vitalian turned to the sixty-six-year-old Theodore and compelled him to accept the post of Archbishop of Canterbury. So it was that a native of Asia Minor made that incredible journey through Rome to Canterbury, where he spent twenty-two years in remarkable service.

Life in three very different cultures must certainly have shaped Theodore for his ministry in a special way. Moving as he did from one very different society to another made many demands upon him; denied many of the conveniences we know, the sheer burden of travel alone was enormous. Vaulting linguistic barriers and learning new customs presented Theodore with experiences and challenges, but shaped him and equipped him to serve the church.

That is why it is so interesting that one of his most important acts was the assignment of definitive boundaries to the English dioceses, greatly improving the ministry of the bishops by limiting the scope of their pastoral attention. Using the ordered forms of canon in synodical gatherings, he slowly introduced reforms and laid the foundations for the parochial organization of the church. Is it not ironic that this man who crossed so many boundaries in his own journey made the imposition of boundaries one of his first priorities? Perhaps because Theodore had crossed so many boundaries in his own lifetime, he knew and appreciated the value of them.

The world has in recent years experienced the removal and reconfiguration of many boundaries; the fall of the Berlin Wall and the opening of the Iron Curtain are both liberating and confusing. European markets are slowly breaking down old barriers, even as we negotiate new trade agreements on this part of the globe. In that respect our world is not so different from what Theodore found when he arrived at Canterbury. Upon his arrival Theodore established a school that quickly gained a reputation for excellence; he obviously understood the importance of education and made it a priority. Leaders of rival factions and people of diverse experience gained the important experience of living in common and working together, experiences that proved far stronger than the old enmities and hostilities that wasted so much of their precious time and talent.

Theodore also went out and visited all of England. He crossed over the many different factional boundaries and entered into the midst of people's lives, working to fashion reconciliations among them. By sheer force of fairness, visiting not just select parts of the nation but by treating all of it equally, he evidenced some of his most powerful teaching and thus brought the country back together again.

But in imposing diocesan boundaries he recognized and acknowledged the truth that we live within limitations; the beginning of order is the recognition of our limits. We cannot do it all. We cannot be it all. This is the human condition, and the gift of God.

We are made of limitations. Boundaries of flesh and time define who we are; limitations of experience and intellect determine what we can know; restraints of ability and opportunity shape our accomplishments. Though we live within the infinite realm of God, we dwell within the finite limitations of this life. We need the hope that infinity inspires, but without the limitations of a singular faith and of particular love, we are condemned to vagueness and paralysis.

Theodore established and blessed the limits. Succeeding generations would make the word "parochialism" the epitome of all that is small and narrow and mean. But Theodore, who had seen much of the world and crossed its boundaries, understood that even God appreciates limits, that God's own power to love and act is manifested within the limitations of Jesus' own mortal frame. Theodore understood that true freedom does not eliminate boundaries; true freedom transcends boundaries.

John Coleridge Patteson

Bishop of Melanesia, and his Companions, Martyrs, 1871   *September 20*

The martyrdom of John Coleridge Patteson is a tragic story of mistaken identity. The stab wounds that took his life were intended for someone else; because he was a fair-skinned Englishman, the Melanesians to whom he came as friend and servant associated him with others who did a lively commerce in slave trading.

"Do not be surprised at the fiery ordeal that is taking place among you to test you, as though something strange were happening to you," Peter cautioned an early assortment of exiled and persecuted Christians (1 Peter 4:12). Some things can and ought to be expected. In a land where men, women, and children had been hunted and trapped, caged and chained, bartered and sold into slavery by fair-complexioned, English-speaking men, any person sharing those physical characteristics could reasonably consider himself endangered. Patteson and his companions may have been taken off guard, but not by surprise. Their Melanesian executioners may be forgiven their mayhem if not their mistake; their anger and their wariness were warranted.

I am sometimes surprised by the violence I meet in others when they learn of my Christian associations. Since I do not always wear a clerical collar, I am not an easy target, but in or out of uniform, affiliation with or affirmation of the church can unleash fury. I ought not be surprised. So much violence and abuse has been done in the name of religion, and of Christ, in particular.

Much of it was well-intentioned, to be sure—the sincere confidence of the righteous who do not grasp the consequences of their pronouncements or programs. Ask those who, having suffered the crushing disappointment of failed marriage, come seeking a blessing upon the promise of hope and love renewed, only to be told that remarriage after divorce is not allowed. Or consider the faithful partner who has daily loved, supported, and nursed a mate throughout a lifetime and into the next, but is denied the recognition of a spouse at the funeral and the hallowing of that grace either because no marriage had been performed, or was never an option. And what of the person who struggles to make peace with genuine affection for another of the same sex, to be met by a church that purports to love the sinner but hate the sin, as though something as essential to one's person as sexuality can be so easily dismissed. And these are just a few of the modern examples; the list extends endlessly into history.

Accepting the anger of those who have been so wronged is not a surprise; it is the burden of baptism, of life in Christ and in community. When we profess to bear one another's burdens, we cannot exempt from that load the burden of collective guilt, the culpability incurred by this community we call the church. When we take on its life, we take on the good and the bad, the grace and the sin. When we are wounded, or even die, as a consequence, it may be a sad tragedy and a lamentable loss, but it is no surprise.

Saint Matthew

Apostle and Evangelist   *September 21*

What kind of person would drop everything and take up with an uneducated, reactionary, itinerant religious teacher? Matthew was probably a very unhappy man; as a tax collector, he was employed by a foreign government of occupation, and thus he was seen as a traitor to his people. It is hardly likely he had much respect for himself, either. Maybe he did not even care that he was hated. So what if he had sold his birthright? So what if no one loved him? At least he could be financially secure, even rich; if no one respected him for what he did, they would at least envy him what he owned.

Maybe it was just one of those days when he was fed up with it all. His spirit was broken, his heart breaking, and his conscience leaking out around the edges when Jesus came by. Or maybe it was just that someone took notice of him, saw him as something other than an imperial functionary on the take. Maybe it was one of those moments when a simple invitation like "Follow me" from someone—anyone—sounds like a good idea, or at least better than what he had and where he was.

After being called by a holy man, Matthew probably expected to be taken to synagogue or at least to have a little Torah quoted to him. Instead, he and Jesus go to Matthew's house, where they sit down to eat dinner with a group of tax-gatherers, Matthew's cronies. Jesus does not reprimand or lecture them; he does not denounce their profession, either. He does not tell Matthew to "get right with God." He just eats with them—his way of saying that taxes or no taxes, people are people and simply because they are people, they demand a little love and respect for what they are in the eyes of God. It did not look much like a revival or a whiz-bang conversion; in fact, it got Jesus in hot water because it looked to outsiders like he was blessing their enemy. He was.

What followed was transforming. Matthew, who once cared so little for his Jewish heritage he could bleed his people dry, became the apostle to the Hebrews. He turned his record-keeping talents from taxes to texts, collecting one of the richest treasuries of Jesus' sayings. And he recorded the journey for us.

He, or someone close to him, or maybe just someone like him, gave it all back to us in a gospel. What kind of person would drop everything and follow Jesus? The kind Matthew described himself in the very first beatitude: "How blessed, how happy are those who know their need of God" (Matthew 5:3, NEB).

Sergius

Abbot of Holy Trinity, Moscow, 1392   *September 25*

In Russia, Sergius is credited with having averted several civil wars and with leading the resistance against the Tartar overlords, thus securing an independent national life for his country. The church remembers Sergius for his contribution to the restoration and revival of Russian Christianity in his Monastery of the Holy Trinity. Forced by civil war to leave their home in the city and to adapt to the simple expediency of farming for their sustenance, Sergius and his brother sought the seclusion of Russia's forests, where they established a monastery.

At one point his authority was challenged by his brother; though he was abbot, Sergius retreated from the conflict until he was prevailed upon to return and take up his leadership again. Offered the see of Moscow and the authority of bishop, he refused the advancement and remained devoted to his simple, gentle work among his monks and their neighbors.

The image drawn from Matthew's gospel of the kingdom of heaven as a net filled with fish is heavy with judgment (Matthew 13:47–50). The picture of fishermen grading and sorting the catch, and the implication that such is the way of the angels of judgment, far overshadows what follows: the householder who brings from his treasure what is new and what is old. What they hold in common is that each is an image of discretion; in each case, choices are being made.

Ecclesiasticus characterizes the truly wise person as one who "seeks out the wisdom of the ancients, and is concerned with prophecies; he preserves the sayings of the famous and penetrates the subtleties of parables; he seeks out the hidden meanings of proverbs and is at home with the obscurities of parables" (Ecclesiasticus 39:1–3). When we plumb the depths of Sergius, we find a person of discretion, of a sound sense of where and how to expend his energies, of one who chose his battles wisely and fought them well.

Sergius is credited with averting at least four civil wars by counseling that warfare among the peoples of the same nation is always and everywhere wasteful. He walked away from threatened conflict with his brother, not because he was particularly averse to contention, but because he realized that warfare between brothers would come to no good end and waste the energies of the community gathered around them. But his greatest wisdom seems to have been in his sorting through the various opportunities of his life and his choosing the ones he truly felt called to undertake.

So he refused an episcopate, and doubtless sorted through a host of other possibilities, for a person of talent had, in his own day as in our own, many opportunities. He opted for a simple life among simple people devoted to simple tasks. The collect for Sergius characterizes both Jesus and Sergius as "poor," when in reality they are the soul of wealth, rich not because they have everything, but because they have discretion, choice. The person who has everything is obviously indiscriminate and eventually comes to know the burden of such indiscrimination; burdened by power, tyrannized by authority, consumed by possessions, they have no life, for they have no choice.

Jesus and Sergius chose, and their gospel to us is the good news that we are free to choose where we shall be, what we shall do, how we shall respond to the gracious gift of life given us by God. Jesus chose his life, and so did Sergius, and so may we. That is not poverty; that is power.

Lancelot Andrewes

Bishop of Winchester, 1626   *September 26*

My political sensibilities bristle at an exhortation that "supplications, prayers, intercessions, and thanksgivings be made for everyone, for kings and all who are in high positions" (1 Timothy 2:1-2). I have been nurtured to be suspicious of power and position.

Bishop of Winchester during the reign of James I and favored preacher at court, Lancelot Andrewes knew how to use influence. Through his erudition and poetic talent, and his king's patronage, the Authorized (or King James) version of the scriptures in the English language was produced. Bishop Andrewes is the more remarkable for his wit, however, his felicitous facility with words. He exemplifies the importance and power of well-crafted language, a significant witness to this age that is fast losing its tongue. It is not that we have grown silent; we are as talkative as ever. But while the power and media to communicate have expanded, our vocabularies and wordsmithing skills have eroded.

Maybe the "dumbing down" of our language is due, in part, to a justifiable suspicion of those "in high positions"—in this case the academics who have lost the ability to communicate or who have cultivated intentional obfuscation. Lacking clarity or wit, they exaggerate and aggravate the social divisions between the haves and the have-nots in a culture where education is as important a currency as money.

By contrast, Lancelot Andrewes represents a thoughtful and generous stewardship of intellect. His gifts, admired at court and at home among the people of his diocese and parishes, were used not to divide but to unite, ultimately introducing the words of scripture into the hands and hearts of all.

While we pray for the genuine and pitiful needs of the world, we need not apologize for prayers on behalf of the powerful and gifted who, like Andrewes, possess gifts to draw those extremes into closer, more productive union. God has need of all.

Saint Michael and All Angels

September 29

A story from the book of Genesis recounting a fugitive's dream of angels descending and ascending upon a ladder extended from the lower reaches of heaven's vault and an incredible account from the book of the Revelation chronicling a war that no one saw, save in the reaches of the mind, are not grounded in our own experience. They do not have the ring of substantiated proof. They are, to be perfectly blunt, make believe.

Make believe. It is a childhood expression, another name for pretending, a practice which has taken on a negative connotation despite its wholesome functions. We no longer appreciate the necessity and the wisdom of pretending. We have lost our imagination. That is why we need this strange festival of angels and archangels. It is a reminder of our need to pretend, to make believe. Jacob, a fugitive, falls asleep in his flight; his concern does not rest, but rises from his subconscious in the form of a dream. He sees an image of angels and knows that God has reached him, found him, touched him. He knows that God is not confined and that no matter how far his flight, nor how long, he will never be far from God, nor God from him.

Similarly, the author of Revelation draws a vivid picture of something that cannot be seen with the eye, but only in the imagination of mind and heart. Living in a time of terrible persecution and turmoil, the vision of victory for God, the belief that God is winning despite all the losses piling up so near at hand, sustains

Revelation's author and gives meaning to a difficult life. The attempt to believe in God's triumph was what made the story of Michael and All Angels.

We think we no longer need imagination, since others make believe for us. We have the camera's eye; it sees for us, even if selectively. We are literalists; we still believe, but only in the tangible. We still practice religion, but only religion that is material; unbounded faith in human progress and in our own accomplishments is faith without imagination, based solely upon what can be seen and measured and calculated and priced.

We need imagination. It was imagination alone that enabled Nathanael to recognize Jesus as the "Son of God" and "King of Israel" when he had no other evidence than his imaginings of a messiah (John 1:49). Nathanael made believe. Nathanael gave voice to his faith and made that which he believed a reality.

Similarly, a beleaguered disciple of the first century, weary of persecution, opened his mind to a vision of cosmic war and eternal victory, a battleground where archangels dispatched demons and the pain and death of life was vanquished. That author made believe, saw a vision of what must surely be. And Jacob, fearful and hiding, fell asleep with his head upon a rock and found himself at the very gate of heaven. "How awesome is this place!" he declared. "This is none other than the house of God, and this is the gate of heaven" (Genesis 28:17). Did he mean the place whereupon he stood, and the rock he placed there to mark it? Or did he mean that place within himself, that wonderful space within the mind where imagination lives—where we see angels, where we imagine a different world and a better one? There it is that we make believe the house of God, and the door by which we enter.

Jerome

Priest, and Monk of Bethlehem, 420   *September 30*

The task of bringing the story of God's people to successive generations lies at the heart of all faithful ministry; there is no religion that does not rely upon the arts of communication, the records of history, the gifts of language, song, symbols, and learning. Reading and hearing the word is essential and central to the Jewish and the Christian liturgies. We believe, at least in part, because other have believed, and have recorded their journeys in faith that others may follow in confidence. Like scouts who move before an advancing army, marking a path, each successive generation leaves traces of God to light the way.

In the scripture readings for this day a letter to a young disciple and an evangelist's attempt to bridge Israel's history and future with the person of Jesus uphold the importance of the written record, but also encourage us to add our own. Paul reminds Timothy that while all scripture "is inspired by God and is useful for teaching," its primary end is our own pilgrimage in faith (2 Timothy 3:16). It does not carry us to truth, or impose truth upon us, but teaches us how to walk on our own legs, that we might ourselves stand in truth's presence. The evangelist Luke reminds his readers that Jesus opened the minds of the disciples to understand the scriptures in order that they might themselves enter, become, and continue the story (Luke 24:44-48).

Jerome tried life as a hermit for a while, but found it unsatisfactory. Instead, his life and career form an exotic itinerary leading from his birthplace in northern Italy, to Syria, to Constantinople, to Rome and service as secretary to a pope, to a grave in Bethlehem. Along the way he translated the Bible from Greek and Hebrew into Latin, the common language of his time and place. Doubtless, he had many a story to tell even as he plumbed the depths of the biblical stories in his numerous commentaries and homilies.

Our journeys do not always seem as exotic as Jerome's, but I suspect he would be spellbound to hear where our paths have led, what we have seen and heard, suffered and endured, celebrated and treasured. And so would others. For such is the stuff of God's continuing story, whose chapters are even now being written in our lives. Jerome understood the importance of the biblical narrative to every believer, stories too precious and interesting to be hidden away. Through his efforts, and those of his successors in translation, we enter the lives of those who have gone before us and allow them entry into our own experiences. There, in the communion of story, we feed, and we are fed.

Remigius

Bishop of Rheims, c. 530   *October 1*

Christianity's phenomenal propagation was at several points in history accelerated by the conversion of influential leaders, challenging the notion that from its earliest days it was a religion that appealed largely to the lower classes of poverty-stricken, uneducated people. Remigius, a French bishop whose life straddles the fifth and sixth centuries, is credited with converting King Clovis and thus changing the history of Europe. Given the choice between several competing religious alternatives, Clovis opted for catholic Christianity. What was it about Christianity that persuaded Clovis? Was it only politics, or did theology play a role?

To believe that Jesus Christ has come in the flesh and is of God affirms the sanctity of all that is human. This facet of Christianity as much as any other has captured the imagination and the loyalties of generations of believers. When we accept as truth the premise that a human being can manifest the fullness of God, we elevate human existence itself to sacred status and, thus, we are elevated.

We are elevated not only in spirit, but are raised whole. The poverty of any spirituality that denies our physicality is manifest in the denial, degradation, and despair to which such ideologies lead. God who is revealed in flesh, who created us as physical beings, pronounced that creation good. Had God desired angels, God could certainly have created us so; but we are of the earth and we are beloved of God. Thus Jesus contradicts Thomas's "Lord, we do not know where you are going. How can we know the way?" (John 14:5). Jesus responds by saying, in essence, there is no difference between his way and their way; Jesus affirms his own humanity and tells the disciples that the way, the truth, and the life which leads ultimately to God is open to them, as it is open to him, because of their humanity.

Jesus assures us that we need look no farther than this life to see and be with God. We are only human, and that is enough.

Francis of Assisi

Friar, 1226   *October 4*

It is often comforting, especially when we are feeling out of synch with the world around us, to celebrate the life of a person who was, even in his own time, an anachronism. Francesco Bernardone definitely marched to the beat of a different drummer. Yet while the rhythm of his walk continues to attract and fascinate, most of us remain apprehensive, preferring Francis on a benign perch in the quiet corner of the garden, a companion to the flora and fauna. Even the brothers that bear his name seldom go abroad in the distinctive brown habit with its simple cowl, but blend in with the vegetation of modern life.

Francis represents an audacious and outrageous challenge; he preaches the gospel not in words, but in images too bold to dismiss and a life that was itself a parable. That is why we both revere and fear him. He speaks the truth by living the truth. In Francis, as in Jesus, the gospel was made flesh and dwelt among us, an incarnation impossible to ignore, so tangible and physical it compels a response. In a world increasingly material, it is the most powerful way—perhaps the only way—to communicate truth.

The Galatians were sated with intellect and skill; they were intelligent and learned, and devoted those gifts to the life of the church. But they presented a daunting challenge to Paul, who was charged to convey the gospel to a people who had placed pride in their own gifts above gratitude for the gifts of God. The frustration is evident and it mounts as he proceeds, revealing at once the marvelously human side of Paul and the maddeningly human demands of his task. He minces no words, and by the time he reaches his epistolary stride, he can contain himself no longer, "You stupid Galatians," he exclaims (Galatians 3:1, NEB). Galatia was hardly any different from Assisi, or America today. It is not that we, any more than the Galatians, wish any intentional evil; it is simply that we are confused and dazzled by our own brilliance, literally stupefied by ourselves.

The Franciscan apostolate is not a rebuke of our gifts; it does not expect us to drop all and run away from the service of the world through our own necessary tasks. It does, however, lay bare the folly of the so-called wise. Traveling without encumbrance, these roving monks have been a constant reminder through the ages that we are not hostages to creation, but the blessed recipients of its bounty, and stewards of its riches. Francis and those who follow in his way preach to us by living as though the gospel were a reality; they live as though the kingdom of God were present, the victory of Christ over this world as real as the closing Dow Jones average and the morning commute. They are an icon of vocation for every Christian, searching us and compelling us to see what we might be, and to live it.

William Tyndale

Priest, 1536   *October 6*

Once he had determined to translate the Bible into English, the challenge William Tyndale set for himself was daunting and deadly. Those whose power derived from their education, namely the priests and politicians, had a vested interest in keeping the people in ignorance. Therefore, Henry VIII and Cardinal Wolsey, and their allies, hunted and hounded Tyndale after he fled England for Germany. Thanks to betrayal by an informant, they finally caught up with him in Brussels, where he was strangled at the stake even before his body could be burned. But before he died, Tyndale managed to complete a translation of the New Testament, the Pentateuch, Jonah, Joshua, Judges, Ruth, and the books of Samuel, Kings, and Chronicles.

In 1526, in his prologue to the epistle to the Romans, Tyndale wrote, "God's mercy in promising, and truth in fulfilling his promises, saveth us, and not we ourselves; and therefore is all laud, praise, and glory to be given unto God for his mercy and truth, and not unto us for our merits and deservings." That is the heart of the gospel for such a people as ourselves, preoccupied with the notion that our salvation rests upon our own accomplishments—that if we fail in any way, or falter, we are forever doomed, or eternally and irretrievably lost. How are we to proclaim a gospel we do not ourselves believe? How are we to commend a gospel we ourselves have never appropriated for our own lives?

What, then, might it mean for us to bear this gospel? It might mean that we ease up on ourselves and measure every day's demands against the reality that God has already saved us, God has already deemed us valuable, lovable, even successful; nothing we can do, whether for good or for ill, can alter that preeminent love of God for each of us. It will certainly mean that when we set out to do anything, we shall enter that experience with the confidence that the outcome is already assured, that our worth and integrity are safe, and that it is not for God's sake that we strive; God has already accounted each of us worthy, therefore we have nothing to prove.

The practical outcome of this gospel is a radical change in our lives. The keen edge of desperation that so often accompanies our work can go. The wary suspicion that comes between us and hones our competitive edge can be set aside. The drivenness that hounds us can be relaxed. And the world, or even this little corner of it, can be a more heavenly place.

William Tyndale was obviously a driven man. He set a task for himself for no apparent reason save his singular passion for the Bible and his equally strong conviction that these texts he so loved should be available to all. He stood to gain nothing material for his labors; instead, his life was in constant jeopardy and his work was more punished than patronized. Only a deep and abiding conviction of his own worth and work could have upheld him in his labors under such conditions.

Consequently, it is not just his wonderful translations that Tyndale bequeaths us, fine as they are. He also leaves us an example of what it means to be so confident of our own relationship with God that we can risk everything on the work we deem most important, the work that is largely a gift to others. William Tyndale believed that the first and best news of God's word is the word of our sure and certain place in God's love and care. Thanks to him, we have read and heard that word in our own language; may it be our will and our pleasure to "do" that word as well.

Robert Grosseteste

Bishop of Lincoln, 1253   *October 9*

"No slave can serve two masters; for a slave will either hate the one and love the other, or be devoted to the one and despise the other. You cannot serve God and wealth" (Luke 16:13). Are we really to choose between money and God, or is something else being asked of us? Can we not uphold the law of Moses that mandates God's place at the head of our lives and still maintain a healthy respect for money? While for some, the drastic language of choice may be appropriate, God and money are for most of us not an either/or, but a both/and proposition.

Robert Grosseteste was a wise and learned man among whose pupils were Roger Bacon and John Wycliffe. He was no bumpkin, but a man of prodigious intellect. Yet, after elevation to the episcopate of Lincoln, he was regularly found in the rural reaches of his diocese among his people. Visiting them all, he taught, engaging them in questions of faith and filling their hearts with the wonder of life. Such behavior does not go unnoticed; his people remarked during his first visitation that he was doing something "new and exceptional."

Robert Grosseteste knew well that what he was doing was hardly new; it was apostolic. The people were astounded, no doubt, that someone as important and learned as their bishop took a lively interest in them and their ideas. His fellow bishops might also have wondered why he gave time and effort to such seemingly small matters, such relatively unimportant people. Occupied as they were with the weighty concerns of office, they were probably very much like the Pharisees cited in the gospel as "lovers of money" (Luke 16:14)—which is but another way of saying they were lovers of power, prestige, and all the other privileges we accord primacy over God.

Yet Jesus maintained that before we can be entrusted with true riches, we must prove ourselves faithful over lesser things: "Whoever is faithful in a very little is faithful also in much," he told his disciples (Luke 16:10). Responsible stewardship over money, or any material good, demands that we keep our priorities in order. We are not to renounce material goods, but rather to serve God as our first priority, and to shape all subsequent actions according to that primary principle.

Robert Grosseteste would appreciate the story of his modern counterparts, the "inventors" of the electronic network called the Internet. Having discovered a practical way to link all people with access to computers, the engineers who designed the system were faced with an enormous question: should they turn this knowledge to their own profit? Returning again and again to their original principle—to encourage the free exchange of information and ideas among the peoples of the world—they realized that there was only one way to ensure this objective: they would have to "donate" the Internet to the world. No one could "license" or in any other way inhibit access to the network, for to do so would defeat the primary objective. They gave the gift created out of their own special gifts for computer programming back to the world. More than a gesture, this act is a parable.

For Robert Grosseteste, who possessed genuine wealth in his day—education, respect, and high office—such privilege meant employing these riches as means to God's ends and not as ends in themselves. People are not cogs in the machinery of life; they are brothers and sisters. The world is not our oyster; it is God's holy creation. Whatever our wealth—and most of us possess at least some, in the form of education, specific gifts and talents, and so on—we are to share it with others. If and when we behave according to these principles, we shall be witnessing to a profoundly different way of sharing wealth, all the while doing new and different, even exceptional things.

Samuel Isaac Joseph Schereschewsky
Bishop of Shanghai, 1906   *October 14*

One look at the name Samuel Isaac Joseph Schereschewsky in a calendar of Episcopal commemorations and you immediately know "there's a story there." He was born of Jewish parents in Lithuania in 1831 and was a candidate for the rabbinate. During his graduate studies in Germany he developed an interest in Christianity that was greatly facilitated by his own reading of a Hebrew translation of the New Testament. As if that were not colorful enough, he then moved to America, considered the Presbyterian ministry, and eventually ended up an Episcopalian.

A student of languages with a rare gift for the same, Schereschewsky responded to the call for missionaries and shipped out to Shanghai. He learned to write Chinese en route, which would still be a spectacular accomplishment, even on the proverbial "slow boat to China." Once there, he settled in Peking and translated parts of the Bible and the prayer book into Mandarin. In 1877, this former Lithuanian Jew became the Bishop of Shanghai. During his episcopate he established St. John's University in Shanghai and began his translation of the Bible into Wenli.

Then came the moment that would secure Schereschewsky's place in the pantheon of heroic figures. He was stricken with paralysis in 1883 and resigned his see. Undeterred by the effects of his illness, he continued to work at his translation, completing over two thousand pages at the typewriter using the one finger he could manipulate. It was a long and arduous labor, but he accepted it gracefully as his true vocation.

We Americans are graced with the blessed optimism of a freedom known to few others in this world. From the ground up we are encouraged by the notion that there is no limit to what we can be, or do, or accomplish. Sad to say, this notion is a lie: there *are* decided limits to what we can be, and do, and accomplish. It is a painful—sometimes even fatal—lesson to learn, when accompanied by despair. Learning our limits can be overwhelming, shutting down all our initiative and creativity. Or it can fuel a competitive spirit that treads always the fine line between positive achievements and the destruction of anyone or anything that stands in our way. For far too many of us, the fear of our limits drives us in an ever-increasing spiral of self-validating behaviors, like the single-minded workaholism that sacrifices everything to the denial of our human limitations.

Yet, Bishop Schereschewsky, sitting at his typewriter, pecking out his translations, saw his limitation in a far more graceful light. The discovery of his limitation was the focus of his life. It was, for him, as though all the other energies and interests and options had been pared away, revealing the singular gift. Perhaps this is what Paul meant when he maintained that "while we live, we are always being given up to death for Jesus' sake, so that the life of Jesus may be made visible in our mortal flesh" (2 Corinthians 4:11). It is not that we are to see our limitations as a sacrifice to be made, but as the gift that they are. We spend a lifetime reducing and refining in order that the singular gift of our most singular life might be added to the whole.

I do not read a word of Mandarin. But Samuel Isaac Joseph Schereschewsky continues to proclaim the gospel to me, sitting at that typewriter for twenty years and, with but one finger, doing what he did well, and gracefully.

Teresa of Avila

Nun, 1582   *October 15*

Teresa of Avila is enjoying renewed interest in these spiritually starved times. Those seeking a deeper knowledge of prayer and a more fulfilling spirituality often turn to her work. Her life was devoted to the formation of the rigorous order of Discalced Carmelites. This is one of the few orders of monastics marked by their sandals, the only shoe acceptable to those who seek to emulate the ancient barefoot orders of the Eastern desert mystics. We would consider them extreme by any measure today and are inclined to wonder just what possible purpose such asceticism serves.

Too, we must acknowledge that the spirituality espoused by Teresa and her ilk represents a most strange time in Christian symbol and custom. Centered upon a theology of the suffering Christ, with its masochistic overtones, it is difficult to comprehend how such a model served a gospel of love and redemption. Nor are we alone in our estimations; Teresa encountered significant opposition in her own lifetime from those who, like us, took issue with her brand of faith.

To encounter Teresa is to encounter passion, not simply sexual passion—though there is more than a little of that type of passion evident in her life and work—but that single-minded devotion and commitment that refuses to be swayed, that pursues its course and defiantly damns any who would divert it. Teresa was a woman of dogged determination who battled great odds to achieve her goals. She was not afraid to venture forth in faith, and her venturing took her into some wild and wonderful places.

A woman of contradictions and paradox, Teresa's love of the disciplined life of monasticism and her passionate devotion to her religious order were necessary to her stability; she was so very far ahead of her time in her thoughtful approach to spirituality, it may have been all the more necessary that she reach into the oldest and most venerable monastic practices to achieve equilibrium. But what astounds most is her sheer audacity. That is what marks her life and makes her stand out against the present landscape of Christianity. Teresa calls us to a passionate faith in a time that is remarkable for its passionlessness.

We do what we have to do in the workplace, in our relationships, in our study, in our religion, and in politics, but we lack that genuine love of our work, that abiding love for the other person, that insatiable love for learning, that ineffable love that gives rise to worship, that passionate love that animates and humanizes politics. This is the characteristic that we see at work in Teresa. It is not the hallucinatory nature or sexual dimensions of her visions, nor the rigorism of her monastic discipline that is off-putting. It is her passion that causes us to raise one eyebrow just slightly. For all the outward manifestations point to just how very much this woman cared. This is what we find so amazing in this nonchalant society of ours—we are thrown off guard by those who find it within themselves to care, passionately.

Teresa is still out there, and we encounter her every once in a great while. She is within us, and she threatens to cut loose when we relax our vigilance. She is even a little crazy at times: God knows what might happen if she prevailed! And because God knows, God bids us let her loose that we might love again, passionately.

Hugh Latimer and Nicholas Ridley, Bishops, 1555
Thomas Cranmer, Archbishop of Canterbury, 1556

October 16

Latimer, Cranmer, and Ridley—not a law firm, but a trio of reformers who had the misfortune to live in perilous times. Their century and their sentiments overlap those of the other great architect of the Protestant Reformation, Martin Luther. But while Luther lost only a job, these three lost their lives.

Thomas Cranmer was made Archbishop of Canterbury in the reign of Henry VIII and became the primary author of *The Book of Common Prayer*, making him the most influential shaper of Anglican theology and polity. Nicholas Ridley was chaplain to the Archbishop and eventually became Bishop of London. Hugh Latimer was an outstanding orator and preacher; Henry VIII named him royal chaplain and then Bishop of Worcester. These three made a lively trio; in those tumultuous times of religious upheaval that followed close on Henry's reign, they lasted through the reign of Edward VI and into the accession of Queen Mary in 1553 (no mean accomplishment in itself), only to be executed by this Catholic queen for their staunch adherence to Reformation principles. Latimer and Ridley died together in 1555 and Cranmer shortly thereafter in 1556.

Was it only obduracy that brought these three to their tragic ends at the stake? Even in the shifting tides of their times, could they not have found a way to survive? Is there, in the end, any faith worth death? For these three men compromise was, after a point, not the operative word in their vocabularies, and it is not the operative word of Christian relationship.

It is not compromise but reconciliation that shapes our life. It is not the compromise of difference, but the reconciliation of difference that we seek. I may ask the person I love to consider my conviction. I may ask the person I love to alter or amend an opinion. But I can never demand that the other compromise if what I mean by compromise is that the other person submits to my will. So long as we insist upon a compromise that is really control and conformity, we shall continue to kill one another. Until we can celebrate a reconciliation that respects differences, we shall not live as I believe God intends us to live.

Each of us is God's worker, said Paul, and each is called to build, some with gold, silver, and precious stones, and others with wood, hay, and straw (1 Corinthians 3:9-14). But Paul makes no distinction between the materials; each builder, each material and each building is as precious as the next. The differentiation is valued; it is we who have lost sight of that distinction in calls to compromise that only thinly mask our selfish desire to have things our own way.

Because they would not compromise their principles, Cranmer, Latimer, and Ridley went to their deaths. Had the spirit of reconciliation prevailed over the demand for conformity, they might have lived and the churches of England and Rome might have been one. The fire that consumed these three did not make them or the church more Christian; like all refining fires, it only separated the elements and heightened the difference.

Ignatius

Bishop of Antioch, and Martyr, c. 115   *October 17*

To know one's finitude is to know one's distance from God; mortality is the companion of humility and vulnerability. Ignatius, aware of his own end and the fragility of his life, knew keenly that he was not God, but he also knew profoundly that he was God's. Ignatius was God's child, and told us that we are God's child, because Jesus was God's child and Jesus, who lived and died as we live and die, was *really* raised from the dead.

Ignatius, who lived in a day when one could probably still hear firsthand accounts of Paul's powerful witness, knew the assurance that nothing of our mortality can ever separate us from the love of God (Romans 8:35-39). That is a lesson that can only be learned, ironically, in embracing all that we are at pains to avoid—living together, working together, suffering together, and even dying together, that sharing of the one loaf which Ignatius called "the medicine of immortality."

Jesus told Andrew that unless a grain of wheat fall to the earth and dies, it can bear no fruit (John 12:24). It is in losing life that life is saved. We are surrounded by many who are saving their lives and preserving their ends, conserving their goods and their energies in living tombs as splendid as any civilization has known; lives are saved daily, but to what end? Ignatius invites us into the shadows of mortality, into an incarnate and dangerous world, lost with that very human Jesus on that road that leads to sure and certain death. Lost, redeemably lost, in God.

Saint Luke

Evangelist   *October 18*

We tend to think of the authors of scripture as religious professionals. The prophets and vast cast of honorable Jews who people the Hebrew scriptures come with flowing robes and flowing beards. They seem always to be engaged in religious dialogue and religious enterprise, so the easy assumption is that this was the central focus and the singular work of their lives. When we turn to the Christian scriptures, those who were attached to the person of Jesus and who carried his work forward into the early years of our history become in our minds the ancient counterparts of the present-day clerical order. We dress them all in clerical collars and set their lives within the confines of sacred courts and hushed sanctuaries. What we lose in the process is any realistic point of connection between their lives and ours.

In his second letter to Timothy the elderly and probably dying Paul addresses a younger member of the faith community. Paul, or others writing in his name, counsels Timothy, or maybe a whole community of youthful Christians to "keep calm and sane at all times." But then the seasoned veteran lists the particular work to which such sanity and calm is to be brought. "Face hardship," advises the older apostle, "work to spread the Gospel, and do all the duties of your calling" (2 Timothy 4:5, NEB). There seems to be a clear separation: "work to the spread the Gospel" is one effort and "do all the duties of your calling" is another. But the two together comprise the whole of Christian living.

The work of spreading the gospel is not set apart for an elite or specialized group. It is not even the sole calling of the disciple to whom this advice is directed. The distinction made in this instance is that one might have some other calling with demands and duties of its own; within that context and in relationship to that work spreading the gospel is undertaken. Evangelism, then, is not a distinct calling, but is the accompaniment to every calling.

This does seem to have been the case for Luke, though the distinction is lost when we replace his vocational title, Luke the Physician, with our ecclesial one, Luke the Evangelist. If we might indulge modern images, we strip him of his lab coat and stethoscope, remove him from the sterile examining room smelling of alcohol, and we dress him in vestments, hand him a Bible, and set him in a church smelling of incense and musty prayer books. Yet his vocation was to medicine and healing; he was educated and trained as a doctor. God calls and works through us all. Within the healing profession and with the tools of that calling, Luke worked to spread the gospel. His gospel has such power because he was a doctor first and because he was able to deploy all the learning and habits of that profession in service to the gospel and its dissemination.

One can imagine that Luke may have actually inspired or urged Paul in this advice to Timothy. The tradition allows us this privilege, for the letter to Timothy indicates that Paul is in the company of Luke, all others having deserted. With the physician there beside him, Paul is reminded that the work of God's gospel is carried out in many places by many diverse people using the abundant riches of God's varied callings.

Jesus, standing in the synagogue of Nazareth, picked up the scroll and read from it the work anticipated of God's anointed: announcing good news to the poor, proclaiming the release of prisoners, recovery of sight for the blind, restoration of those who are broken (Luke 4:18). When Jesus declared that all of that had been accomplished he did nothing more than erase the line drawn between the gospel—God's work—and his own work. That is evangelism. It is the assumption of the gospel, the appropriation of the gospel, into one's life and work. The only inhibition to the full realization of the gospel, according to Jesus, is our failure to assume its truth as the operative context of our life and work. Closing the gap may be as simple as acknowledging that Luke was both physician and evangelist—as simple as remembering and realizing in our own lives that today the fullness of God's gospel has come true, and living that truth in all the duties of our callings.

Henry Martyn
Priest, and Missionary to India and Persia, 1812   *October 19*

When Jesus converses with the Samaritan woman at the well he assumes that he is talking to an infidel—she is, after all, a Samaritan—and proceeds to lecture her, telling her that she does not know what she worships, that she could not possibly know, for she is not a Jew and salvation is confined to the Jews. The time is coming, he tells her, when her eyes will be opened. Then, in a most astounding reply, she announces that she certainly does know that the Messiah, who is called Christ, is coming and then all things will be revealed (John 4:21-25).

Jesus' erroneous assumption, and the Samaritan woman's challenge, serve as a point of education in the life and ministry of Jesus. In this encounter Jesus is thrust beyond the limits of his mission to a wider consideration of the expanse of God's reach. Even in Samaria Jesus finds that God has been before him.

Just as Jesus assumed that a woman of Samaria could not possibly understand the tenets of the Jewish faith, so we tend to assume that beyond the limits of Christianity lies an abysmal ignorance, a vast darkness awaiting our illuminating candle. We Christians have slighted and uprooted traditions of worship and spirituality the world over—and then we wonder why anyone should ever feel enmity toward our well-intentioned reforms! While we have improved considerably in the area of foreign mission, in our personal witness and evangel we have not come terribly far from these impulses.

Henry Martyn was a marvelous exception to the rule. A young and enthusiastic clergyman of the Church of England, in 1806 he traveled to Calcutta as chaplain of the East India Company, commencing a story of remarkable vocational synchronicity, a fascinating exposition of the mysterious ways in which talents, tasks, and time are ordered in propitious ways.

Unusually gifted with a facility for languages, Martyn accomplished much in his five years in India. He translated the New Testament and *The Book of Common Prayer* into Hindi. Then he began a study of Persian and completed a Persian translation of the New Testament as well. In 1811 Martyn realized a dream to go to Persia and found himself appointed the first English clergyman in the city of Shirmas, where he engaged in theological discussion with learned Muslims and, subsequently, amended and corrected his Persian translations. His dream expanded; he moved to Arabia where he hoped to add an Arabic translation of the

New Testament to his accomplishments. But he died in the city of Tokat, en route to Constantinople, at the age of thirty-one.

What was most remarkable about Henry Martyn was his respect for others. In every culture he entered, he took up the burden of learning another people's language and worked to comprehend their way of seeing the world. He seems never to have assumed that those different from himself represented anything other than the rich possibility to learn something new about the richness of God.

The moment by the well in Samaria was most rare; seldom do we see Jesus encounter the good news of God in such terms. From his presumption, Jesus learned that his mission would extend well beyond the Jews. But he learned something more, something that many of us learn when we open ourselves to receive from those who see the world, and God, from a different perspective. He learned that God had already been there. In the supposed darkness of Samaria, in the person of that woman by the well, Jesus encountered God as surely as the woman encountered the Christ. In that most unlikely place each met within the other the God whom each was seeking.

That is mission, and ministry; it is meeting God in one another. It was certainly so for Henry Martyn, who seems to have undertaken his travels not so much to promote God, as to meet God. Our most fruitful witness and ministry come not from preaching God, but from seeking God, from venturing forth and reaching out to one another, to discover all the places and the many ways that God has gone before us—and comes out to meet us.

Saint James of Jerusalem

Brother of Our Lord Jesus Christ, and Martyr, c. 62   *October 23*

W here did this man get this wisdom and these deeds of power? Is not this the carpenter's son? Is not his mother called Mary? And are not his brothers James and Joseph and Simon and Judas? And are not all his sisters with us? Where then did this man get all this?" (Matthew 13:54-55). With these questions the people of Nazareth greeted the return of one of their own. Jesus, teaching in the synagogue, seems to have had no standing with his own townsfolk. Where did he get all this, they wanted to know, as though knowing the answer would supply the credibility Jesus lacked.

Thus we come to a familiar problem: upon what basis are we to cast our faith? In what teaching shall we trust? Whose witness is the true witness, and whose wisdom reliable? We have been taught, and wisely so, that we ought to research and consider carefully where we place our trust. We want to know as much as we can before we decide; we want to make knowledgeable decisions. And this is all well and good. But if we rely too much and too long upon the opinions of the experts, the sources of our knowledge, after a time we come to distrust ourselves.

That is why we need the example of James of Jerusalem. Said to be the brother of Jesus, seated at the head of the Christian church, this James was Bishop of Jerusalem. It was hardly a cushy job, for the episcopate had not yet achieved the splendor it would eventually attain. It was and still is a very messy job. And there before his chair, in the midst of that assembly—the first official council of the gathered elders of the Christian faith communities—was a major muddle. The community was divided over the requirements of membership in the Christian assembly. Were new Gentile converts to be required to submit to the full letter of Hebrew law, or would faith and baptism alone suffice?

Lesser leaders might well have resorted to established precedent, to tradition. Instead, James did a most creative thing: he made a decision. He rendered a verdict, and it became the accepted practice, shaping for all time the institution of which he was head. In that moment, James revealed himself to be the genuine brother of Jesus.

Both Jesus and James were decisive. The teaching of Jesus, as he related his own perceptions of God, and the direction of James, as he rendered his opinion in the assembly, were both clear examples of authority based upon personal experience. The only authority that either of them had was the authority of their own perceptions, perceptions formed by their very human reason and experience.

Like the townspeople of Nazareth, we are suspicious of such authority. The personal witness of other Christians, or those of differing faiths, is easily discredited as lacking authority. Our own witness and faith is prone to a leaning dependency upon tradition—be it the scriptures or the historical church—or upon the opinions of others. Unless we can cite chapter and verse, or ecclesiastical canon, or the latest poll, or the currently accepted experts in the field, we tend not to venture forth at all. We want always to be right, to be safe and sound. And when carried to extreme, we find ourselves perilously near death. For then we bear someone else's faith, someone else's story, someone else's experience; beneath such a burden, how can our own life be sustained?

The liberating word of the gospel is that we are responsible creatures. We are free to hold our own faith, to make our own judgments, and to value our own experience. Those who rejected the authority of Jesus did so on the basis of his humanness; because he was one of them, they discredited his witness. What they revealed was not simply their mistrust of him, but their own lack of respect for themselves. They were saying, in truth, that because Jesus was no different from them his word could have no value, his witness no authority.

Yet it is in that very humanness that we see the sanctity of our responsibility—that as creatures of God we are endowed with the ability to respond in faith and hope and love to the life that is ours and the world in which we live it. In Jesus, whom we believe to be all that God desires of humankind, we see the high regard of God for the human race, a regard that is obviously far higher than what is revealed in the townspeople of Nazareth.

When James was called upon to arbitrate the dispute that divided the community, he acted upon no other authority than his own experience, experience informed by tradition and shaped by scripture, but a departure from both. As he pondered his decision, I wonder if James recalled the day they had rejected his brother in Nazareth. They had rejected Jesus because James was his very human brother. That day so many days later, in Jerusalem, James's word was respected because Jesus was his brother. It was an irony too sad to be savored.

Alfred the Great

King of the West Saxons, 899   *October 26*

Names like Aethelwulf and Guthrum sound like a Tolkein fantasy, replete with knights in armor and enchanted forests. It is difficult to believe such people existed, much less that they should encounter problems and issues familiar to us. If we get past our impressions stoked by too much Walter Scott, too many tales of Robin Hood, too many scenes of dinner parties involving whole roasted pigs and ruffians and the absence of silverware, we discover a real people and a real king who was respected for his courage and, far more rare in his day, for his Christian virtues.

Alfred was a reconciler with a huge task; wars and tumults had left England and her culture devastated. Alfred saw education as the pivot necessary to move the leaden weight of a defeated and degraded nation. He brought his considerable forces to bear, waging war on ignorance and restoring education in his land. Alfred took seriously the commandment that we should love God not only with heart, soul, and might, but with our minds as well.

"The multitude of the wise is the salvation of the world, and a sensible king is the stability of any people" (Wisdom 6:24). Alfred certainly exemplified these words, whether he knew them or not. For out of his labors grew one of the most impressive educational systems in the world, and a people whose leadership has, in its finer moments, been the salvation of the world.

We seem to have lost our appreciation for the inherent holiness of education, for we do not give our energies much to the advocacy of education as a good, as an essential component of stewardship. Must we wait for war and devastation to teach us?

Saint Simon and Saint Jude

Apostles   *October 28*

Like Neil Simon's "Odd Couple," Simon and Jude were mirror images of one another. Something of their opposing personalities is captured in the prayer that characterizes them as "faithful and zealous." Jude was more likely the one remarkable for his steadfast faith; Simon was so hotheaded that his name comes down to us in its more familiar form, Simon the Zealot. About all we know of them is that they shared ministry and martyrdom in Persia. Why and how they ended up together is not known. That they ended up together, however, is a point rich in meaning.

The lives of saints Simon and Jude raise the possibility that balance and well-roundedness may not be virtues at all, but evidence of our sinful tendency toward self-sufficiency. The well-rounded person is capable of doing many things well, and can get along awfully well on his or her own. We all love balanced folks who can be trusted to take care of themselves with a minimum amount of support. In fact, were we all as well-rounded as our institutions would like, we would need no mental health clinics or tutoring services or support groups. That is the little giveaway to this kind of balance: because it promotes a kind of self-sufficient independence, it represents the oldest sin in the book—that old sin of Adam and Eve, the sinful impulse to be like God.

In Simon and Jude we see something different. I suspect that Jude, the peaceful and reconciling half of this team, was one of those people for whom life just lies in wait. He is easy prey, the kind that gets steamrollered, a human doormat. But it is just as likely that people loved him dearly, called him the very milk of human kindness, and openly praised his graciousness. And Jude, being the person he was, probably found reinforcement in their words.

Simon the Zealot, on the other hand, was that kind of person who needs a keeper. I suspect he was the smaller of the two men, and the more pugnacious for it, outspoken and prone to rapid shifts of mood. He was probably as passionate as Jude was passive, seizing every moment with a kind of rapacious intensity. In any argument, Simon could be trusted to be up front. Many simply settled back and let him go to the front lines with their cause. He was the risk-taker, and they rewarded him for it, constantly praising his zeal and urging him on.

Without one another, Simon and Jude would likely have been martyred far earlier in their lives. Together they were a formidable pair, each bearing the gifts necessary to the life of the other. Jude was always there to mediate and reconcile the abrasions created by Simon's zeal; Simon was always there to speak on behalf of Jude and protect him from those who would take advantage of his gentleness. Neither was what we could call "well-rounded."

Jesus told his disciples that the world would hate them (John 15:18-19). He never exhorted the disciples to seek out the world's approval, nor to curry its favor; he never once suggested that discipleship demanded the well-rounded personality, but rather prepared them to be hated, to be misfits within the established social order. They were misfits not simply because they believed in the gospel of Jesus, but because, like Simon and Jude, they were encouraged not to self-sufficiency but to interdependency.

They were bonded together not because each was self-sufficient, but because, in Jesus, their irregularities fit together. Like odd-shaped stones carefully set into a solid foundation, the very irregularities made their bond far stronger than a course of regular bricks; it takes far greater force to destroy the well-made stone structure than to topple a brick wall.

Simon and Jude, in their curious mix of faith and zeal, remind us that we need not be all things to all people even some of the time, that what we need is a deeper appreciation for our own unique gifts, and for the strange and exciting gifts of others. They remind us that our greatest need is not comprehensiveness but integrity; not the ability to be all things, but rather to be the very best of what we are. But ultimately, they remind us of our need for each other—the need that binds us one to another, and builds the house of God.

James Hannington

Bishop of Eastern Equatorial Africa, and his Companions, Martyrs, 1885 October 29

It was James Hannington's misfortune to share the fate of Edwin Arlington Robinson's Miniver Cheevy: he was born into the wrong time. It was Hannington's sad fate to be seized by the missionary impulse at the very height of British colonialism, the Victorian era. He is truly a martyr, a sacrificial victim, a Christian who died not so much for his actions or even his words, but simply because he was who he was, where he was, when he was.

On his first trip to Africa, Hannington was sent to a place tellingly named Victoria, in Nyanza. Illness sent him back to England, but he returned later as Bishop of Eastern Equatorial Africa and took up a mission on the shores of Lake Victoria (the name seemed to follow him). Attempting a mission to Uganda, Hannington and his party were apprehended by emissaries of King Mwanga, who feared foreign penetration into his territory. That fear swiftly killed Hannington and his party, less than a year from their arrival in the country. Still, we owe King Mwanga the benefit of the doubt.

Jesus admonished his disciples to be "wise as serpents and innocent as doves" (Matthew 10:16). It could be argued that King Mwanga was as wise as Bishop Hannington was naive, that King Mwanga was as innocent as Bishop Hannington was culpable. James Hannington was sincere in his desire to bring the gospel to people who had never heard it; King Mwanga was sincere in his desire to protect his tribe and their land from a people who went around naming things "Victoria."

Peace and harmony are bought at great price. It is heresy to maintain that all roads lead to the cross; it is gospel to proclaim that all roads lead *through* the cross. The bloody intersection of James Hannington and King Mwanga is but one cruciform juncture in the ongoing reconciliation of the peoples of the earth. The gospel planted in Uganda and the church that grew painfully out of it is now an indigenous, native Christianity of considerable vitality. In ways that can only be described as mystery, the children of Mwanga and the children of Victoria are united in the struggle to bring greater reconciliation to that part of the human family.

We are right to fear one another, and we are commanded to fear God; both are the beginning of wisdom. King Mwanga's fears were to be respected; apparently Bishop Hannington was incapable of assuaging those fears. It is to Hannington's credit that he met King Mwanga's fear with sacrifice; he did not call out the Queen's troops, but sacrificed his own life. The road to Uganda was purchased with *his* blood, not the blood of the Ugandans—or so Hannington claimed in his dying words, "Go, tell Mwanga I have purchased the road to Uganda with my blood."

But the truth is that Uganda was long ago purchased for God with the blood of Jesus, in order that no more blood be shed. It remains to be seen in this strife-ridden, suspicious world whether Christians can learn from the sacrifice of the martyrs, or simply repeat endlessly and with ever-increasing magnitude this sadly fearsome scenario.

All Hallows' Eve

October 31

This meditation is a "bonus," for All Hallows' Eve does not appear in the cycle of lesser feasts and fasts. Provision is made for this observance, however, in *The Book of Occasional Services*, and some parishes do celebrate the occasion. It occupies an important place in what was probably intended as a three-part cycle of liturgies encompassing All Hallows' Eve, All Saints' Day, and the commemoration of All Faithful Departed.

Among the several readings appointed for this commemoration is a reading from Samuel (1 Samuel 28:3-25), the curious story of Saul's visit to a very strange advisor. In the modern translations, the woman to whom Saul went is fashioned a medium or a seer, but in the older renderings she is known by her more familiar name, "the Witch of Endor." Strange as it is that Saul should seek her out, we all know people whose integrity we respect but who still check the horoscope every morning, or who will admit over hors d'oeuvres that they have had their palm read. The very strangeness of this story seems to lie in its matter-of-factness, the very ordinariness with which it is set forth in scripture.

According to our creed the God we worship is the God who made everything that is, seen and unseen, and having made it all is capable of deploying it all according to will, purpose, and some design which remains just beyond our comprehension. To deny or denigrate such experiences as that of Saul and the Witch of Endor is to maintain that God communicates only in the ways we dictate and deem tasteful. Because Saul's source is suspect in our eyes, we are perplexed by its intrusion into our religious sensibilities. Like the festivities of Halloween, it remains somewhat fantastic and even a little laughable.

Laughter is a common component of Halloween, the crazy laughter that comes of surprise and of fear. We would rather not talk about the fear, yet it is fear that we commemorate in these latter days of October, when the chill of winter wafts in and around the dying warmth of summer, when the trees and all nature seem to echo the theme of death. All the little hobgoblins in sheets, emulating the spirit world as ghosts and skeletons, as vampires and all manner of horrid creatures move us to laughter, for laughter is our way of averting the fear.

But lately it is harder to laugh. We live in a world that has taken on an uncanny and unsettling resemblance to the ballroom of Edgar Allan Poe's "The Masque of the Red Death," a world of elegantly attired sybarites whose party masks obscure the reality of the plague they carry. It is not just AIDS; it is all the afflictions of our mortal bodies, of which we become more cognizant as our peers and contemporaries, in increasing number, relate to us their own experiences with radical surgeries, radiation, and chemotherapies.

Halloween affords us a time to snicker at death, to race through the graveyards with our friends, to dress up in disguise as though the ruse might fool the grim reaper and protect us for yet another year. But we need not run from the fear or disguise it with costumes or ritualize it away in parties and laughter; it was that fear that drove Saul in desperation to find the Witch.

It was abject fear that reduced Saul to soothsaying; because he was petrified Saul rescinded his own edict and sought solace in Endor. Why does it surprise us that Samuel appeared to Saul in Endor? Why not? God appears in many media in scripture, so why not fear? In fear, our defenses are strung so tightly they are of no use to us. Fear can literally paralyze, rendering the victim helpless and thus defeated. Surrendering to his own fear, Saul learned he was not rejected by God; Saul was oblivious to God. Through Saul's fear and defeat God spoke—in a vision of Samuel, and more.

There was more for Saul at Endor than a vision; there was care. That is the greater surprise, the surprising turn at the end. For Saul, whom the woman had feared for his power, was reduced by his fear to one in need. It says that when she saw that Saul was terrified, this woman—this "witch"—was moved to minister to him. She urged him to rest and to take food. She prepared him a meal and gave him what he needed most, which was care.

The good news of the story is that fear does not remove us from the reach of God. Fear may be the point of vulnerability through which God actually reaches and touches us. In our own very arrogant and confident generation, fear may be one of the few places remaining through which the light and the love of God may shine. It has already made many of us more careful; it may yet make us more fully Christian.

Whistling as we walk past the graveyard will in no way exempt us from the eventuality of one day residing there. Dressing for success cannot protect us from the failures to which we are prey. Smiling cannot avert the genuine pain that comes of contemplating our own certain end in the face of our friends or in the bathroom mirror. It may do us much good to face into the fear; Saul did, and found there the face of God.

All Saints

November 1

I have known the power and the pain of both AIDS and cancer in the bodily presence and the palpable absence of endearing and enduring friends. Having kept company with disease and death, anger and absence, I have come to suspect that the commemoration of All Saints is a problem for us American Christians, who have an uncanny knack for dealing with the public manifestation of our discomfiting theology in an increasingly predictable way.

We have lost All Saints in the increased trivialization of Halloween. This is not a diatribe against commercialization; commercialization is only the symptom of which trivialization is the disease. What I protest is taking what were once robust adult commemorations and infantilizing them, pushing them into the realm of the child so we can conveniently distance ourselves from them. This is an insult to theology and an insult to children.

All Saints' Day is the centerpiece of an autumn triduum. In the carnival celebrations of All Hallows' Eve our ancestors used the most powerful weapon in the human arsenal, the power of humor and ridicule, to confront the power of death. The following day, in the commemoration of All Saints, we gave witness to the victory of incarnate goodness embodied in remarkable deeds and doers triumphing over the misanthropy of darkness and devils. And in the commemoration of All Souls we proclaimed the hope of common mortality expressed in our aspirations and expectations of a shared eternity. Yet all that is reduced to toddlers dressed as mutant Ninja turtles extorting candy and ubiquitous pumpkins grinning like so many happy faces.

I used to think that this trivialization masked the embarrassment of our fear of death. Being the death-denying culture that we are, we know full well how difficult it is for us to look death in the face. But we have no choice these days. When the doorbells of our lives ring we do not meet a child in funny disguise. We meet the faces of friends and family who are mortally ill, the face of death incarnate.

But there is something else at work in our trivialization of these marvelously important days—some other embarrassment. Is it that we are embarrassed to admit to the hope that is in us? To be fearful of death is natural and ageless. But we have gone beyond that fear; that we shall die we cannot deny. That we shall live, however, is a matter of faith we indulge at tremendous peril. Death shall not disappoint us; we can be sure of its coming, but of life we are less sure.

We want to believe that human flesh and human being is blessed, but we are not so sure of incarnation, so Christmas is a thing of material gifts and nostalgic ephemera. We want to believe that the power of life and love will triumph over the power of death, but we are not so sure of resurrection, so Easter is a thing of fashion and fuzzy little bunnies. We want to believe that life is eternal, but we are not so sure of eternity, so this autumn season of spooks and saints and souls has become a thing of leering pumpkins and sugar candies.

But it is not incarnation we fear, nor resurrection, nor eternity—it is disappointment. We do not want to hope in vain. That is why this commemoration of spooky death and of saints and souls is so precious. We Christians have no unique perspective on love; there are many gospels of love and most all the world's religions instruct as well as we can—or better—in the matter of love. We have no unique perspective on faith; it is the basis of all religion and the very substance of government and economy, for no God can inspire, no government can rule, no commerce can work without genuine faith—faith in God's authority to guide, faith in those who govern, faith in the value of goods and services. But where else is hope?

We Christians dare to hope beyond the constraints of mortality. For others hope is hedged, hope is where most draw short. Some constrain life to this earthly plane by hope in reincarnations depending upon fleshly, time-bound existence. Others hope in the painless consignment of the soul to everlasting nothingness. But we Christians hope beyond mortality, our hope embodied in saints and souls, a vast company and communion dwelling beyond time and forever.

It is an embarrassment, to be sure; we have no evidence to produce beyond our stories. It seems frivolous, even dangerous, and marks us as suspect. In a realm that bows to tangible security as once it bowed to stone idols, we are the gamblers who stake all that we have on unproven supposition. In a culture that seeks its own gratification at any cost, that spends its produce and its people as though there were no tomorrow, we alone dare to live as though there *is* a tomorrow and more—a place within which and a people with whom to share that tomorrow.

That is why we need these precious days of All Hallows, All Saints, and All Souls. For we know how hard it is. It is hard to look death in the face and say to death, "I know I shall see you again." But it is harder still to scan the flickering light of life's vitality in the face of a dying friend and say, "I know I shall see you again."

If our experiences of death give rise to renewed witness to such hope, it would not be the first time that the course of history is diverted by the force of epidemic disease. For us Christians, the obstacles of this time may redirect the springs of eternal life, bringing life to the arid landscape of our hopelessness. But let us be clear about one thing: it is not the plague of terminal illness that is the obstacle—it is our embarrassment. It remains to be seen in our own lives whether that relentless and irrepressible stream of living water promised by God will find its way to the desert around us, or through us.

All Faithful Departed

November 2

I grew up in the South, that part of the country where birth is the most important determinate to all relationships. Long before anyone ever dreamed of asking "what do you do?" as a means of establishing worth or place in community, folks in our part of the country wanted to know first of all "who are your kin, who do you come from, who are your people?"

To be born to landed wealth, to people of good reputation, and of white skin was to be afforded advantage and privileged relationship. To be born of lesser resources, to people only lately come to the region, or of any darker hue was to be regarded with skepticism at best and rejection at worst. Thus, in a cruel imposition of the most rigid determinism, all relationship was predicated upon divisions. And we who prided ourselves on free democracy and viewed the monarchies of Europe and the castes of India with haughty disdain maintained and nurtured a system all the more vicious for its cloak of virtue and smug righteousness. As one was born, so one might be expected to die, passing through this life in rigid conformity to the narrow path dictated by the social order.

A subtle and dangerous distinction lurks in a tragically flawed collect for All Faithful Departed—the feast we once called All Souls. For when we pray, as we do in this particular collect, to a God who is "the Maker and Redeemer of all *believers*," we have stopped short of credible truth and faith's reality. This is not paradox; this is contradiction.

We maintain in our creed that God has made everything that is, seen and unseen. But we pray to a God who is "the Maker and Redeemer of all believers." What happened to everyone else? Well, they went the way of All Souls. Now we pray only for the *faithful* departed; everyone else be damned—literally. We then ask that God "grant to the faithful departed the unsearchable benefits of the passion" of Jesus. Only to the faithful departed? What happened to our confidence that at least one of the "unsearchable benefits of the passion" is that the passion of Jesus is "the atoning sacrifice for our sins, and not for ours only but also for the sins of the whole world" (1 John 2:2)?

The prophet Isaiah proclaimed that everyone is born of God and everyone is gathered up in God at death:

> On this mountain the Lord of hosts will make for all peoples a feast of rich food, a feast of well-aged wines, of rich food filled with marrow, of well-aged wines strained clear. And he will destroy on this mountain the shroud that is cast over all peoples, the sheet that is spread over all nations; he will swallow up death forever. (Isaiah 25:6-7)

The point which scripture seems consistently to make is that everything, and everyone, belongs to God always. Let our prayers this day be, as once they were, for *all* souls, for all belong to God always. Neither prenatal circumstance nor posthumous judgment shall ever shake that faith. And thus believing, we may see the world and each other anew.

Richard Hooker

Priest, 1600   *November 3*

Richard Hooker remains the quintessential, archetypal Anglican. A parish priest and a distinguished scholar, Hooker authored *Laws of Ecclesiastical Polity*, his comprehensive defense of the Reformation settlement under Queen Elizabeth I. After *The Book of Common Prayer*, it is probably the most important repository of the essence of Anglican tradition and practice.

Among the treasures of this work is Hooker's understanding of the church, which he characterizes not as an assembly but as a society. He makes this important distinction: that while the assembly may bear the name of a church, and while any multitude of Christians congregated may be identified by the name of a church, assemblies actually are a property of the church, and not the church itself. Assemblies exist, says Hooker, for the performance of public actions. After the actions have ended, the assembly may dissolve and no longer have being. But the church gathered by Christ continues no less after the dissolving of its assemblies than when gathered.

This distinction provides an insight into the spirit of Anglicanism which, for all its appreciation of liturgical assembly, has long held and practiced a peculiar life, a life remarkable for its refusal to draw strict boundaries around its gathering or to draw sharp distinctions between secular and sacred. Regard for the difference between assembly and society explains, at least in part, why Anglican assemblies are notorious for their sociability. That which transpires upon and proceeds from the floor of our conventions has traditionally borne greater resemblance to an exchange of ideas in society than the proceedings, pronouncements, and platforms of the legislative assembly.

It is of the nature of the assembly, and its political agenda, to be partisan. That is perhaps why in our recent assemblies we have tended to act as parties unified around particular ideologies, and why we have so much difficulty in conceiving of ourselves as belonging to some larger organic whole. While some believe that unity is found in conformity to a single ideology or polity, such designs for unity among Christians are quite unlikely, and even undesirable. It is far more likely, and more consonant with the gospel as understood by Hooker, that any future unity will be based not upon unified public assemblies of partisans (or Christians), but rather in a spirit—a sociability, if you will—that transcends the limitations of assemblies.

This Spirit is elusive. Throughout history, from the congregational struggles in Corinth on down to the internal struggles of Southern Baptists, Episcopalians, and all those assemblies divided over issues and ideologies ranging from creationist theologies to the ordination of women, this has been our way of life. But Paul suggests, as does Hooker, that there is another way.

It is of the nature of the Spirit of God, says Paul, to behave differently. "'What no eye has seen, nor ear heard, nor the human heart conceived, what God has prepared for those who love him'—these things God has revealed to us through the Spirit" (1 Corinthians 2:9-10). And what is the distinctive nature of that Spirit? The Spirit searches everything. Therein lies the difference.

The assembly stops short, confines itself to the limitations of its own interests and ideals. The assembly considers only those things that support its own ideology or interests, often rejecting competing information or considerations. Thus such public action as proceeds from any assembly is reflective only of a portion of humankind. Though we struggle in vain to apprehend and propound ultimate truth, such truth as we proclaim or codify or worship is ultimately partial. And being partial, such truth is always partisan. Our public actions then, and the works of our assemblies, shall never be other than partial and partisan.

The Spirit of God, and the spirit intended for our own living, searches everything; it is inclusive. To live within that spirit means that we shall never be able to rely upon our assemblies for definitive truth, but must live in society. It means that we shall not likely arrive at answers, but shall rather make our lives in unending dialogue.

Hooker was described as a man of moderate, patient, and serene character, because he lived within that spirit who searches all things and knows that in the searching there is no arriving. Freed from any need to arrive, he was the more capable of that patient, serene moderation that comes of the journey. His was the spirit of Anglicanism; some would even say the Spirit of God.

Willibrord
Archbishop of Utrecht, Missionary to Frisia, 739   *November 7*

L ord," the eager disciples asked Jesus, "is this the time when you will restore the kingdom to Israel?" (Acts 1:6). Will this be the age, will ours be the decisive act, that ushers in the glorious kingdom of God? This question has made mission a task linked with the establishment of a tangible goal: the kingdom of God on earth. When we do not achieve the desired results we deem our work a failure because we have equated the coming of God's kingdom with the mutable circumstances of our own lives. Thus we lose heart—even become heartless—in our attempt to force the desired end.

Appointing seventy missioners, Jesus sent them out two by two—a strange strategy. He divided them into small, unarmed units without purse or bag or shoes, thus reducing an impressive force to vulnerable pairs. He told them he was sending them among wolves without so much as a staff to beat off an attack, to be laborers of a harvest without a tool to cut the ripened grain. He told them to salute no one on the road, lest they dally in conversation or be otherwise diverted, but to move quickly. Moreover, in their mission they were not to do a thing *to* anyone. They were to take their place in the midst of the life of the people, to live side by side with them, taking whatever came patiently and gratefully.

They were to live at the mercy of others, not to bring others under subjection or dependence. They were not to convert but to subvert the life of the community they entered, changing everything the hard way—from the bottom up, from the inside out. And they were to do it only by living day by day, side by side with others in such a way that others would know the kingdom of God had come near them. They were not then to *bring* the kingdom of God; they were to *be* the kingdom of God.

What little we know of the work of Willibrord indicates a ministry that was, for the most part, unremarkable. We know that he was Archbishop of Utrecht in the eighth century and that he was a missionary to Frisia, the land we now know as Holland. We know that his work was sometimes disturbed by conflicts, but we also know that, from time to time, Willibrord simply pulled up stakes and went elsewhere until the conflict died down. He died a natural death, presumably peacefully and in his own bed. That alone would distinguish him among Christian missionaries.

Willibrord's life, like our scriptures, suggests that our work as missionaries, as bearers of God's will, is to simply *be* with others. We are to take our place beside them, put our arms around them, walk with them in our clumsy, halting way through this troubled time, this confused and angry land. It is not a particularly remarkable thing we do, except for its ordinariness, its regularness, it unremarkability.

But as we live and pray, we remember; and as we remember, we take unto ourselves those so easily forgotten in the course of every day. And if we remember often enough, we shall be witnesses not only to those we embrace, but to the ravening wolves who lurk around us, who do not or will not understand—witnesses to the truth that is in us, that the kingdom of God is come near.

Leo the Great

Bishop of Rome, 461   *November 10*

W hy would Jesus describe his disciples as the salt of the earth (Matthew 5:13)? Salt was historically associated with purity; the Romans maintained it came from the purest of all things, the sun and the sea. Salt was the most primitive of all offerings to the gods, including the God of Israel. Salt was a preservative; the great slabs of bacon and ham stored in my grandfather's smokehouse were protected from contamination and decay by immense quantities of salt.

Purity and preservation—two qualities associated with Leo the Great, the pope who presided over a time of factionalism and doctrinal struggle in the fifth century, when the Roman Empire was in shambles. Leo not only had to negotiate with Attila and his Huns, but he had to mediate with Genseric and the Vandals, whom he barely dissuaded from burning and slaughtering the cities they nevertheless pillaged.

The life and witness of Leo stand in stark contrast to the image of Christianity as something sweet or sentimental. Leo certainly knew that true sweetness in life in not found in the heavy use of sugar; true sweetness is often found in the salt. Salt is the most effective sweetener when the taste is bitter. We put salt on the grapefruit to make that acrid fruit palatable; we put salt in the cocoa to cut its biting edge and render it sweet chocolate. When we are sapped and depleted by hard exertion, it is not sugar we need, but salt, to replace what we have lost. The body can live without sugar; it cannot survive without salt.

The world can often be a bitter place—a place of defeated lives, frustrated goals, people ground to pieces by systems over which they have no control and people within those systems who agonize that they are part of something they are powerless to change. For Leo it was Attila the Hun; for us it is promotional pressures, research mired in futility, a marriage that no longer supports, a child that taxes every nerve. The possibilities for creative bitterness abound.

Into this life we are sprinkled. Crazy people who find something to sing about in the midst of every age. Crazy people who find someone to sing with in the midst of every nation. Crazy people who build cathedrals in places like Harlem and soup kitchens in the Bowery. Crazy people who will give up part of a lunch hour to pray because they believe souls have to be fed, too. Do not think others do not notice. Anyone that crazy draws attention, like a light set on a hill that cannot be hid no matter how hard we try.

God uses salt, and right liberally, too—sometimes raising the blood pressure of a whole nation, and sometimes restoring and retaining the waters of life. God uses salt, uses you and me, to add a little spice to life, sometimes to sweeten it, sometimes to purify it, sometimes to help preserve it. Lumped too closely together, we cannot be shaken from the shaker, or we become so potent as to induce nausea. But sprinkled around we sweeten the bitterness of life and help to heal its pain—a humble task, and a high calling.

Martin

Bishop of Tours, 397   *November 11*

Legend has it that while still a catechumen preparing for baptism into the community of Christians a young man named Martin was approached by a poor man who asked for alms in the name of Christ. Martin, who was a military man and uniformed for the part, removed his sword from its scabbard and cut his ample cloak into two portions, one for himself and one for the beggar. It is said that the following night Jesus appeared to Martin. Jesus was clothed in half a cloak and claimed to have gotten it from a young catechumen named Martin.

The quaint little legend about the cloak was intended, I suppose, to convey the spirit of Martin. But the images are misleading; they distract from the greatest of Martin's sacrifices. For if Martin was of the temperament portrayed in the legends that surround him, such acts of kindness constitute hardly any sacrifice at all. The fact that the young soldier shared his cloak or eventually opted for a spare monastic life tells us only that Martin was of a kind and gentle nature, and these acts were expressive of that temperament.

Martin remains a lively and living example of sacrifice for entirely different reasons, for sacrifice that had little to do with cloaks and even less to do with asceticism. Martin's sacrifice was his service as a bishop of the church. The measure of his success is suggested by the fact that Martin was unpopular among many of his fellow bishops because of his defense of and care for the poor and helpless, and his opposition to the bishops' violent efforts to repress heresy.

Giving his cloak and living in a hermitage were things that Martin wanted to do. They were freely chosen expressions of his character. Serving the church as bishop was what Martin was called to do. The wonder of his service is that he steadfastly refused to shape his character to the office; he resolutely remained himself and thus shaped the office to himself.

"Is not this the fast that I choose: to loose the bonds of injustice, to undo the thongs of the yoke, to let the oppressed go free, and to break every yoke?" (Isaiah 58:6). The prophet's priorities and preaching sound a very modern note. There is a contemporaneity in this listing and one that ought not be lost on us. For we have come too easily to associate sacrificial giving and Christian service with the stuff of kindly action, dishing up food in soup kitchens, staying up all night to manage shelters for the homeless, and collecting and distributing clothing for the poor. All of these are worthy missions and necessary ones. But these are not sacrifices, not in this land where food, clothing, shelter, and leisure are abundant.

Martin would sooner have taken a beating, I would wager, than don a miter and sit in the assembly of the elders of the church. Yet it was there, in the midst of a system that was itself the symbol and sometimes source of human oppression, that Martin's sacrifice was most needed. After all, how shall we "loose the bonds of injustice" except by changing the institutions that tie our world and the human family in knots? How shall we "undo the thongs of the yoke" except by wrestling with that yoke and those who impose it? How shall we truly "let the oppressed go free" except by liberating the systems? How shall we "break every yoke" except by striking at the hands that make them?

In his ascetical and exemplary simplicity, in his opposition to the heretic-hunters, and in his evenhanded compassion Martin's episcopate challenged the church and all the institutions influenced by the church. In that sacrifice he probably clothed hundreds of beggars of all sorts and conditions, and in hundreds of different ways. For Martin's gifts, deployed in his episcopate, had the power to alter systems.

Martin points us to the ministry of service that demands not the repression of our gifts, but the expression of them, not a repudiation of our institutions but a reformation of them. The legend says, interestingly, that Martin gave the beggar only half his cloak, keeping something for himself. Throughout his life he held something for himself; he held fast to convictions he would never surrender to the will of the others, not even to insure his own popularity. The portion he reserved constituted his gift and his sacrifice for God.

Charles Simeon
Priest, 1836   *November 12*

Simplicity is not a trait normally associated with theology, or the church. Charles Simeon brought the gift of clarity to bear on both. In his preaching, this priest's commitment to the elegant simplicity of the gospel and the uncomplicated truth of the Christian imperative resurrected a moribund church and revitalized it for service in nineteenth-century England. Simeon and his followers formed the Evangelical movements of the Anglican Church, giving rise to the Church Missionary Society and sermons renowned for their teaching of scripture, their simplicity, and their passion.

There are many ways and reasons to complicate the message of Jesus. One is the lack of skill in preaching, a failing with a long past, if we are to judge from Paul's own words: "How are they to call on one in whom they have not believed? And how are they to believe in one of whom they have never heard? And how are they to hear without someone to proclaim him?" (Romans 10:14).

Another complication is the corruption of human nature itself. Our possessive and controlling nature inclines us to hoard what we ought freely to share—not just our possessions, but the precious possession of the gospel itself. Left to our own devices, our churches (and the larger church of which they are a part) can become a secret society, with its own vocabulary and rites of initiation and a jealously guarded membership. Thus doctrine replaces documentary and the gospel is, if not lost, at least constrained.

Jesus freed the gospel in stories and freed his hearers to find their place within them. Interestingly, the Episcopal hymnal contains no lyric reference to "story" or "telling," while the old evangelical hymnals boast "Tell Me the Old, Old Story," "I Love to Tell the Story," "Tell It Again," "We've a Story to Tell," and numerous other songs emphasizing the importance of the personal narrative. Our most memorable and life-changing experiences of God and the gospel are linked to stories—stories we have heard, and stories within which we have been active characters.

It is not in formulating moral rules, making official doctrine, or even creating ritual that the church is faithful to preaching and proclamation. It is our stories, shaped and shared together, that make our morality, that define our doctrine, that animate our art, music, movement, poetry, and prayer. Our life is a story and our story is a living evangel, waiting to be told.

Consecration of Samuel Seabury

First American Bishop, 1784   *November 14*

On March 25, 1783, a secret meeting of Connecticut clergymen in Woodbury named Samuel Seabury or Jeremiah Leaming, whoever would be willing or able, to seek episcopal consecration in England. Leaming declined, citing age and poor health; Seabury accepted. Duly consecrated after some struggle, this gift of the episcopate was presented to the fledgling post-revolutionary church which eventually took the name of that office—episcopal—for itself. It was not a gift universally desired, then or now. Its imposition by a secret meeting of clergy acting without lay input, by one diocese out of a loose confederation of colonial churches left in the aftermath of revolution, represents all the worst aspects of church polity—including the very arrogance associated with the monarchy in England the war had challenged. Yet we have this "gift" and on this day we give thanks for it. We struggle, as we often do in the face of such gifts, to know how best to use it.

Once a gift is bestowed, it becomes the prerogative of the recipient to dictate the gift's place and function. I may be given a coffee mug but choose to drink tea from it, or use it to hold toothbrushes or pencils, or even set it on a shelf and admire it. So it is with the episcopate; we may deploy the bishop as a pastor, or an administrator, or a spiritual director, or as a liturgical ornament. Indeed, we often ask all that and more of those in the office. But the one thing we cannot do is neglect our responsibility to the giver of the gift itself.

If, indeed, God has given us the episcopate as a gift, then it is up to us to put that gift to use. The episcopate is the creation of the church (not the other way around) and the church—which is you and me—is challenged to put the gift to service. Our responsibility is to direct the talents and energies of our bishops, asking neither more than they can accomplish nor less than they are able. If we wait always upon them (either dallying in expectation of their lead, or catering to their every whim), then we fail to provide the direction every good servant needs to fulfill his or her office.

Like every gift entrusted to us, the episcopate evokes our stewardship. We ought to measure prayerfully and shrewdly the resources—the men and women—we elect to this office. And once elected, we must be prudent investors, alert to the dangers of deploying these resources too cautiously or too prodigally, of asking too much or too little of them. They depend upon us, and we are as much accountable *for* them as we are held accountable *to* them. Spend them wisely and well.

Margaret
Queen of Scotland, 1093   *November 16*

Brought by marriage to foreign soil, Margaret was the wife of Malcolm, whose associations with Duncan, Macbeth, and Macduff are memorialized in Shakespeare. But Margaret belongs also to the church, revered for her efforts to discipline the unruly church in Scotland while also opening its communion to a wider circle. Perhaps because of her own status as an alien, she was all the more sensitive to the need for reconciliation of diverse peoples.

Some, said Jesus, stumble upon the reality of God's love as "treasure hidden in a field" (Matthew 13:44). They suddenly unearth the truth as an unexpected gift found in the midst of ordinary activity. Others, said Jesus, may go after truth with a connoisseur's devotion, searching exotic ideas and places, weighing and measuring until perfection is found. Both are acknowledged as legitimate. The kingdom's inclusiveness is then summarized in the parable of the expansive net of God's love, encompassing everyone and everything (Matthew 13:47-50); those swept into the net will find themselves in the company of many a weird fish and not a few crabs. The network of God's love draws all together. Matthew's gospel is addressed to those who have felt rejection, those beyond the net, or deemed insignificant—the ones who have been strained out, beyond the embrace of love and adrift in the depths of a lonely sea. But they are also words of discomfiture to those who fancy themselves fishermen, but who are themselves just fish, like all the rest of us (it is no accident that this trio of parables immediately precedes the tale of Jesus' rejection in his own hometown).

To those who plied the seas with nets, the images held particular power. They fashioned the initials of the title "Jesus Christ, the Son of God" into the acronym ICTHUS—the Greek word for fish. Those who had been fishermen took upon themselves the sign of the fish, and within the net they took their places, rejoicing as the catch grew ever wider, the haul heavier. There they were joined by Margaret and now us, praising the skill of the One who casts the seine, praying for a bountiful harvest of creation's seas in joyful expectation of the time when the net is gathered in, and God's day upon the waters is complete.

Hugh
Bishop of Lincoln, 1200   *November 17*

Born to the nobility in France, Hugh departed from the road of grandeur for the contemplative life of the Carthusians, the strictest order of the church. Sequestered within the walls of that fortress of contemplation, the Grande Chartreuse, Hugh came to the attention of Henry II, who invited him to become prior of a new Carthusian foundation at Somerset in England. Reluctantly he went, and with equal reluctance, later accepted appointment to the episcopate of Lincoln.

Maintaining the strict disciplines of his order, Hugh actively supported the poor, the oppressed, and the outcast with humility, tact, and a cheerful disposition. Despite his humility—and because of it—Hugh was free to reprove Henry for his unjust taxations. He even refused to exact money from the people for the wars mounted by Richard, Henry's successor. Had it come from a more pompous or power-conscious person, such opposition might have aroused the anger of the king; heads did roll for lesser offenses in those days. Instead, Richard openly expressed his admiration for Hugh.

In his letter to Titus, Paul exhorts him as a Christian to be a "model of good works, and in your teaching show integrity, gravity, and sound speech that cannot be censured" (Titus 2:7-8). Likewise, Jesus urged his disciples to be prepared always for the day of the Lord's coming, remaining watchful, faithful, and wise (Matthew 24:42-47). The most effective witness is sometimes the quiet, sustained, and ever-present one, ready at any moment for the Lord's return. Translated into our experience, it is to be consistent and continual in our witness so that anyone who looks at any time might recognize the gospel we represent.

The magnificent accomplishments, the grand gestures, are but echoes now—dim visions of empires won and lost, built and destroyed. We are inheritors of a quieter revolution in a long line of small voices and tiny gestures. In these noisy times, Hugh reminds us that to be heard, we need only to lower our voice.

Hilda

Abbess of Whitby, 680   *November 18*

In one sense, Hilda of Whitby was an unwed mother; she never married, though she was called "mother" by many who knew her. In East Anglia, the country we know as England, at the age of thirty-three, she entered monastic life. Eventually she founded the abbey at Whitby and ordered it by her own rule of justice, devotion, chastity, peace, and charity. Hilda was graced with gifts of justice and prudence; she was a woman of uncommon common sense.

The more one learns, the more complexity one sees. But learning cannot be said to be wisdom until, seeing through the complexities, one discerns the foundations. When her own community was divided over the differences between the practices of Celtic and Roman Christianity, a synod was called at Whitby. Hilda was personally sympathetic to the Celtic tradition, just as some of us have loved various aspects of our own tradition like the prayer book or certain hymns or particular styles of worship. But the synod did not choose the Celtic tradition; they opted for the Roman position. Hilda adapted to that decision and was one of the strongest proponents of peace. She knew that there were far more important considerations, that the difference of the two traditions was only a symptom of a much deeper issue—the fundamental issue of a united community.

Peter seems the very opposite of Hilda in the story Matthew tells of him, when in his self-serving style Peter casts what little social graces he may have had to the wind and with all the delicacy of a Sherman tank simply puts the matter of discipleship to Jesus plainly: "Look, we have left everything and followed you. What then will we have?" (Matthew 19:27). Look at what we have sacrificed, says Peter. What might we expect in return? Jesus tells Peter that the disciples will sit upon twelve thrones, judging the twelve tribes of Israel. And Jesus tells the disciples and anyone else concerned to know what recompense is coming that "every one who has left houses or brothers or sisters or father or mother or children or fields, for my name's sake, will receive a hundredfold, and will inherit eternal life" (Matthew 19:29).

That is a very nice package, and not a bad return on the investment. Not only do the disciples get their thrones, but everyone gets a hundredfold increase on all that has been left for the sake of the gospel. Taken at face value that seems more than a fair wage, a bounty well worth the effort. Countless interpreters have derived from those words a gospel of success, a promise of abundance of the type preached all over this land, not only by the media evangelists, but by every manufacturer who promises effective results from the use of perfumes, pie crusts, or polishes.

But common sense, and a literal reading, can also lead to a different conclusion. For what Jesus promises the disciples is not just an honorable place. He promises them twelve thrones, to be sure, but they are thrones of judgment, not easy chairs. Jesus promises the disciples not greater leisure, but greater responsibility—the task of judging the tribes of Israel. It would be their lot to negotiate the gospel through the treacherous waters of jealousy and suspicion that locked Jews and Gentiles in struggle well beyond their own deaths.

And what of the hundredfold increase? Anyone who knows the burden of love that comes of maintaining a single house, loving but one family of siblings, caring for one set of parents, parenting one litter of children, managing one piece of real estate, must shudder at the thought of having it all magnified a hundred times over, with eternity thrown in for good measure. Jesus promises that we may expect no escape, but an increase in responsibility. So it was that a woman who never wed became the mother of many, lived justly and wisely, practiced a homely common sense and fulfilled the promises—and the responsibilities—of discipleship.

Elizabeth

Princess of Hungary, 1231   *November 19*

Power and money seem mysteriously to have escaped the power of redemption. The rich are castigated and held in contempt, as though their resources predispose them to damnation; it is good to find a word of kindness for the occasional person of wealth and high standing. Elizabeth of Hungary was a princess, daughter of King Andrew II of Hungary. Living in the thirteenth century, she possessed as much as any modern could want. She married well and maintained a family, and her life seems always to have been remarkable for her generosity.

Elizabeth was drawn to the ideals of the Franciscans. She received spiritual direction from them and, after the death of her husband, she embraced the Franciscan ideal as a member of the Third Order. Elizabeth did not retire, in the usual sense, to a monastic life of simple comfort. She chose affiliation with a religious order that allowed her to continue living within the society she knew best. She did not renounce her past, nor did she renounce her wealth. Instead, she continually gave of her resources for the sake of others. She gave her dowry as alms. She sold her jewels and established a hospital. She opened the royal granaries in time of famine to feed the poor. After her husband's death, her generosities were the scandal of the court. When her material resources were reduced to a subsistence, she trimmed her living and gave all of herself to her work. She died of exhaustion—an appropriate end to the life of one giving all she had.

The desire to do good for others may stem from many a different impulse. The spending of money, talents, and vital energies may be motivated by expectation of reward. Charitable giving in this country is rewarded with tax incentives, and it is no secret that most modern philanthropy is but thinly-veiled public relations. Each of us is willing to donate a little something in the way of money or time in those places where our gifts can be seen and admired by others.

We may also be moved to give for fear of loss. We are reluctant to pass the beggar on the street, or to throw the little mailing labels with the annual appeal from some charity into the garbage, for fear that we are breaking some cosmic chain letter to God, that our failure to give of our time, treasure, or talent is somehow noted—as though we are being graded in a vast book of life, and that we shall be found wanting.

But the gospel provides a new perspective on the old problem of our relationship to those things we own: "Do not be afraid, little flock, for it is your Father's good pleasure to give you the kingdom." That little sentence prepares us for the words that follow: "Sell your possessions, and give alms. Make purses for yourselves that do not wear out, an unfailing treasure in heaven, where no thief comes near and no moth destroys. For where your treasure is, there your heart will be also" (Luke 12:32-34).

"Do not be afraid, little flock, for it is your Father's good pleasure to give you the kingdom." The joyful good news is that the kingdom for which we labor so hard, and so fear to lose, is given us by the God who made us. We are, in a happy sense, robbed of our anticipation and relieved of our anxiety. And out of that state all charity is to proceed. The kingdom is secured in God's promise; we can proceed to give away our riches and share our bounty, freed from fear.

Secure in her understanding of the gospel, Elizabeth was freed from giving for self-gain and from fear, freed to give all; in the promise of the gospel she already possessed all that she needed for herself. Her giving was, if we are to guess by her life, an act of thanksgiving. In this season, we gather in families around laden tables in the midst of the greatest comfort in the modern world and we render thanks for the fruits of our labor in an annual ritual of self-congratulation. The one thing we forget is the prelude to all thanksgiving, the foundation of all our living and our giving—the gift of the kingdom, delivered to us out of God's good pleasure. Possessing this treasure we need none else.

Edmund

King of East Anglia, Martyr, 870   *November 20*

Commemorating Edmund is not without its problems and its puzzlements. King of East Anglia in the ninth century, his reign is described as an equitable one, albeit a rather short one. Ascending the throne in 865, he was in 869 confronted with the invasion of the Danes under Hinguar and Hubba. Taken captive by the invaders, Edmund was promised his life would be spared if he would share his kingdom with Hinguar. Edmund refused. As a Christian, he could not and he would not associate himself in such a manner with a pagan. For his refusal he was, in the rather colorful description of one biographer, "made the target of the Danes' archery practice, and finally beheaded."

Jesus counsels his disciples to be "wise as serpents and innocent as doves" (Matthew 10:16). With all due respect for Edmund and for those who revere his memory, Edmund might well have rehearsed this gospel before rendering his resounding refusal. He was right to be wary of promises made by invading armies, but inasmuch as he feared for his life in any case, Edmund seems to have chosen the more cowardly course.

In his pristine and proper refusal to soil his reign by association with a so-called pagan, Edmund declined an opportunity to reconcile the differences that separated him from his enemy. After all, the purity of the established religion of Israel was threatened by Jesus' association with sinners, with outcasts; it was cited as one of the several ways in which Jesus profaned the faith of Israel and defamed it.

In fairness to Edmund, the mingling of Christian and non-Christian was not always fortuitous for the Christian community. There was always the threat that the Christian might, by association with the non-Christian, be enticed to return to pagan patterns, or to abandon the Christian faith altogether. There were then, as there are now, those who sampled every religion and dabbled in each, practicing a kind of religion that could be best characterized as "hedging one's cosmic bets." By dabbling in each cult, coven, or congregation one could claim at least nominal association with them all and when, in the end, all truth is revealed and the "right" one acknowledged, all the bases are covered.

Edmund disappoints in the missed opportunity; who is to know how far the Danes could be trusted in their offer to share the rule? There was always the risk that they might be deceptive, but there was an equal chance that their offer was sincere and might well have led to a most instructive period in the history of the faith. It was an opportunity lost, an opportunity to rule side-by-side with one of another culture and tradition, and in that rule, to expand that love and justice for which the nations have long prayed and worked.

For our own time, the lesson of Edmund is instructive. Fear of contamination cost us a decent king in Anglia in the ninth century; what opportunities do we miss in our separateness? What do we communicate to others when we tell them in word and deed that they are not of us, nor we of them, nor shall we ever meet? To what do we witness in a stubborn insistence upon our own way, to the exclusion of all others? And how is it that we worship a God whose love for us was so intense that it could not stand apart but rather risked and suffered all that is human for the sake of drawing closer, but would ourselves die before we would share a throne or a thought with another?

Edmund lost his head well before the Danes took it. But he also lost an opportunity that might well have turned out far better and could certainly have turned out none the worse. Pray for Edmund, and for the Edmund who lives in us.

Clement

Bishop of Rome, c. 100   *November 23*

A letter from this bishop of Rome to the church in Corinth, called "First Clement," addressed a youthful group of Christians at Corinth who had rebelled against the elder clergy and deposed them. Because of the influence of these fledgling communities upon one other, such upheaval could spread. Clement cracked down. In his response he left no doubt that the order of the church was to be hierarchical, using as his defense a lineage that traced the gospel from God through Jesus, to the apostles, to their followers, who were appointed bishops and deacons—as had Clement been himself.

Clement's theology was shaped of a different understanding than our own, but nearly two thousand years later we perpetuate much of his theology of holy orders and its attendant structure, both of which were shaped by particular events. Clement, responding to crisis, dictated a hierarchical structure and demanded obedience to it.

Whether we ought to perpetuate Clement's order and its clericalism is open to question. Clement used the terms "bishop" and "presbyter" as synonyms but left no doubt that these orders constitute a higher rank, even calling some of them "rulers" of the church. Clement's response reflects the tendency of authority to respond to any threat to its order with authoritarianism. Clement acted instinctively to shore up any erosion of power with a massive imposition of authority from above, buttressed by tradition—tradition itself ranked in hierarchy over present experience.

In some instances, authoritarianism is a proper response to crisis. A focused authority can serve to impose sufficient order to allow the reasonable conduct of business. And tradition can offer counterpoise to our inexperience. But authority and the offices by which order is authorized, especially within the church, are properly a means, and not an end in themselves. So I wonder why Clement seems neither to have questioned nor respected the dissatisfaction of those in the congregation who demanded new leadership.

In his second letter Paul instructs the younger Timothy to "be strong in the grace that is in Christ Jesus"; what Timothy has heard from Paul in the presence of many witnesses, Timothy is to entrust to others of the community of faith who, in turn, may carry it on to others (2 Timothy 2:1-2). Timothy himself may have succumbed to the youthful arrogance of authoritarian control. By not entrusting ministry to others, Timothy is an obstacle to the propagation of the gospel. Timothy apparently has "strong control needs," and lacks the ability to delegate; Paul urges him to share.

Paul mixes a list of metaphors: the soldier's obedience to command, the runner's responsibility to rules, the farmer's claim to the harvest. He urges Timothy to think about these metaphors, that the Lord would grant understanding. Such rumination raises fascinating possibilities. The soldier of Christ is subject to the community of Christ's risen body which is the church. Thus those in any ministerial office serve not only at the call of God, but also of God's people and are thus answerable to God through the community itself. The athlete is subject to rules; beating the other persons in the competition is not always the same thing as winning the race. The true winner must do more than best competitors; the victor must win honestly, not by cheating.

The last instruction is the most troubling. Paul says that the hardworking farmer ought to have the first share of the crops, but in the Christian community reward is not always consonant with labor, a point made by Jesus in his parable of the eleventh-hour workers who were paid the same as those who had worked all day. It is not for our own reward that we labor nor always for our benefit, but rather that all may have equal share in the bounty of God.

With these instructions encouraging shared ministry in mind we may be grateful for Clement's legacy, but somewhat guardedly. Clement's solution, like his very name, brought mildness and calm that allowed a fractured and chaotic community to carry out its ministry together. But Clement's solution can become a cure worse than the disease it seeks to remedy. Knowing more of how and why we have ordered our ministry will provide a deeper understanding and the possibility to learn from our past and benefit the future, but it does not exempt us from responsibility for our own time or task, a point with which even Clement would agree.

Thanksgiving Day

Fourth Thursday in November

"Consider the lilies of the field" (Matthew 6:28). It is the wrong time of year to think of those lilies, for they have crumbled into brown heaps now covered over with dead leaves. When we consider the lilies, the ones we see in our minds are in full bloom, swaying in the summer breeze in lush meadows or richly-planted gardens.

The life of the lily begins not as a flowering blossom, but as a seed that matures into a rather ugly tuber, a brown bulb whose soft and vulnerable interior is covered by a layer of dead amber skin. Within that unseemly bulb lies only the dormant idea of the blossom. Buried within the ground, the bulb endures darkness and cold before it can respond to the warmth of the springtime sun. To consider only the lily's bloom is to overlook the greatest portion of its life.

Thanksgiving is something of a Mardi Gras of the autumn season, a last fling before the lights of the church are dimmed in Advent, in anticipation of Christmas. The lily was chosen by Jesus as the metaphor of life under God's care; centuries later it became the symbol of Mary, his mother. Advent belongs uniquely to her, the final weeks of her pregnancy, a time of waiting and worry as she bears a new life. Her blossom endures the cold and dark realities of the embalming myrrh at her baby's cradle, Herod's wrath, and Egypt's desert; it endures the chilling concern for a son's uncertain future and the grief of his premature death. All this it endures until some distant Easter's warmth coaxes it into bloom. Consider the lily, but consider it whole—and be thankful for it all.

James Otis Sargent Huntington

Priest and Monk, 1935　　　　　　　　　　　　　　　　　*November 25*

While on retreat in Philadelphia James Huntington discerned his call to a monastic vocation. He considered the Society of St. John the Evangelist, an order with strong English antecedents and a province in the United States, but he ultimately determined to establish an indigenous American community. He found two other priests willing to join him, and they began their life together at the Holy Cross Mission on the Lower East Side of New York City, where they worked alongside the Sisters of St. John the Baptist, serving poor immigrants. Demands upon them were constant, and their pastoral and personal resources were taxed to the limit. One priest resigned for reasons of health, and the other left soon after. Despite these reversals, in November of 1884 Huntington presented himself to Bishop Potter of New York, who received his life vow to the religious life.

Desertion is a common theme in ministry. Paul's impatience with Galatia courses through his letter to that trying community, and the end has the unmistakable ring of exasperation: "From now on, let no one make trouble for me," he exclaims in closing (Galatians 6:17). Jesus struggled with his own frustration with those who, though they had seen abundant evidence of God's power in their lives, were nonetheless unbelieving that Jesus could be the bread of life (John 6:34–38). Still, Jesus did not reject or demean them, but said that he would in no way disparage or turn away anyone who comes—even those who come only to try him.

From one perspective, Huntington seems to have been very much alone in his ministry. But that overlooks the obvious: all those people among whom Huntington lived and worked. He was never alone. Huntington was constantly in the presence of God, incarnate in each of those among whom he ministered. He found constant companionship in those who called upon his gifts and stretched him to his limits. When others came to join him, it was not to keep him company, but to give themselves.

These realities are slow in coming to us; our notions of evangelism and ministry are calculated otherwise. We want to attract people, and preferably attractive people. But those who are difficult or questioning or skeptical invite us into their own lives and experiences, even at the most profoundly intimate level; we do not easily reveal our difficulty, our insecurity, or our doubt to just anyone. God is present not only in those who share our work and our perspective, but is also present in those who challenge us and call us beyond our own self-imposed limits.

The evangelical example of James Huntington is his abiding assurance of God's presence—a spirituality not only of silence and solitude, but also of the joyful recognition of God in that marvelous company of witnesses surrounding us, and summoning us, in the everyday.

Kamehameha and Emma

King and Queen of Hawaii, 1864, 1885   *November 28*

The Christian year in the Episcopal calendar ends with the commemoration of a nineteenth-century king and queen of Hawaii. Kamehameha IV and his wife, Emma Rooke, had just turned twenty when they ascended the Hawaiian throne in 1855. Kamehameha and Emma inherited a monarchy with all the trappings of ceremony and circumstance. But they also inherited a nation laid low by smallpox. The people were astounded by this king and queen who took their places among them and raised the money to build the largest civilian hospital in Hawaii.

But this unselfish charity is not the only reversal of custom we encounter in the story of King Kamehameha and Queen Emma. On a boyhood tour of England, the king had experienced the Anglican liturgy, which resonated with his native Hawaiian spirit. In 1860, King Kamehameha and Queen Emma asked the Bishop of Oxford to send missionaries to Hawaii to establish the Anglican Church there.

Imagine a proclamation of the gospel so memorable and compelling that a childhood brush with it issued forth in an invitation to bring that gospel to a new world. It is an image of evangelism we do not often see, and a path of evangelism nearly lost in the luxuriant abundance of schemes promising renewal and growth. It is an evangelism of integrity, offering the love of God and the substance of the gospel freely.

The apostle Paul, stumbling across the altar in Athens erected to an unknown god, saw within the deep conviction and sacred impulse of those who worshiped there a faith at one with his own. Paul was obviously and deeply touched by their desire to worship, their confession of need, and their humility before the unknown. Paul wisely and gently commended their faith, a faith of such integrity that even Paul is humbled; he is neither didactic nor dogmatic, neither condemning nor condescending, but evinces genuinely Christ-like behavior. It is also one of the most compelling visions of evangelism in all of scripture, this vision of Paul gently and graciously sharing the story of his own faith with those committed people of Athens.

The invitation of Kamehameha and Emma tells us much about the integrity of the Anglican liturgy in their own day; a king and queen saw within it a gift worthy of the people they loved and served. Our witness and our evangel will be seen and measured not in what comes to us, but rather in the places we are invited to go.

Index

Cowley Publications is a ministry of the Society of St. John the Evangelist, a religious community for men in the Episcopal Church. Emerging from the Society's tradition of prayer, theological reflection, and diversity of mission, the press is centered in the rich heritage of the Anglican Communion.

Cowley Publications seeks to provide books, audio cassettes, and other resources for the ongoing theological exploration and spiritual development of the Episcopal Church and others in the body of Christ. To this end, it is dedicated to developing a new generation of theological writers, encouraging them to produce timely, creative, and stimulating publications of excellence, and making these publications available widely, reaching both clergy and lay persons.